The Literary Qur'an

The Literary Qur'an

Narrative Ethics in the Maghreb

Hoda El Shakry

FORDHAM UNIVERSITY PRESS
New York 2020

This book was a recipient of the American Comparative Literature Association's Helen Tartar First Book Subvention Award. Fordham University Press is grateful for the funding from this prize that helped facilitate publication.

Fordham University Press also publishes its books in a variety of electronic formats. Some content that appears in print may not be available in electronic books.

Visit us online at www.fordhampress.com.

Library of Congress Cataloging-in-Publication Data available online at https://catalog.loc.gov.

Printed in the United States of America

22 21 20 5 4 3 2 1

First edition

FSC www.fsc.org MIX Paper | Supporting responsible forestry FSC® C013604

In loving memory of Zaynab Shahata (1911–1998),
who never learned to read the Qur'an,
but for whom the Qur'an offered other ways of reading.

For my parents, Aida Nawar and Sayed El Shakry

Contents

Note on Translations and Transliterations

Arabic words and names have been transliterated into the Latin alphabet using a modified system based on the *International Journal of Middle East Studies* (IJMES). Arabic names of authors who publish predominantly in French or English have not been changed for the sake of consistency (for example, Abdelwahab Meddeb, Assia Djebar, Driss Chraïbi). When available, I have cited from existing translations into English; modifications to published translations are indicated. Unless otherwise noted, all other translations from Arabic and French are my own.

Acknowledgments

Like many students of the Qur'an, I began my studies in childhood, when its esoteric message and opaque language seemed immeasurably beyond my comprehension. My Qur'anic teacher in Cairo, *ustaz* Saeed, patiently trained me as he himself had been trained: supplementing rote recitation and mimetic repetition with *tartīl* (hymnody), *tajwīd* (elocution), and *tafsīr* (exegesis). Studying with *ustaz* Saeed shaped not only my understanding of the Qur'an but, more crucially, how I came to think about pedagogy, reading, and hermeneutics in ways that I continue to unpack. The Qur'an became an internalized palimpsest and embodied intertext that inflected my literary sensibilities and fostered a critical curiosity about the ethics of reading.

This book would not have been possible without the valuable contributions of numerous individuals and institutions. The research and writing of this book were funded by generous support from the American Institute for Maghrib Studies (AIMS), Penn State Center for Global Studies, Penn State Institute for Arts & Humanities, Penn State Africana Research Center, as well as the ACLA Helen Tartar First Book Subvention Award.

A modified version of Chapter 3 was published as "Revolutionary Eschatology: Islam & the End of Time in al-Ṭāhir Waṭṭār's *al-Zilzāl*," *Journal of Arabic Literature* 42.2–3 (2011): 120–47. Portions of Chapter 2 appeared in "Abdelwahab Meddeb and the Po/Ethics of Sufism," *Expressions Maghrébines*, 16.2 (Winter 2017): 95–115. I thank the *Journal of Arabic Literature* (Brill) and *Expressions Maghrébines* for permission to reprint and for the gracious feedback offered by their anonymous reviewers.

This book has benefited from engaging conversations and audiences at the American Comparative Literature Association (ACLA), Modern Language Association (MLA), Middle East Studies Association (MESA), Harvard University, University of Texas at Austin, Pennsylvania State University, University of Pennsylvania, Graduate Center at City University of New York (CUNY), and UNC Chapel Hill.

I am exceptionally grateful to Michael Allan and Tarek El-Ariss, who workshopped an early draft of the book manuscript and offered immensely generative feedback for its revision. Omnia El Shakry, Leah Feldman, and Magalí Armillas-Tiseyra provided insightful comments on the Introduction, and our conversations across the writing process have profoundly shaped this book. The anonymous reader reports for the manuscript were extremely gracious and constructive. Kareem James Abu-Zeid proved a phenomenal translations editor. Tom Lay, my editor at Fordham University Press, immediately understood the investments of this project and has patiently supported its realization.

My interest in the Maghreb began as an undergraduate at Rutgers University, and I am indebted to the outstanding scholars and mentors with whom I worked there: Janet Walker, Elaine Chang, Richard Dienst, and Richard Serrano. UCLA's Department of Comparative Literature provided a rigorous intellectual community for my graduate studies, and I am grateful to the faculty, staff, and colleagues who supported my research, particularly Eleanor Kaufman, Kirstie McClure, Susan Slyomovics, Michael Cooperson, Ali Behdad, Stathis Gourgouris, Françoise Lionnet, Aamir Mufti, and Lia Brozgal. I owe a particular debt of gratitude to the generous and continued support of Nouri Gana and Gil Hochberg.

I was fortunate to spend a year as a Faculty Fellow at NYU's Gallatin School of Individualized Study, where I worked alongside an inspiring group of scholars and educators. I thank Sinan Antoon, Maria Cruz Soto, Rosalind Fredericks, Lisa Goldfarb, A.B. Huber, Vasuki Nesiah, Jacques Lezra, Susanne Wofford, and Valerie Forman—who continues to be a singular mentor and friend.

My colleagues, students, and the staff at Penn State's Department of Comparative Literature have been a consistent source of intellectual and professional encouragement. While at Penn State, I have had numerous opportunities to share my work and exchange ideas across a variety of formal and informal spaces with Jonathan Brockopp, Nina Safran, Samar Farage, Benjamin Schreier, Samuel Frederick, Christopher Moore, Emmanuel Bruno Jean-François, Jennifer Boittin, Michael Berubé, Janet Lyon, Sarah Townsend, Maha Marouan, Alicia Decker, Jonathan Eburne, Jonathan Abel, Shuang Shen, Sophia McClennan, Thomas Beebee, Rosemary Jolly, Adrian Wanner, Eric Hayot, Charlotte Eubanks, Nergis Ertürk, Anna Ziajka-Stanton, Gabeba Baderoon, Caroline Eckhart, and Robert Edwards. The African Feminist Initiative, Modern and Contemporary Studies Initiative, and Dr. Sisters group are spaces that have fostered intellectual and social community during my time at Penn State. The insights and intellectual voracity of my graduate students—Anouar El Younssi, Beyza Lorenz, Merve Tabur, Alex Fyfe, Rebekah Zwanzig, Rana Ghuloom, Deena Al-halabieh, Lubna Safi, and Derek Gideon—influenced both my critical pedagogy and this project.

Ideas grow and develop in the margins of conversations, and this book is no exception. It was enriched by innumerable thinkers, particularly David Fieni, Gretchen Head, Anne-Marie McManus, Annette Damayanti Lienau, Sarah Eltantawi, Amir Moosavi, Ghenwa Hayek, Yasmine Ramadan, Dina Ramadan, Benjamin Koerber, Ayoub El Mouzaïne, Fernanda Fischione, Brock Cutler, Anita Husen, Nahrain Al-Mousawi, Elizabeth Marcus, Roger Allen, Muhsin al-Musawi, Dina Al-Kassim, Waïl S. Hassan, Mohamed-Salah Omri, Ellen McLarney, Rudolph Ware, Yoav Di-Capua, Suad Joseph, Susan Gilson Miller, Achille Mbembe, Paul Amar, Nadia Yaqub, Eve Troutt Powell, Samer Ali, Elizabeth Holt, Olivia Harrison, Fatima Sadiqi, Hala Halim, Samer Frangie, Zeina Halabi, Fadi Bardawil, Jeffrey Sacks, William Granara, R. A. Judy, Edwidge Tamalet Talbayev, Yasser Elhariry, Shaden Tageldin, Tarek El-Ariss, Michael Allan, and Samira Haj. The late Saba Mahmood has shaped my intellectual development since graduate school, and her groundbreaking scholarship on agency as an ethical formation inflects this entire manuscript. Stefania Pandolfo's work first introduced me to Maghrebi literature as an undergraduate, and she continues to be an unparalleled inspiration.

Martín Perna, Marco Martinez, Justin Clark, Beniamino Ambrosi, Marites Naca, Elizabeth Gelber, Kyle Waneberg, Daniel Stern, Stephen Sykes, my brother-in-law Nadeem Haj, and the incomparable Nassie Elzoghby have shared meals, ideas, and laughs over the years, and I'm grateful for their friendships. David Simpson graciously provided support and companionship while I was writing this manuscript. Andrea Devita guided me to trust my instincts, a truly singular gift. Shaoling Ma, Ariane Cruz, Courtney Morris, Judith Sierra-Rivera, Magalí Armillas-Tiseyra, and Ebony Coletu have enriched my life in State College in immeasurable ways, and I'm humbled by the friendship and support that have accompanied their numerous intellectual contributions—from writing groups to proofreading. Leah Feldman embarked on this journey with me from the beginning and has provided consistent academic, emotional, and culinary sustenance over the years. My nonhuman companions Cholula and Mirin joyfully fill my writing days with furry snuggles.

My maternal grandmother, Zaynab Shahata (1911–1998), was an exceptional woman whose narrative creative license cultivated in me an early love of storytelling. My niece and nephew, Selma and Jed, are an unparalleled magical presence in my life. My sisters, Omnia, Marwa, and Leila, have served as intellectual interlocutors, mentors, confidants, and friends. I am continuously in awe of their brilliance, and their love fuels all of my life's successes.

For their constant support and faith, I dedicate both my love and this manuscript to my parents, Aida Nawar and Sayed El Shakry. Their tireless work ethic and intellectual curiosity have left an indelible mark on this book and my life. Through them, I came to see the ways in which the Qur'an traverses ethical and literary spaces.

Preface: The Ethics of Reading

اقْرَأْ بِاسْمِ رَبِّكَ الَّذِي خَلَقَ {١}
خَلَقَ الْإِنسَانَ مِنْ عَلَقٍ {٢}
اقْرَأْ وَرَبُّكَ الْأَكْرَمُ {٣}
الَّذِي عَلَّمَ بِالْقَلَمِ {٤}
عَلَّمَ الْإِنسَانَ مَا لَمْ يَعْلَمْ {٥}

READ in the name of thy Sustainer, who has created
—created man out of a germ-cell!
Read—for thy Sustainer is the Most Bountiful One
who has taught [man] the use of the pen
—taught man what he did not know!

—"Al-ʿalaq" ("The Germ-Cell") (Qurʾan 96:1–5 trans. Asad)

The Qurʾanic sura "Al-ʿalaq" ("The Germ-Cell" or "The Clot") is documented as the first sura to be revealed to the Prophet Muhammad. When commanded *iqraʾ*—signaling both reading and reciting—by the Archangel Jibrīl (Gabriel), the then forty-year-old Prophet, who is reported to have been unlettered, responded twice that he was not a reader. Upon being asked for a third time, the Prophet came to *know* these first five verses as if they were emblazoned on both his mind and heart. This account appears in a hadith attributed to the Prophet's beloved wife ʿĀʾisha, who was a renowned *muḥadditha*, or transmitter of the apostolic tradition of hadith (M. M. Ali 1–15).

Hadith literature refers to the sayings and practices ascribed to the Prophet Muhammad that were largely compiled in the eighth and ninth centuries.[1] Their authentication relies upon a complex verification system in which each hadith needs to be genealogically traced directly to the Prophet, often through one of his wives or companions. The veracity and ranking of a given hadith is based upon its ability to document and justify an uninterrupted chain of transmission—a process referred to as *isnād*. While it is a body of religious scripture distinct from the Qur'an, hadith literature offers an important narrative supplement for Qur'anic exegesis.[2] Since the Prophet Muhammad is the archetype of Muslim ethics, it also serves a valuable function in Muslim spiritual life.

As the Prophet's first revelation, the sura "Al-ʿalaq" is significant for what it discloses about the Qur'an as both a text and spiritual guide for Muslims. Imbuing the creation myth with physiological and epistemological overtones, the sura forges a direct link between the physical act of creation—in its reference to a clot, interpreted by most exegetes as either a human embryo or an atom—and the pursuit of knowledge. As the direct word of God, the Qur'an is divine providence as well as the foundation of Muslim ethics and knowledge formation. The semantic ambiguity and polysemy of the word *iqra'* within Islam's spiritual lexicon lends the act of reading the *embodied* dimension of recitation. To "read" in the Islamic tradition, then, is to engage not only the faculties of the mind and spirit but also those of the body. The Qur'an's textual dimensions are emphasized by the repeated use of the word *qalam*, meaning a writing implement such as a quill, reed, or pen. The sura's simultaneous emphasis on reading/reciting and writing demonstrates the centrality of pedagogy to Islam, as well as the diverse forms of literacy valued in the production and transmission of Qur'anic knowledge.

Centuries after the death of the Prophet Muhammad, the Moroccan novelist Driss Chraïbi reimagined the first revelation. His 1995 novel *L'Homme du Livre* (The Man of the Book; translated into English as *Muhammad*) mirrors the Qur'an's complex narrative construction, at once invoking and transforming the holy text. The work partakes in the tradition of *sīra*, or religious biographies on the Prophet Muhammad, but does so within the literary form of the novel. While it brings together Qur'anic suras, hadith, *sīras*, Islamic history, and philosophy, *L'Homme du Livre* is nonetheless a fictional portrayal of the first days of the Prophet's revelation. Elaborating on these codified records, the novel focuses on Muhammad's emotional and psychological state during the revelations. It describes the Prophet's fear, confusion, and doubts over his prophetic destiny, as well as the importance of his wife Khadīja, eventually his first convert, to the early history of Islam. Mirroring the Qur'an's narrative multivocality and asynchronicity, Chraïbi's dramatic retelling moves temporally across centuries, as well as between narrative perspectives, historical contexts, and geographical locales.

In addition to foregrounding the intimate relationship between the Prophet Muhammad and the Qur'an, *L'Homme du Livre* is interspersed with references to reading, writing, and the *qalam*. The novel is bookended by accounts of the first revelation and closes with a lengthy description that moves in and out of the Prophet's consciousness:

> Forty years later, in a cave, a man died to himself. The wings of the past closed behind him like the last page of a familiar book that will never be read again. Somewhere, another Book had opened between the shadows and flickering light of reality. Pens had been set aside and the ink had dried since astral times. And it was said that the Book's last word was written even before the first was given expression in any language. Someone was turning the pages, moving from the last to the first, from "he" to "I," and the first word was written:
>
> "*READ.*"
>
> The word achieved the power of speech as soon as it was uttered. He said—he said in a voice so peaceful that it was terrifying:
>
> "*READ.*"
>
> Revelation was there, surging from the rock, and it was simple, so simple and pure beyond sense and reason. And, because it was there, Muhammad immediately gathered together all his past and future doubts and collected his disbelief like so many stones for the raising of an enduring wall that would stand between the earthbound man he had been since birth and the Man of the Book he was being summoned to become. (Chraïbi, *Muhammad* 88–89, translation modified)[3]

This passage is marked by a series of metaphorical bookends: past/future, reason/faith, writing/reading, text/orality, the first/last pages of the Book, the death/birth of the Prophet, as well as the intersubjective switch between he/I. Muhammad's transition from human to prophet, and earthbound to enlightened, is echoed in the materiality of revelation that comes not from the heavens above but, rather, from a humble rock. His transformation into a prophet is itself likened to an act of reading, in which a familiar book is replaced by the wonders of The Book. Straddling at once the past and the future, the suspended temporality of revelation has an almost eschatological overtone. Moreover, spiritual knowledge is inextricably bound to critical questioning—as the Prophet moves from disbelief, to doubt, faith, and eventually, embodied knowledge.

L'Homme du Livre is part of a broader literary tradition, which this book charts across twentieth-century Maghrebi literature, that engages with the Qur'an's formal, literary, and spiritual registers. In addition to its narrative, rhetorical, and hermeneutical qualities, these works invoke the Qur'an's extradiscursive dimensions of praxis and embodiment. The Qur'anic sura "Al-ʿalaq" is a critical intertext to this corpus, insofar as it places the pursuit of knowledge—particularly as embodied in the acts reading, writing, and interpretation—at the very heart of Muslim ethics. This study subsequently theorizes the Qur'an as a living literary archetype that shapes and is shaped by literature.

The Literary Qur'an

INTRODUCTION

The Qu'ran as (Inter)text: Embodiment, Praxis, Critique

وَلَوْ أَنَّمَا فِي الأَرْضِ مِن شَجَرَةٍ أَقْلَامٌ وَالْبَحْرُ يَمُدُّهُ مِن بَعْدِهِ
سَبْعَةُ أَبْحُرٍ مَّا نَفِدَتْ كَلِمَاتُ اللَّهِ إِنَّ اللَّهَ عَزِيزٌ حَكِيمٌ

> And if all the trees on earth were pens, and the sea [were ink], with seven [more] seas yet added to it, the words of God would not be exhausted: for, verily, God is almighty, wise.
>
> (QUR'AN 31:27 TRANS. ASAD)

Literary scholars have long noted Goethe's fascination with Islam and the influence of the Qur'an—which Goethe had access to in English (Sale), French (Du Ryer), and German (Arnold and Megerlin)—on his theories of literary creation, circulation, and translation.[1] He read and compared multiple translations of the Qur'an, even citing suras in his personal correspondences and diaries. Goethe's insights in *Divan* (1819) on poetic prophecy and the relationship between the worldly and the divine, as well as the literary and the theological, centered on the figure of the Prophet Muhammad—who was also the protagonist of his unfinished play *Mahomet*. He began working on the sympathetic portrayal of the Prophet while translating Voltaire's incendiary 1736 play *Le fanatisme, ou Mahomet le Prophète* (Fanaticism, or Mahomet the Prophet) into German.[2] In other words, Islam, and the Qur'an specifically, inspired Goethe's understanding of literary archetypes, systems, and relations within his theorization of *Weltliteratur*.[3]

Yet, the Qur'an has largely been absent from disciplinary debates in the field of world literature and has only recently garnered sustained critical attention.[4] This lacuna speaks to the broader oversight of Islam in Euro-American literary studies, as well as the canonization of particular models of secular reading—by which I mean the occlusion of religious epistemes, practices, and intertexts.[5] While scholars of world literature may only just be discovering "the Qur'an's fundamentally comparative nature," it has long served as a literary exemplar and intertext across a diverse range of literary traditions (Damrosch 4).[6] Interrogating the relationship between the Qur'an and narrative calls attention to the differential valuation of literary and critical reading practices. It compels us to critically reexamine not only conceptual binaries of the secular/religious but also questions of methodology (close/distant reading), genre (literature/theory), and discipline (area studies/comparative and world literature).

This study does not intend to advance a totalizing theory of the relationship between religion and literature; nor to mold the Qur'an's multivalent narrative traditions into a generalizable world literature methodology. *The Literary Qur'an: Narrative Ethics in the Maghreb* interrogates how the Qur'an—that is, its formal, narrative, and rhetorical qualities as a text, as well as its attendant embodied practices and hermeneutical strategies—enriches our understanding of literary sensibilities and practices in the context of the Maghreb. My use of the term "ethics" refers to Islam's intersecting moral and epistemological dimensions, in which the critical pursuit of knowledge is inseparable from the spiritual cultivation of the self. At once in dialogue with and against the grain of debates surrounding secularism, secular critique, and postsecularism, I read critique as intrinsic to the very practice of Islam as a philosophical, intellectual, and spiritual tradition.[7]

Redirecting our attention to the narrative possibilities embedded within and afforded by theological discourse, this study explores how the Qur'an models and invites *critical* modes of textual and embodied engagement. To that end, my reading of Islam bridges critical hermeneutics and hermeneutic phenomenology. The former speaks to a methodology of active critical interpretation that accounts for semiotic ambiguity and multivocality, while simultaneously attending to broader ideological concerns.[8] Meanwhile, hermeneutic phenomenology detranscendentalizes fixed notions of truth by moving from description to interpretation as an inherently phenomenological experience of the world, consciousness, and knowledge.

Foregrounding questions of form and praxis, *The Literary Qur'an*'s organizational logic echoes my reading of the Qur'an as a textual object and literary intertext. The book is structured around a series of pairings that invite paratactic readings across texts, languages, and literary canons. Each section highlights a conceptual node in the book's broader theorization of narrative ethics in Tunisia, Algeria, and Morocco—I: "Poetics of Piety"; II: "Ethics of Embodiment"; and III: "Genealogies of Transmission." Reflecting both critical methodology and argument, the pairing of canonical Francophone and lesser-known Arabophone novels (from the 1940s to 1980s) further confronts the disciplinary impasses of Maghrebi studies. Disrupting the geopolitical, philological, and ideological divisions that silo Arabophone and Francophone literatures, these pairings reveal the multilingual and polysemic nature of Maghrebi literature both across and within languages. This draws attention to Maghrebi studies' asymmetrical distribution of literary value across the false binary of "secular" Francophone and "religious" Arabophone literary traditions.

This book's comparative praxis is staged rather than explicated: paired works appear in autonomous side-by-side chapters, each of which is committed to the practice of close reading. This marks a methodological divergence from the largely antiformalist tendencies of world literature and postcolonial criticism, which tend to rely upon critical distance and world-systems or networked readings. My attentiveness to form, however, is not intended to obscure the multitudinous forces and actors that shape Maghrebi cultural formations. By including the Francophone canon and focusing on the novel, this study confronts the ideological biases that have shaped the Maghreb as an epistemic object. The genres of poetry or the short story would be more obvious choices were I concerned simply with questions of cultural autochthony. The novel lends itself to comparative analysis with the Qur'an, insofar as both operate at the scale of narrative totality and world-building while also fostering close textual readings.

My close readings across this book call attention to literature as a site in which the process of entextualization occludes ethical practices. To read ethics back into literature, I argue, one must attend to narrative, citational, and hermeneutical practices that have largely been disciplined out of Euro-American literary studies and canon formation. My analysis builds upon a vast body of Islamic scholarship that blends together literary and theological methodologies, conceptual vocabularies, and reading practices. In their intertextuality with the Qur'an and Islamic philosophy, the novels in this study disrupt the bifurcation of secular and religious discourses. Their intertextuality relies upon an understanding of the fundamental *literariness* of the Qur'an, and inversely, the ethical imperative of literature more broadly. These works are not simply citing from a fixed corpus or heteronomous tradition; rather, I argue that they work dialogically with the development of Islam's polyvalent textual practices. Returning to my discussion of the sura "Al-ʿalaq" in the Preface, the Qur'an's narrativity encompasses a range of aesthetic and ethical practices that mobilize the faculties of the mind and the body. This includes the Qur'an's formal qualities (linguistic register, code-switching, polyphony) as well as hermeneutical and embodied practices (memorization, recitation, transcription, citation) associated with scripture as a model for spiritual life.

The Literary Qur'an challenges the prominence of postcolonial approaches to the study of the Maghreb by examining how its writers at once theorize and cultivate forms of cultural capital that move beyond the binary of "cultural authenticity" and "colonial mimicry." There is a tendency to treat "theory and method . . . as naturally metropolitan, modern, and Western," whereas formerly colonized states are interpellated through "the idiom of cases, events, examples, and test sites in relation to this stable location for the production or revision of theory" (Appadurai, "Grassroots Globalization and the Research Imagination" 4). This book is part of a broader critical effort to *theorize from below*—namely, to decentralize Euro-American historical frameworks, periodizations, and critical methodologies mobilized in the study of non-Western cultural practices and forms. This informs my own close reading practices, in addition to the book's theoretical scaffolding—which extracts a model of narratology and poiesis from the Qurʾan.

The critical framework of narrative ethics brings together and expands upon the concepts of *adab*, *ijtihād*, and poiesis. Before the term was secularized in its codification as "literature" during the late nineteenth century, *adab* signaled the genre of belles lettres, as well as the moral dimensions of personal and social conduct. Meanwhile, *ijtihād* refers to the practice of individual "reasoning independent of precedent" within Islamic jurisprudence and Muslim spiritual life more broadly (Haj 9). Poiesis, or *shāʿiriyya/shiʿiriyya*, alongside the concept of *ibdāʿ* (creation, innovation, or creativity), speak to the artistic drive as an ethical act of creation—one that I read as intimately tied to Muslim subject formation.

The lens of *adab* brings questions of pedagogy, embodiment, and ethics into dialogue with theorizations of literature, literariness, and critical reading. Islamic pedagogy—at both madrasas (Qurʾanic schools) and institutions of higher education that specialize in Islamic studies, such as al-Zaytūna (Tunisia), al-Qarawiyyin (Morocco), and the Ben Bādīs Institute (Algeria)—is crucial to understanding the influence of the Qurʾan on the literary figures in this book. These institutions were foundational to the intellectual formation of Maḥmūd al-Masʿadī, Abdelwahab Meddeb, al-Ṭāhir Waṭṭār, Assia Djebar, Driss Chraïbi, and Muḥammad Barrāda. From the study of the Qurʾan, hadith, *tafsīr* (exegesis), to the fields of Islamic philosophy, jurisprudence, and history, these courses of study generated a shared vocabulary and intellectual archive within a particular model of Islamic education and edification. In the context of this study, Islam represents a multivalent set of beliefs and habits that are inextricably linked to social and cultural practices. The works examined in this book reflect diverse interpretations and articulations of Islam and therefore do not subscribe to a singular political project or ideological orientation.

In what follows, I begin by outlining the history of the Maghreb as it pertains to the methodological orientation of Maghrebi studies, particularly around the bifurcation of Francophone and Arabophone literatures. Arguing for the multilingual accenting of Maghrebi literature both within and across languages, I connect the lack of critical attention to Qurʾanic intertextuality to the privileging of Francophone works. Turning to the question of secular criticism, I expound my mobilization of the term "critique" in relation to the Qurʾan. I engage scholarship in the anthropology of Islam in order to parse out the ways in which the term "secular" is often deeply inflected by its own orthodoxies. I then consider how the secularization narrative has impacted the study of literary forms and practices, especially the genre of the novel. I propose that the concept of *adab* provides a valuable corrective, by offering a more generative and inclusive model of literature. I subsequently bring in both historical and current debates within Qurʾanic studies on the narrative, stylistic, and literary dimensions of the Qurʾan. From Qurʾanic aesthetics I turn to how Qurʾanic hermeneutics and Sufi poetics can be mobilized in literary criticism. Theorizing the Qurʾan as a literary object, process, and model, I argue, introduces ethical ways of approaching questions of writing, reading, and literary hermeneutics.

Imagining the Maghreb

In his 1983 work *Maghreb pluriel*, Moroccan novelist and literary critic Abdelkébir Khatibi (1938–2009) theorizes "the Maghreb as a horizon of thought" (*le Maghreb comme horizon de pensée*), arguing that it "self-globalizes" because of its ethnolinguistic diversity and geopolitical location on the threshold of Europe, Africa, and the Middle East (38–39).[9] Beyond problematizing West-(Arab) East trajectories of cultural modernity, intellectuals like Khatibi have long theorized the Maghreb as a linguistically unstable site.[10] Maghrebi literature for them is not only multilingual but is polysemically accented within any given language.[11] Both Arabophone and Francophone Maghrebi literatures disrupt essentialist narratives of decolonization in which Arabic signifies the language of origin and return. In fact, much of twentieth-century Maghrebi literature problematizes the relationship between Arab ethnic identity, the Arabic language, and Islam. Some writers in this study, such as Assia Djebar, have even framed the Maghreb's Arabization and Islamicization as a colonial project akin to Ottoman, Spanish, and French imperialism. Others, like Abdelwahab Meddeb and Driss Chraïbi, uncouple Islam from the Arabic language in order to disrupt their imbricated codification within postindependence nationalist discourse.

The Maghreb is a particularly rich site for exploring the Qur'an and literature, insofar as its fiction denaturalizes Arabic as the privileged currency of both Arab cultural capital and Islam. This is particularly the case with Francophone Maghrebi literature in which the Qur'an functions as both a literary intertext and a textual object mediated through its circulation in translation. The obfuscation of Qur'anic intertexts in critical literature on the Maghreb can be read in relation to the region's complex colonial histories and their impact on cultural, linguistic, and literary practices, as well as the periodization of Arab cultural modernity within narratives of the *nahḍa*, or Arab cultural awakening.

The Maghreb is a geopolitical as well as an imagined space, the contours of which have been defined by a series of interconnected historiographical, ideological, and colonial narratives.[12] Both etymologically and geopolitically, the Maghreb (from *gh-r-b*, or "to set") is structurally interdependent with the Mashriq (from *sh-r-q*, or "to rise"), used to designate the countries east of Egypt. The term began circulating with the spread of Islam around the seventh century, when it was mobilized to indicate the westernmost territories that were subject to the expansion of the Arab-Islamic empire. It acquired another connotative layer in its adoption by French imperialist discourse to indicate their territories in the region: Algeria as a settler colony (1830–1962), Tunisia as a protectorate (1881–1956), and Morocco as a protectorate (1912–1956). Unlike the anachronism "Indochine," however, "the Maghreb" is a term still in active circulation, in both Arabic and French, across academic as well as civil society contexts. As such, it brings to the fore the complex relationship between the Maghreb as the final frontier for the Islamization as well as Arabization of the region, and as a repository for the French imperial imagination.

While in its transnational circulation the term "Maghreb" encompasses Tunisia, Algeria, and Morocco, it has a broader signification in the Arab/ic context, where it can include Libya and Mauritania. The Arab Maghreb Union (Ittiḥād al-Maghrib al-ʿArabī), for example, was ratified by Algeria, Libya, Morocco, Tunisia, and Mauritania in 1989. Created as a forum for postindependence economic and political cooperation, the union was centered around pan-Arab identity—suggesting a very different mode of transnational affiliation than the (post)colonial Francophone Maghreb.[13] This study follows the French-accented "Maghreb" in order to historicize and trouble its relationship to Islamicization, French imperialism, and decolonization. That said, I am sensitive to the ways in which these discrepant investments are replicated in the critical biases of Maghrebi studies scholarship. As the structure of this book—pairing canonical Francophone novels with lesser-known Arabophone ones—reflects both method and argument, my use of the term "Maghreb" is delimited by the very politics of canon formation.

The French colonial civilizing mission (*mission civilisatrice*) entailed a drastic reconfiguration of the social, cultural, and economic constitution of Algeria, Morocco, and Tunisia. Practices such as the enforcement of the French language in education, government, and public-sector spheres irrevocably impacted cultural production in the region. This influenced the language politics of Arabic and indigenous Berberophone languages under French occupation, as well as in the aftermath of independence.[14] The "language question," as it came to be known, was propelled by colonial efforts to control the region, in addition to postindependence attempts to unify the Maghreb under the signifiers Arab and Muslim.

The cultural Arabization of the Maghreb occurred in concert with its Islamicization—both during the expansion of Islam and as part of the consolidation of national identity upon independence. Moreover, French colonial policies differentially racialized and governed indigenous Berberophone populations, Arab Jews, and Arab Muslims. The dichotomy between Arab Muslims and Kabyles/Berbers, for example, was manipulated by the colonial state to insidious political ends in what is referred to as *le mythe Kabyle*. Historian James McDougall notes that "an elaborate system of oppositions was contrived between 'Arabs' and 'Kabyles,' with the former generally denigrated as civilizationally unimprovable, the latter as 'closer to Europe' in race, culture, and temperament" ("Myth and Counter-Myth" 67).[15] These narratives not only informed divisive colonial policies and subsequent nationalist persuasions, but they further influenced how questions of religion, ethnic identity, and language shaped Maghrebi cultural practices.[16]

Crucially, French colonial policies separated the Islamic courts and legal systems from state institutions in ways that essentially privatized religious practices. Subsequent postindependence legal reforms—such as the largely Sunni Mālikī *mudawwana* personal status code ratified in Morocco in 1956—merged precolonial models of jurisprudence with nationalist agendas, often overwriting colonial policies of legal pluralism. French legal codes, for example, accounted for Berber customary law under the 1930 Berber *dahir*, or decree (*ẓahīr* in Arabic), an act perceived by many as an attempt to undermine the legal power of sharīʿa.[17] France's control over the status and power of religion across its empire, particularly through "the simultaneous isomorphism of race and religion in the figure of the Muslim," sheds light on the divisive question of *laïcité*, or French secularity, in metropole France (Fernando 18).[18] The unholy marriage of "racialization and secularization" in the figure of the unassimilable Muslim exposes *laïcité* as a political project that expands upon and extends colonial policies and practices (ibid.). It subsequently lays bare the entanglement of religion, culture, and politics within French (post)colonial ideology, which sought to "to secularize Islam by turning it into religion, distinct from culture and politics" (ibid. 22).

In addition to contextualizing some of the complexities of Maghrebi cultural practices, these histories inform the academic inclinations that have shaped Maghrebi studies. The Maghreb does not sit comfortably within the organizational logics that govern scholarship on Arab, African, and Muslim populations. Critical studies on the Maghreb rose to prominence in the US academy during the mid-1990s to early 2000s, facilitated in large part by the flourishing of Francophone studies and its associated academic press imprints, alongside the increased translation and publication of Francophone fiction into English.[19] Maghrebi studies has largely remained under the disciplinary auspices of French and Francophone studies departments, with limited attention devoted to the region's Arabophone traditions. By virtue of its disciplinary conscription within Francophone studies, Maghrebi literature has historically been examined through a postcolonial framework. It is more likely to be geopolitically linked to sub-Saharan Africa rather than the Middle East and North Africa—exposing the privileging of the French language and culture as a metric of cultural modernity. This further divorces Maghrebi literature from the heterogeneity of Arab/ic and Muslim cultural histories and narrative practices.

On the other hand, canonical narratives of Arab/ic cultural production either document the unidirectional flow of cultural capital from colonial metropoles, or they privilege the countries of the Mashriq—as in the adage "Cairo writes, Beirut publishes, and Baghdad reads." The omission of the Maghreb speaks to the canonization of literary practices and reading publics along normative ethnonational and linguistic demarcations. These biases replicate broader problematics within Arab/ic literary studies in the United States and Europe. The dominant periodization of Arabic literature traces a

Eurocentric developmental arc that begins with the pre- and early-Islamic periods, followed by the four-century-long Golden Age (al-ʿaṣr al-dhahabī), the Age of Decline/Decadence (ʿaṣr al-inḥiṭāṭ)—which coincides with the "Arab Middle Ages" and encompasses the fall of the Abbasid dynasty, the Mongol invasion, the Crusades, the rise of the Mamluk dynasty, and much of the Ottoman Empire—concluding with the *nahḍa*, or "Arab renaissance," which is itself bookended by Napoleon's invasion of Egypt in 1798 and the close of World War I. This epochal timeline clearly credits European (colonial) modernity with the resuscitation of Arab literary, cultural, and scientific production. Heralded as the peak of Arab cultural modernity, accounts of the *nahḍa* are frequently inflected by orientalist and colonial rhetoric that rely upon dichotomies of the religious/secular and traditional/modern.[20] It is no coincidence that this period also corresponds with the flourishing of the Arabic novel—read, on the one hand, as a European (colonial) cultural import, and on the other, as the exemplar modern secular genre.

My focus on the Qur'an confronts the secularizing and Eurocentric tendencies of Maghrebi studies. The field's simultaneous delimitation along linguistic and regional lines has resulted in the hypertrophy of Francophone criticism on the one hand, and the atrophy of Arabophone criticism on the other. The relative paucity of scholarship on indigenous Berberophone cultural production further underscores the divisiveness of French colonial policies, as well as their indelible imprint on subsequent academic practices and the canons they engender. It is striking how few studies of Maghrebi literature employ a comparative framework that seriously addresses both Arabophone and Francophone texts. Rather than trying to fill an empirical lacuna, this book troubles authoritative narratives about the meetings between East and West, and Islam and post-Enlightenment secular Europe that underpin the study of Maghrebi cultural production.

Desecularizing Critique

Literary scholars, philosophers, anthropologists, and political theorists have long grappled with the association of critique with secularism, tracing intellectual genealogies through Diderot, Kant, Hume, Hegel, Mill, Marx, and Foucault.[21] Many attribute secularism's conflation with antireligious thought to Enlightenment rhetoric that privileged reason, rational knowledge, and scientific truth as the torchbearers of modernity. This logic pits the secular real against specious religious opinion, faith, or belief in the divine (read: unreal). If the secular is fundamentally skeptical, religion, or so the argument goes, is inherently speculative.

In the context of literary studies, much of the debate surrounding these questions has centered on Edward Said's notoriously slippery concept of secular criticism in *The World, the Text, and the Critic.*[22] Without explicitly defining the terms "secular" and "criticism," he theorizes a practice of literary criticism at once distant and situated, whose "political, moral, and social judgements" expose the chasm between "culture and system" (26). Describing criticism as profoundly *oppositional,* Said writes that it is

> reducible neither to a doctrine nor to a political position on a particular question, and if it is to be in the world and self-aware simultaneously, then its identity is its difference from other cultural activities and from systems of thought or of method. In its suspicion of totalizing concepts, in its discontent with reified objects, in its impatience with guilds, special interests, imperialized fiefdoms, and orthodox habits of mind, criticism is most itself, and if the paradox can be tolerated, most unlike itself at the moment it starts turning into organized dogma. . . . [C]riticism must think of itself as life-enhancing and constitutively opposed to every form of tyranny, domination, and abuse; its social goals are noncoercive knowledge produced in the interests of human freedom. (29)

While the word "religion" is largely absent from much of the essay on secular criticism, the use of the charged terms "orthodox" and "dogma" imply a fraught relationship between secularism and religion.[23]

In "Religious Criticism," the brief concluding essay to the volume, Said notes that religious discourse "serves as an agent of closure, shutting off human investigation, criticism, and effort in deference to the authority of the more-than-human, the supernatural, the other-worldly" (290). Religion, Said avers, "furnishes us with systems of authority and with canons of order whose regular effect is either to compel subservience or to gain adherents" (ibid.).[24] Read with the essay on secular criticism, the conclusion appears to inflect secularism with an antireligious tone. However, Said maintains a semantic and conceptual ambiguity, insofar as he tells us *what religion does* rather than *what religion is.* In this sense, the diverse critical readings of Saidian secular criticism are particularly informative.[25]

Bruce Robbins argues that "perhaps the most crucial meaning of *secular,* in his usage, is as an opposing term not to religion but to nationalism" (26). Wendy Brown similarly operates from the starting point of "secularism as an instrument of empire" (n.p). Aamir Mufti, on the other hand, highlights the centrality of "minority culture and existence" to the Saidian concept (96). Meanwhile, Stathis Gourgouris notes, "Its most important dimension is not battling religion per se but dismantling theological politics of sovereignty in favor of radical conditions for social autonomy" (*Lessons in Secular Criticism*, jacket). He calls for "de-transcendentalizing the secular," suggesting that the true labor of secular criticism is the dialectical critique of both secularism and antisecularism ("Detranscendentalizing" 439). If, as these scholars propose, secular criticism opposes nationalism, imperialism, hegemony, and sovereignty, then its theological accenting suggests a very different understanding of religion—and specifically its ideological or political instrumentalization—from this book's reading of Islam.

Theorizing the Qur'an as a literary intertext, I argue that it functions as an ethical mode/l of knowledge production that fosters critical reading practices. By not treating belief and critique as mutually exclusive practices, I avoid the binary logics that oppose freedom and coercion, or heterodoxy and orthodoxy. Such dualities run the risk of modeling agentival activity along a progressive political formulation in which "the normative political subject . . . remains a liberatory one, whose agency is conceptualized on the binary model of subordination and subversion" (Mahmood, *Politics of Piety* 14). Returning to Said's definition of criticism as "noncoercive knowledge produced in the interests of human freedom," this study's formulation of Islam shifts emphasis to the critical pursuit of (spiritual) knowledge as an ethical praxis.

My use of ethics is informed by studies on the anthropology of Islam that argue against the distinction between ethics and morality as reflecting private and public modes of conduct respectively. This model, based in Aristotelian ethics and reiterated across Foucault's oeuvre, suggests that ethics operates outside of the realm of social or political agency. As Talal Asad aptly observes, the relegation of religion to the private sphere is a fairly modern phenomenon that is largely rooted in the Protestant tradition. He reads the universalization and privatization of a series of beliefs, practices, and discourses under the transcendental category of "religion" as a by-product of the modern formulation of secular power.[26] Religion as such is "conceptually and practically tied to the emergence of 'the secular' as a domain from which it is supposed to be normatively independent but to which it is indelibly linked" (Mahmood, "Ethics and Piety" 225). In other words, religion is defined and delimited by the secular state apparatus and not the other way around. Hussein Agrama describes this as the *active principle of secularism*, whereby the state is "promoting an abstract notion of 'religion,' defining the spaces it should inhabit, authorizing the sensibilities proper to it, and then working to discipline actual religious traditions so as to conform to this abstract notion, to fit into those spaces, and to express those sensibilities" (503).

Expanding upon Asad's delinking of religion from the framework of belief in an a priori theological ontology, Mahmood theorizes the ethical dimensions of spiritual praxis as a series of embodied acts. More than a phenomenology of religion, Asad and Mahmood break from the bifurcation of mind and body within theorizations of piety, in order to consider their coconstitutive dynamic. Mahmood frames agency as an *ethical formation* in which ethics is intrinsic to the constitution of the self. It is "a product of the historically contingent discursive traditions in which [these subjects…] are located," but not categorically delimited by these conditions (Mahmood, *Politics of Piety* 32). She thus uncouples "the notion of agency from the goals of progressive politics" in favor of a model in which "agentival capacity is entailed not only in those acts that resist norms but also in the multiple ways in which one *inhabits* norms" (14–15).

Within the context of Muslim subjectivity, Mahmood's reading of agency beyond the binaries of suppression and subversion, or reiteration and resignification, calls attention to the ethical potentiality of iterative acts. Mayanthi Fernando similarly argues that the "framework of religion as culture cannot conceptualize Islam as an authoritative system of norms that engenders deep ethical and moral commitments on the part of the practitioner" (16). In this study, the iterability of the Qur'an serves both a discursive and an ethical function. On the one hand, it is a literary intertext and mode/l of hermeneutic analysis. On the other, in order to fully engage with the Qur'an—as both a practitioner and reader—it must be inhabited, embodied, and performed. Bearing in mind the Maghreb's fraught relationship to Islamicization, Qur'anic intertextuality illustrates the ways in which agency as an ethical formation entails the simultaneous inhabiting of and resistance to norms.

Mahmood's and Asad's critical interventions provide a valuable corrective to the influence of the secularization narrative on contemporary literary criticism. The privileging of secularism as the engine of cultural modernity is deeply embedded within taxonomies of narrative practices and forms, particularly the novel. Susanna Lee's study on narrative and secularism defines secularism as "a narrative structure, even a narrative strategy" reliant upon "the idea of the absence of a supreme structuring power" (13, 12). This relationship, she posits, is intrinsic to the epistemic construction of modernity and the power relations that reside therein. The coconstitutional reading of modernity and secularism challenges "The notion of a God who controls the entire world, who inscribes all people and all moments in a narrative of divine providence or of divine punishment and reward" (12). In this formulation, religion functions as a narrative ontology that structures human existence while simultaneously foreclosing critical forms of agency. It is worth noting that there is an ironic structural symmetry in the displacement of theological logocentrism in the name of a monolithic conception of modernity. By problematizing the relationship between secularism and critique, the framework of narrative ethics extricates literary forms and practices from a liberatory model of secular modernity.

A World Abandoned by God

The secularization of literature, and of the novel in particular, is predicated on a teleological understanding of cultural modernity that marries linear historical progress with the evolution of literary forms. Problematizing the novel as the penultimate genre of literary modernity, however, serves another crucial function. It calls attention to the fraught relationship between modernity, orientalism, and capitalist imperialism—or what Arjun Appadurai dubs the "hegemony of Euro-chronology" (3).[27] It is no coincidence that a generation of social and cultural theorists, including many from the Frankfurt school, were heavily influenced by the classical Weberian modernization thesis. Weber's sociology of religion posits that modern capitalist society emerged from a disenchantment with religious discourse and institutions. On the one hand, proponents of the thesis fail to account for "the concrete ways in which European and American forms of secularity are indigenized in particular times and places around the globe, as well as to the ways 'Western' secularity was shaped by Latin Christendom's colonial and postcolonial encounters with religious difference" (Neuman 16). On the other hand, postcolonial criticism has often overcorrected in its undervaluation of critical practices that take seriously questions of religion and piety.

Imagining cultural practices beyond a singular emancipatory political project brings to the fore a host of critical modes, ethical imperatives, and subjectivities easily obscured by postcolonial studies approaches. As Timothy Mitchell reminds us: "Modernity, like capitalism, is defined by its claim to universality, to a uniqueness, unity, and universality that represent the end (in every sense) of history. Yet this always remains an impossible unity, an incomplete universal" (24). This is precisely why the language of alternative modernities only serves "to revise the narrative of the West and to provide an alternative history of origins and influences" that remains predicated on the spatial logic of center and periphery (ibid.). Mitchell's framing of modernity as a historiographic and discursive *staging* rather than a *stage* is helpful for thinking through the developmentalist periodization of literary forms. Frequently read through the lens of belated modernity, the Arab/ic novel is often treated as an adaptation of the European genre—whereby a "universal" literary form is imbued with "local" content.

Theorizations of the novel across Euro-American literary criticism and continental philosophy largely conceive of it as a modern and inherently secular genre. In the oft-cited words of the Marxist literary critic Georg (György) Lukács, "The novel is the epic of a world that has been abandoned by God" (88). On the one hand, this formulation speaks to a post-Enlightenment moment in which religious ideology had waned within social, cultural, and political spheres of life. On the other, the novel, for Lukács, embodies an antitheological ontology. It seeks to answer the existential concerns of its age, namely a loss of faith in ideological totalities—religious or otherwise. And yet, the novel itself is an attempt at narrative totality, albeit an inherently heteroglossic and polyphonic one, as Mikhail Bakhtin reminds us. These centripetal and centrifugal forces create a productive tension in which totality is at once harnessed and unsettled.

Within canonical periodizations of the genre, the postmodern novel builds upon its modernist predecessor's debunking of universalist truth. By collapsing master narratives, these works are said to resist the totalizing aspects of narrative world-building afforded by the genre. These antifoundationalist tendencies fuel the conflation of the novel with a distinctly secular project. Describing the secular nature of the postmodernist novel, Roland Barthes writes: "In the multiplicity of writing, everything is to be *disentangled*, nothing *deciphered*; the structure can be followed . . . but there is nothing beneath. . . . [B]y refusing to assign a 'secret,' an ultimate meaning, to the text (and to the world as text), [literature] liberates what may be called an anti-theological activity, an activity that is truly revolutionary since to refuse to fix meaning is, in the end, to refuse God and his hypostases—reason, science, law" (147). Barthes, alongside a number of poststructuralists and deconstructionists, views the codification of the word of God as antithetical to radical critical thought. As with Lukács, the novel here is metonymic of a world/ly cosmology in which meaning is unstable, rhizomatic, and polyphonic. Barthes's Nietzschean treatise on the death of the "Author-God" posits that the author/god denotes foreclosure and the imposition of "a final signified" (ibid.). To kill the author is therefore to unshackle the significatory potential of a text. This liberatory rhetoric presupposes a model of reading in which the presence of an author-figure (secular or divine) restricts the interpretive possibilities of a text.

According to many Qur'anic scholars and Islamic philosophers, Islam invites nonheteronomous modes of critically reading scripture. The concept of *ijtihād* references individual reasoning independent of precedent; it is contrasted with *taqlīd*, or imitative reliance on legal precedent. Within Sunni Islamic jurisprudence, *ijtihād* is generally applied to a jurist's ability to deduce religious truths by employing their own intellect and training in *fiqh* (jurisprudence), scripture, as well as the Arabic language—rendering them a *mujtahid*. Islamic reformers, such as Jamāl al-Dīn al-Afghānī (1838–1897), mobilized the concept to account for the critical faculties of individual spiritual praxis, as well as to keep apace with social changes.

The authors featured in this book, alongside their interlocutors across Islamic thought, invoke the concept of *ijtihād* in their critical engagements with the Qur'an. Their literary works, as well as my own close readings, resist the enshrinement of narrative texts within revelatory hermeneutical frameworks. Rather, writing and reading function as meditative, reflective, and embodied acts. This model of narrative ethics frames literary and scriptural texts as formally multivocal and hermeneutically open. These imbricated registers invite reading practices that rely upon phenomenological experience, contextualization, close reading, and the critical faculties of the individual. This renders legible a complex nexus of moral, spiritual, and intellectual concerns at the heart of my reading of Islam—namely, as an intrinsically critical practice that cultivates ethical modes of subjectivity in the pursuit of knowledge.

Undisciplining Literature

One of the major figures signaling the intersection of the Qur'an and literature is the theologian Abū Ḥāmid al-Ghazālī (1058–1111), who is referenced across the literary works in this book. His interdisciplinary approach to Islamic philosophy and Qur'anic exegesis, coupled with his poetic narrative style, inspired theologians and literary scholars alike. Framing his poetics through the Aristotelian concept of poiesis (*shāʿiriyya*), Islamic scholar Ebrahim Moosa writes that he "employed the very materials used by his predecessors, such as verses of the Qur'ān; prophetic report (*aḥādīth*); philosophical, legal, and theological discourses; and the narratives of mystics . . . so that they constituted an organic unity. Not only was the whole of the new narrative very different from the sum of its parts, but the narrative also transformed the whole" (38). Like the authors in this study, al-Ghazālī paid homage to the Arab-Islamic heritage, or *turāth*, while simultaneously transforming it through its very recontextualization.

Transcending the rehashed debates surrounding *aṣāla* (cultural authenticity) and *taqlīd* (imitation), these writers reorient the very temporality of cultural innovation. This antiteleological understanding of historical time, what Moosa refers to as "heterotemporality," undergirds not only the work of al-Ghazālī but many other Muslim thinkers cited in these novels—such as Ibn Khaldūn (1332–1406), Ibn ʿArabī (1165–1240), and Manṣūr al-Ḥallāj (858–922) (39). This temporal manipulation is further reflected in the formal construction of all six novels, in which the narratives are extratemporal (al-Masʿadī), eschatological (Meddeb, Waṭṭār), palimpsestic (Djebar), proleptic (Chraïbi), or asynchronous (Barrāda).

Syrian poet and critic Adonis (b. Ali Ahmad Said Esber) addresses these concerns in his Janus-faced theory of modernity, which he argues exists recursively "both of time and outside of time" (*An Introduction to Arab Poetics* 99). Troubling progressivist notions of linear historical time, he reimagines the very chronotopic nature of aesthetic representation:[28]

> Modernity . . . [is] of time because it is rooted in the movement of history, in the creativity of humanity, coexisting with man's striving to go beyond the limitations which surround him; and outside time because it is a vision which includes in it all times and cannot only be recorded as a chronological event: it cuts vertically through time and its horizontal progress is no more than the surface representations of a deep internal movement. In other words, modernity is not only a process that affects language; it is synonymous with its very existence. (99–100)

Poiesis, in this context, entails the process of narrative creation rather than the body of work it engenders. Twentieth-century Maghrebi intellectuals generally framed their literary projects through the lenses of *ibdāʿ* (creation), *tajrīb* (experimentation), *tajdīd* (renewal), or *taṭawwur* (development/evolution)—terms themselves originating in Qurʾanic exegesis.[29] While these concepts address literary innovation, they do so within a notably different register than the categories of the avant-garde or postmodern. The future temporality of the avant-garde and postmodern suggests a disavowal of historical precedent that emerges from their mutual reliance upon periodization and generic taxonomies. With the concepts of *ibdāʿ*, *tajrīb*, *tajdīd*, and *taṭawwur*, however, the artistic process entails simultaneous creation and re-creation: reimaginations of the Arab-Islamic heritage work dialogically with cultural innovation. This productive tension derives from the unique ways in which literature and literariness have been conceived at once diachronically and synchronically through the concept of *adab*.

While the term *adab* first appeared in Arabic print around the eighth century, it did not become a subject of orientalist fascination until the 1940s, when the Italian scholar Carlo-Alfonso Nallino gave a lecture on the subject at Cairo University. Before *adab* was codified as the literary genre of belles lettres, it encompassed a broad range of genres and textual practices, in addition to carrying the valence of moral and intellectual refinement. Distinct from other fields within Arab and Islamic thought—such as *fiqh* (jurisprudence), *ʿilm* (knowledge; science), *tārīkh* (history), *falsafa* (philosophy), *manṭiq* (logic), *naqd* (criticism), *balāgha* (rhetoric), *ʿilm al-lugha* (lexicography; linguistics; philology), *ʿarūḍ* (prosody), and *al-bayān* (eloquence)—*adab* nonetheless overlaps with many of the methodologies from these disciplines.[30] It also includes poetry and prose, works about *adab*, historiography and geography, as well as some encyclopedias and biographies. Derivative fields include the formalist precursor *ʿilm al-adab* (the science of *adab*), often attributed to the fourteenth-century polymath Ibn Khaldūn, and *tārīkh al-adab* (the history of *adab*).

Due to its ideational ambiguity, *adab* resists conceptual or semantic codification. This polysemy is foundational to its history and application across Arab/ic and Muslim intellectual traditions. The etymology of the term is itself disputed; some philologists and historians argue that *adab* derives from the plural *ādāb*, which comes from *daʾb*, meaning "custom" or "habit." Others still posit that *adab* comes directly from *ʾdb*, meaning "marvelous thing" or "invitation" (generally to a meal). According to *Almawrid*, the term signifies (1) hospitality, entertainment, hosting, or giving a banquet; (2) manners, etiquette, breeding, civility, decorum, or propriety; (3) culture or cultural refinement; (4) to educate, to cultivate, or to culture; (5) literature, letters, or belles lettres; and (6) ethics, morals, decency, or standards of behavior (64). *Hans Wehr* similarly defines an *adīb* as "cultured, refined, educated; well-bred, well-mannered, civil, urbane; a man of cultured and refined tastes; man of letters, writer, author" (9–10). Across these various definitions, the concepts of ethics and aesthetics are often in dialectical relationship with one another.

Adab carries a valence of both interdisciplinarity and intersubjectivity: it covers the moral and intellectual qualities of the *adīb*, the corpus of and about *adab*, in addition to the readers' engagements with this body of work and its community of producers as well as fellow readers. As a pedagogical tradition, *adab* frames cultural creation and education as a collective process that moves across mediums, individuals, and historical times. Islamic intellectual historian Nadia al-Baghdadi notes the multiple possible translations of the term: "It is rendered most closely as 'educational literature,' 'etiquette,' '*Bildung*,' or '*paideia*'; others would go for '*humanitas*'" (439). While they cannot fully capture *adab*'s polysemy, *Bildung*, *paideia*, and *humanitas* do account for its interwoven pedagogical and moral dimensions—particularly as a practice directed at the cultural edification of a community around shared values.

Ira Lapidus argues that *adab* is a pivotal concept in Islam for articulating "the relationship between knowledge and action—to the inward flux of intellect, judgement, and emotion in relation to outward expression in speech, gesture, ritual, and action—as the key to the very nature of man's being and his relationship to God" (40).[31] Bridging inward comportment with outward behavior, *adab* stretches across aesthetic, spiritual, and existential registers: "Implicit in the study of *adab* are not only issues about literature and the role of literature in moral, religious, and social life, but also fundamental Muslim ideas about how life is to be lived to fulfill the religious goals of human existence" (ibid.).

Covering a broad range of disciplines and fields, *udabā'* (plural for *adīb*) were held to high aesthetic and ethical standards. *Adab* reflected both the intellectual labor of the *adīb*, as well as their erudition and moral standing. It further echoed the social and intellectual community surrounding the production of works of and about *adab*. Put otherwise, "*Adab* and the role of *adīb* came to represent both process and product: the process of contributing to the corpus of materials that would maintain and enhance the status of *adab* and the aesthetic norms of its practitioner, and the products of the education, diversion, and somewhat precious self-fulfillment that the corpus provided" (Allen 238). Across much of its history, *adab* entailed literary emulation of the elevated register of Qur'anic Arabic and was linked to a literate elite. As access to education and literature gradually extended beyond the royal court and religious intelligentsia, works of *adab* began to serve a broader reading public.

The distinction between form and content was a literary heuristic many orientalist scholars imposed onto *adab*. While some, such as Gustave E. von Grunebaum, "stressed that *adab* was a principle of form and not an 'array of materials,'" others argued for the importance of content, alongside such concerns as style, tone, and intention (Malti-Douglas 10). Ilse Lichtenstädter, for example, claimed that despite its formal and thematic diversity, *adab* was united by the common purpose "of bringing knowledge to the people in an entertaining fashion" (Lichtenstädter qtd. ibid. 9–10). Attempts to disentangle form, content, style, and authorial intent suggest a fundamental misreading of *adab* within orientalist scholarship.

In a frequently cited entry in the *Cambridge Encyclopedia of Arabic Literature*, S. A Bonebakker offers a reading of the early usage of *adab* that addresses some of these tensions. He writes that it "may refer either to literary creativity, or else to literature as an object of philological study or to knowledge of literature as a mark of erudition. However, these two senses, with their respectively active and passive connotations, are not always clearly distinguished" (Bonebakker 19–20). *Adab* challenges hierarchies of objects, subjects, and acts within literary epistemologies, long before the critical interventions of formalism, structuralism, poststructuralism, and deconstruction. It enriches the concept of narrative ethics precisely because of this ambiguity between creative acts, agents, and works. *Adab* thus opens the door to interdisciplinary and comparative modes of analysis for the study of cultural materials that cut across literary and theological discourses.

The concept of *adab* offers an alternative genealogy for understanding literary practices, tastes, and forms. In so doing, it troubles the seeming universality, across both historical time and geography, of the category of "literature." Historicizing *adab's* conscription within literary rather than religious institutions of higher learning in fin-de-siècle Egypt, Michael Allan exposes the institutional forces—from universities to printing presses—behind its generic transformation.[32] The dismissal of *adab*'s ethical and embodied dimensions disavows other modes of literacy, reading practices, or textual forms. As Allan demonstrates, contemporary discourses of world and comparative literature can similarly codify ways of reading tied to the universalization of secular modes of knowledge production and subject formation. Reframing literary reading as a nexus of embodied practices, habits, and sensibilities directs us away from generic understandings of literature as a mere taxonomy of texts. This allows us "to consider how secular criticism defines religion as seemingly inimical to critical analysis" and to "begin to ask how secularism frames investments in particular definitions of what constitutes literary reading and sanctions ignorance about modes of textuality, dissent, and discussion within traditions deemed religious" (Allan, *In the Shadow of World Literature* 137). As a literary (ur)text, the Qur'an introduces a unique set of formal and aesthetics concerns, not to mention directives on how to read. In the sections that follow, I examine these in order to consider how the Qur'an can be mobilized in literary analysis.

Qur'anic Aesthetics

Due to the overlapping qualities of knowledge production, cultural edification, and ethics, *adab* shares a complicated relationship with the broader Islamic sciences. The Qur'an's introduction in the seventh century challenged the then-reigning dominance of poetry as the literary form par excellence.[33] The theological doctrine of *i'jāz al-Qur'ān*, or the inimitability of the Qur'an as a uniquely divine act of aesthetic expression, impacted the aesthetic standards of the pre-Islamic period while prompting some Muslims to look upon poetry with moral suspicion. Islam also introduced a number of fields related to the hermeneutical study of the Qur'an and hadith that both developed upon, and contributed to, existing literary methodologies. This dialogic relationship between Islamic intellectual traditions and literary practices was largely overwritten by European orientalist scholarship, which sought to secularize the concept of *adab* by noting its clear distinction from the Islamic sciences. Similarly, *adab* became conflated with secular humanism, or was divested of its holistic origins, in order to be partitioned into "moral, social, and intellectual" domains (Malti-Douglas 9).

Adab is by nature highly referential and often entails multivocality, as well as the weaving together of various narrative styles, voices, and sources—not unlike the Qur'an, hadith, and their surrounding scholarship. Similarly, integrating the Qur'an into works of *adab* through allusions, quotations, and veiled references can be traced to embodied spiritual practices such as rote recitation, memorization, and citation. Even the Qur'an's inimitability was integrated into existing theories of literary criticism, insofar as Muslims consider the holy text to be the highest form of literary eloquence. The Qur'an's literariness is said to be the impetus behind a renewed interest in literary arts, driving the documentation and collection of pre-Islamic poetry.[34] Crucially, the critical analysis of poetic form and language helped Qur'anic scholars "interpret opaque words and phrases in the revelation" (Holmberg 195).[35] Introducing novel "moral and metaphysical concepts," the Qur'an expanded existing aesthetic standards, formal categories, and cultural modes of expression (bin Tyeer 3). The text's generic ambiguity elevated existing poetic modes of expression within a format that exceeded the parameters of prose. Its structural complexity, linguistic artistry, and profound interdisciplinarity, in turn, generated "a new type of reader, a new critic, and a new taste" (5). Poetic discourse and literary analysis thus functioned in concert with the development of Qur'anic hermeneutics.

The Qur'an's narrative style is distinct from that of the Bible or Torah: "As opposed to divinely-inspired compositions, translations, and redactions," it represents God's direct speech through the Prophet, hence its intimate bond with the Arabic language (El-Desouky, "Between Hermeneutic Provenance and Textuality" 12). It has been described as "the most meta-textual, most self-referential holy text known in the history of world religions. There is no other holy text which would refer so often to its own textual nature and reflect so constantly and pervasively its divine origins" (Abdul-Raof, *Schools of Qur'anic Exegesis* 2). The Qur'an is also notable for its nonlinear arrangement: the presentation of suras (chapters), in addition to the individual *āyas* (verses) therein, do not coincide with their historical chronology or the order in which they were revealed to the Prophet. Allegories, histories, edicts, prophecies, liturgies, and juridical proclamations are intermixed rather than formally, thematically, or chronologically grouped. The narrative logic of the Qur'an's final presentation is thus distinct from its existence as a sacred object of revelation.

The Qur'an's history is intimately tied to the existence and life span of the Prophet Muhammad; the dominant view being that verses were memorized and eventually written by scribes across the twenty-three-year period of prophetic revelations. The collation of the first written version of the Qur'an—a consonantal skeleton (*rasm*) absent of voweling—is often dated to the era of the third caliph 'Uthmān (ruled 644–656) (Sinai 273). Guidelines for the final arrangement of the Qur'an are said to have been left by the Prophet after he received all of the revelations, in addition to being well-known to his companions (Von Denffer 23–28).[36] The codified version of the Qur'an, arranged roughly based on sura length from longest to shortest, has long been a subject of orientalist fascination. Early Qur'anic translators and scholars were frustrated by its "disjointed" organization, with some even describing it as incoherent or poorly written (Esack 64).[37] Many subsequently divide the Qur'an into the "Meccan" and "Medinan" periods, in reference to the Arabian cities across which the revelations were received. These categorizations map conceptual and ideological readings onto geohistorical periodization, such as the popular distinction between the philosophical or existentialist tone of the early Meccan suras and the more overtly political Medinan suras.[38]

German orientalist scholar and translator Theodor Nöldeke's canonical revisionist chronology was published in *Geschichte des Qorâns* (History of the Qur'an) in 1860. Expanding upon the earlier Islamic tradition of grouping the Meccan and Medinan suras, he elaborated on the system by marking three chronological divisions within the Meccan period. This trend began "to acquire a heuristic monopoly in Western research on the Qur'an. . . . The strong and undeniable sense of coherence and, particularly to Western eyes, reassuring linearity which it grants to the Muslim sacred text was greatly appreciated, while its historical and methodological assumptions were little, if at all, brought into question" (Stefanidis 1). The imposition of temporal linearity onto the Qur'an has been both a tool for its contextualization as well as an imposed hermeneutical strategy. It privileges the academic study of the text alongside literary criteria of narrative "legibility." While Nöldeke's revised model lost some traction in the mid-twentieth century, the division between the Meccan and Medinan revelations remains active within Euro-American Qur'anic studies.

The Qur'an's largely length-based arrangement assists with the rote-recitation and memorization of the text, which is often performed in reverse order from shortest to longest. Recitationality is central to the Qur'an as both divine logos and a textual object: in addition to the divine command to the Prophet Muhammad *iqra'*, the name Qur'an itself connotes reading/recitation. Appearing throughout the text, the word Qur'an is the *maṣdar*, or verbal noun, of *qara'a* (قرأ): to declaim, to recite, to read, to study, to teach, to investigate, to examine, to explore, or to study thoroughly (*Hans Wehr* 753).[39] It blends questions of pedagogy with reading/reciting—not unlike *adab*'s valence of cultural edification. Alongside recitation, practices such as mimetic pedagogy, Qur'anic talismans, the physical ingestion of ink from Qur'anic memorization tablets, "service, personification and physical example" all highlight the centrality of "corporeal knowledge practices" to Muslim spiritual praxis (Ware 57). These embodied forms of knowledge are central to a theological ontology in which the Prophet Muhammad, to borrow historian Rudolph T. Ware's metaphor, is the *walking Qur'an*, or a kind of Islamic urtext.[40] Ware's argument echoes scholarship on the anthropology of Islam by Asad and Mahmood, in which Islam functions as both a "discursive tradition" and "a dense web of fully embodied encounters" (76).[41]

Within the Qur'an itself, there are frequent references to the importance of reading, recitation, and memorization to comprehending the text as a source of spiritual knowledge. One is "not simply learning something by rote, but rather interiorizing the inner rhythms, sound patterns, and textual dynamics—taking it to heart in the deepest manner" (Sells, *Approaching the Qur'an* 11). Michael Sells argues that recitation and memorization work hand in hand with the narrative complexity of the Qur'an: "The actual stories, which seem fragmented in a written version, are brought together in the mind of the hearer through repeated experiences with the text" (12). In this sense, the sonic texture of the Qur'an—what Sells refers to as "sound-vision," "lyrical meditation," or "sound figures"—plays a significant role in spiritual praxis and Qur'anic hermeneutics (16, 19, 27). Moreover, it reveals the different registers on which the Qur'an's narrativity operates: reading, copying, reciting, hearing, and memorizing the Qur'an each foster a unique experience of the text.

Returning to the Qur'an's intense self-referentiality, the text frequently invokes its own symbolic narratology. The term *āya*, which is used to reference verses, also means sign, token, miracle, wonder, marvel, exemplar, utterance, or word (*Hans Wehr* 36):

بَلْ هُوَ آيَاتٌ بَيِّنَاتٌ فِي صُدُورِ الَّذِينَ أُوتُوا الْعِلْمَ وَمَا يَجْحَدُ بِآيَاتِنَا إِلاَّ الظَّالِمُونَ

> Nay, but this [divine writ] consists of messages clear to the hearts of all who are gifted with [innate] knowledge—and none could knowingly reject Our messages unless it be such as would do wrong [to themselves]. (Qur'an 29:49 trans. Asad)[42]

Moreover, the Qur'an refers to itself as *al-ḥadīth* (18:6), which, besides referencing the prophetic tradition, also means: speech, utterance, discourse, report, account, tale, or narrative (*Al-mawrid* 458).[43] Rhetorical concepts—largely derivatives of *m-th-l* (to resemble, imitate, compare, represent, or signify)—similarly appear across the Qur'an, highlighting the significance of its symbolic and allegorical devices (*Hans Wehr* 891–92).

Theorizing the Qur'an's distinct narrative techniques as *discontinuous naẓm* (syntactic and textual arrangement), Ayman El-Desouky argues that its "unique styles of direct modes of address, sound and syntax, and temporal discontinuities" reflect "the form of its divine voice" while further signaling "a radical aesthetics of the untranslatable literary thrust of the Qur'an" ("Between Hermeneutic Provenance and Textuality" 29–30).[44] The Qur'an's grammatical stylization, particularly the principle of *iltifāt*, is central to its untranslatability. *Iltifāt* references the frequent rhetorical and grammatical shifts in the Qur'an, which can include changes in the speaker, subject or addressee, verb tense, number (single, dual, plural), gender, case marker, personal pronouns, and even the use of nouns in place of pronouns.[45] Qur'anic code-switching can simultaneously be read across theological and literary registers, insofar as it precludes God's anthropomorphization as "a reified deity" while reflecting the symbolic limitations of language: "In the Qur'an the divine voice is heard in a variety of manners through an extraordinary range of emotions and tones, but the form or image of the speaker is never defined—a literary feature that mirrors the Qurʾanic affirmation that the one God is beyond being fixed in any delimited form or image" (Sells, *Approaching the Qurʾan* 20). Demonstrating the spiritual significance of Qurʾanic narrative devices, *iltifāt* highlights how the Qurʾan can serve as a model of ethical narratology in literary analysis.

Orientalist arguments on the supposed unintelligibility of the Qurʾan need not venture beyond the text itself. The Qurʾan affirms its theological and aesthetic inimitability in a number of suras: (12:2), (13:37), (16:103) (Esack 68). The impulse to narratively tame the Qurʾan is particularly relevant when considering the periodization of literary modernity within an antitheological ontology. Critiques and revisionist rewritings of the Qurʾan discount qualities such as multivocality, nonlinearity, asynchronicity, and narrative code-switching—the very aesthetic stylizations privileged in (post)modernist writing.

Hermeneutical Po/Ethics

Islamic scholars and exegetes have offered diverse points of entry into the analysis of the Qurʾan that account for both its divine revelatory origins and its aesthetic beauty as a text. This dialectic between the sacred and the sublime, as well as revelation and hermeneutics, haunts the methodological concerns that frame Qurʾanic studies. Qurʾanic *tafsīr* (exegesis/hermeneutics) entails "the literary activity whose function is the elucidation of the clear and ambiguous aspects of the Scripture and its major principles" (Abdul-Raof, *Schools of Qurʾanic Exegesis* ix). On the one hand, the Prophet Muhammad is often considered the first Qurʾanic exegete, insofar as the Qurʾan outlines his role in explicating the text to his followers. On the other hand, the Qurʾan is said to self-elucidate, or to "have explained itself via intertextual reference within it (*al-qurʾānu yufassiru nafsahu*)" (xv).

Qurʾanic scholars mobilize a variety of taxonomies, frequently dividing exegetical scholarship into formative and modern periods, as well as mainstream and nonmainstream schools of thought—each with their own branching subclassifications.[46] Hussein Abdul-Raof notes that "the mainstream school of exegesis . . . takes into account the exoteric (non-allegorical, literal) meaning of the Qurʾān," while nonmainstream exegetes—which for him include Shiʿa, Ismāʿilī, Ibādī, Muʿtazili, and Sufi approaches—"all resort to the esoteric (allegorical, underlying) meaning of the multi-faceted meanings of Qurʾanic expressions" (Abdul-Raof, *Schools of Qurʾanic Exegesis* xvi). These divisions are compounded by "whether an exegete advocates or rejects independent reasoning" or *ijtihād* (ibid.). Integrative approaches to Qur'anic exegesis bring the Qur'an's literary and formal qualities into dialogue with its philosophical message; blending holistic methodologies with textual analysis, they combine surface, close, and distant reading.[47]

Challenging textual or atomistic approaches, Amina Wadud's holistic Qur'anic hermeneutics reimagines traditional Qur'anic exegesis through the principle of *tawḥīd*, which she defines as "the unicity of Allah, harmony in and unity of all creation under a single Creator" (xxvi).[48] Wadud's *hermeneutics of tawḥīd* "emphasize[s] how the unity of the Qur'an permeates all its parts" through a holistic framework that balances the complex "dynamics between Qur'anic universals and particulars" (xii). Applying the foundational Islamic principle of *tawḥīd* to the textual and conceptual analysis of the Qur'an serves a number of crucial functions. Primarily, it forges a relationship between the aesthetic qualities of the Qur'an and its ethical, spiritual, or philosophical dimensions.

This imbrication speaks to the practice of *ta'wīl*—an interpretive approach that scholars and practitioners distinguish from *tafsīr*—that is aimed at unearthing "the allegorical and esoteric significations" of the Qur'an (Abdul-Raof, *Schools of Qur'anic Exegesis* 102).[49] The term *ta'wīl* appears in the Qur'an (3:5–7) in reference to verses that are *muḥkamātun* (clear or literal) versus those that are *mutashābihātun* (allegorical, figurative, or metaphorical).[50] Qur'anic translator Muhammad Asad writes that "since the Qur'ān aims at conveying to us an ethical teaching based, precisely, on the concept of God's purposeful creativeness, the latter must be, as it were 'translated' into categories of thought accessible to man" (Qur'an trans. Asad 1132).[51] Premised on the symbolic nature of the Qur'an, the concept of *ta'wīl* is simultaneously phenomenological and imaginative. In his study on Ibn 'Arabi, Henry Corbin defines *ta'wīl* "not [as] an allegorical exegesis but a transfiguration of the literal texts" that relies upon "the pre-eminence of the Active Imagination" (Corbin 88). This "symbolic exegesis" entails a kind of esoteric hermeneutics most profoundly articulated in Sufi philosophy (50). My own reading practices are informed by esoteric and Sufi hermeneutics, which rely upon a literary close-reading approach deeply invested in the symbolic. This aligns not only with the narrative strategies employed in the novels themselves but also with the intertextual figures and texts cited therein.

Sufism functions as one of the many modalities through which I read the expression of Islam as a polyvalent set of practices, beliefs, and doctrinal as well as hermeneutical approaches. In this sense, I push back against the Manichean rhetoric that bifurcates peaceful/heterodox Sufism from violent/orthodox Islam. While the entrenched distinction between "moderate" and "extreme" Muslims has become a defining feature of contemporary public discourse on Islam, the romanticization of Sufism originates in orientalist colonial discourse. Islamic scholar Carl W. Ernst historicizes the term "Sufi-ism" in the late eighteenth century, writing that "British colonial officials . . . maintained a double attitude toward Sufism: its literary classics (part of the Persian curriculum required by the British East India Company until the 1830s) were admired, but its contemporary social manifestations were considered corrupt and degenerate in relation to what was perceived as orthodox Islam" ("Between Orientalism and Fundamentalism" 110). Their records, which informed much of the orientalist scholarship on Sufism in the nineteenth century, maintained "that Sufism had no intrinsic relation with the faith of Islam" (ibid.). Sufi literature was exoticized, while its practice was divested of social, political, or ethical value. The anticolonial resistance of various Maghrebi Sufi orders against French imperialism, for example, is often whitewashed in the fetishization of Sufism as an apolitical mystical practice.[52]

My own usage of Sufism echoes Islamic scholar Saʿdiyya Shaikh's thoughtful framing of the heterogeneous tradition:

> Springing from the heart of Islam's spiritual reservoir *Taṣawwuf*, or Sufism, can be described as the process by which a believer embraces the full spiritual consequences of God's oneness (*tawḥīd*). The goal of the Sufi path is to enable a human being, through the cultivation of virtuous excellence (*iḥsān*), to commune directly and experientially with her Creator. In the historical development of Sufism, one encounters varied and increasingly sophisticated notions of the mystical path, or *ṭarīqa*. Such a path generally entails that the Sufi aspirant, under the guidance of a spiritual master, follows a practical method of purification and refinement of the self, undergoing many states (*aḥwāl*) and stages (*maqāmāt*) that lead to progressive unveilings of the divine reality (*ḥaqīqa*). (35)

Shaikh's definition maintains Sufism's internal heterogeneity as both a philosophy and an individual spiritual praxis. Her emphasis on the personal cultivation of virtue, often under the spiritual guidance of a more advanced practitioner, reiterates its simultaneous phenomenological and pedagogical orientations. Across the various theorizations of Sufism, there is a shared conceptualization of *taṣawwuf* as a path or process toward communion, and eventually unification, with God—a divine presence manifested in all of creation.[53] While the precise terminology and ordering of these steps varies according to individual Sufi orders, they generally encompass *shawq* (yearning) or *ṭalab* (searching); *maʿrifa* (knowledge/gnosis); *ʿishq* (love/desire); *riḍāʾ* (contentment) or *istighnāʾ* (detachment); *ittiḥād* (union); *ḥayra* (ecstatic wonderment) or *duwār* (vertigo); and conclude with *fanāʾ* (the annihilation or dissolution of the self)—often alongside *faqr* (material and existential impoverishment).

Sufi poetic discourse, or what I have elsewhere theorized as "Sufi po/ethics," encompasses the aesthetic dimensions of *taṣawwuf*, in which spiritual experience is at once enacted and expressed through conceptual language and symbolization (H. El Shakry, "Abdelwahab Meddeb and the Po/Ethics of Sufism" 98). As a philosophical ethos premised upon the hidden, concealed, or transcendental nature of spiritual life, Sufism resonates with the representational qualities of literary expression. It mobilizes the dialectic within Qurʾanic exegesis between the *bāṭin*, or esoteric, and *ẓāhir*, or exoteric meaning of divine revelation. In Sufism, the *ẓāhir* references the external and material world manifested in the body, while the *bāṭin* is the realm of the soul and inner knowledge. The pairing appear across the Qurʾan, particularly in the sura "Al-ḥadīd" ("The Iron"), in which they reference two of God's ninety-nine names/attributes (57:3), and the gate separating true believers from those of weak faith on the Day of Judgment (57:13).[54] The dialectical concepts of *bāṭin* and *ẓāhir* reveal the overlapping registers of Qurʾanic hermeneutics, divine providence, and phenomenological spiritual experience. Calling attention to the Qurʾan as both a revelatory and a literary object, they trace a formal and methodological relationship between aesthetic expression and divine truth.

Adonis argues that Sufi poetics have the potential to disrupt both epistemic structures and ontologies of being. His critical study *Al-ṣūfiyya wa-l-sūriyyaliyya* (*Sufism and Surrealism*) examines the uncanny intersections between Sufism and surrealism as philosophies rooted in the transcendental, the ineffable, the unknowable, dream-states, and the unconscious. They share, on the one hand, a mutual suspicion of dogmatic orthodoxy, and on the other, a defiance of "traditional aestheticism" (Adonis, *Sufism and Surrealism* 16). Concerned with interrogating the nature of existence, both participate in symbolic orders unmediated by the binaries of spirit/matter, thought/action, or material/immaterial. Their antipositivism foregrounds the relationship between aesthetic, phenomenological, and transcendental experiences. This pairing highlights Sufism's aesthetic qualities while simultaneously unsettling the ways in which avant-garde movements such as surrealism are often tethered to secular epistemes.

The tension between representation and phenomenological experience is central to the aesthetic philosophy undergirding Sufism. Sufi literature explores "the limits of language and the sayable, that which can and that which cannot be said, written, spoken of, in relation to desire, belief and the sacred" (Elmarsafy, *Sufism in the Contemporary Arabic Novel* 8). Not relying upon a one-to-one correspondence between the signifier and the signified, Sufism offers a conceptual vocabulary for conveying sublime experience. In this dynamic "relationship between mysticism and apophasis," symbolic excess works dialogically with representational absence (ibid.). The opacity and intense symbolization of Sufi poetic language enables spiritual knowledge, since Sufis "use art in their doctrines about God and existence and man: figurative language and style, symbolism, metaphor, imagery, rhythm, wordplay; the reader experiences the experience, and has a glimpse of their horizons through their art" (Adonis, *Sufism and Surrealism* 18). This poetic language works through "allusion rather than explanation," insofar as "everything in it is symbolic: everything in it is itself and something else" (ibid.). As Sufism relies upon figurative language and symbolism to express embodied spiritual experience, it has generated a rich repository of conceptual imagery that fosters very particular ways of reading.

As a hermeneutical practice, Sufism does not assume a direct equivalence between revelatory texts and their meanings. This echoes Adonis's privileging of the process of textual production over the archive that it engenders. More than a corpus of "written dogma," Sufi philosophical literature models a path of writing intimately connected to its "gnostic domain" (20)—hence the significant role that writing plays within many of the novels in this study. This highlights its methodological significance to both theological and literary practices: "the importance of the Sufi contribution lies in its re-reading of the religious texts and the attribution to them of other meanings and dimensions; this in turn permits a new reading of the literary, philosophical and political legacy, which has led to a fresh look at language, not only in the religious context but also as a tool of revelation and expression" (ibid.). Sufism's hermeneutical privileging of the ineffable, unknowable, and unimaginable fosters an embodied and experiential semiotics for approaching narrative texts. It serves as a model for ethical modes of knowledge production that informs not only the fictional works in this book but also my own close-reading practices.

The Literary Qurʾan

Written between the 1940s and 1980s, the six novels in this study offer diverse points of entry for examining the relationship between the Qurʾan and Maghrebi literature. Each of the three sections pairs a canonical Francophone and lesser-known Arabophone novel from Tunisia, Algeria, and Morocco respectively. More than simply shared national contexts, the pairings speak to overlapping thematic and formal topoi that emerge in and through these side-by-side readings. The book's narrative arc traces a trajectory from Tunisia through Algeria and Morocco, an organizational logic that deliberately moves from the least to the most commonly theorized cultural archives of the Maghreb. In many ways, Tunisia is considered the most "Arab" country of the Maghreb and is more commonly absorbed into Middle Eastern than Francophone or postcolonial studies scholarship. Morocco, on the other hand, is frequently interpellated as the most cosmopolitan (read: French) country of the Maghreb, while also occupying a privileged space within the American global imaginary.[55] Meanwhile, as the only settler colony and longest-occupied, Algeria simultaneously reads as the most colonial and anticolonial of the three.

Section I, "Poetics of Piety," explores Sufi poetics in Maḥmūd al-Masʿadī's *Mawlid al-nisyān* (The genesis of forgetfulness, 1945) and Abdelwahab Meddeb's *Talismano* (1979). Section II, "Ethics of Embodiment," theorizes Muslim ethics amid the fraught ethnolinguistic tensions of (post) colonial Algeria in al-Ṭāhir Waṭṭār's *Al-zilzāl* (*The Earthquake*, 1974) and Assia Djebar's *L'amour, la fantasia* (Love, fantasia, 1985; translated into English as *Fantasia: An Algerian Cavalcade*). Finally, Section III, "Genealogies of Transmission," uses Qurʾanic intertextuality and narratology to challenge periodizations of literary (post)modernity in Driss Chraïbi's *Le passé simple* (*The Simple Past*, 1954) and Muḥammad Barrāda's *Luʿbat al-nisyān* (*The Game of Forgetting*, 1987).

The study opens with two experimental novels from Tunisia, including the earliest work in this book: Maḥmūd al-Masʿadī's 1945 *Mawlid al-nisyān* (The genesis of forgetfulness). The highly philosophical work is the most conceptual of the six under examination. It offers a meditation on the phenomenological dimensions of Islamic praxis that is inflected by Sufism, existentialism, and humanism. The chapter frames these concerns within al-Masʿadī's broader philosophical writings on Islam and literature. The second chapter, on Abdelwahab Meddeb's experimental 1979 novel *Talismano*, moves into the more contemporary context of postindependence Tunisia. I examine Meddeb's polemical attack on Bourguiba-era Tunisia, in which hegemonic power is simultaneously concentrated in state and religious institutions. The novel counteracts these forces in its rescripting of the Qur'an as well as its invocation of Sufi figures, texts, and rituals.

Al-Masʿadī and Meddeb shared similar pedagogical training, which is quite explicitly reflected in their philosophical orientations and literary preoccupations. Both studied at the elite al-Ṣādiqiyya, which was founded in 1875 by the reformer Khayr al-Dīn Pasha al-Tunisī—just five years before the official start of the Protectorate. The school diversified the educational offerings of Qur'anic madrasas and was eventually brought under the administrative auspices of the Protectorate, when it shifted from a reformist approach to Islamic studies toward a curriculum that better served French colonial interests (Perkins 69).[56] Al-Masʿadī and Meddeb both then studied at al-Zaytūna mosque and university, followed by the Sorbonne. Meddeb's grandfather, Shaykh Mukhtār Meddeb, was a Qur'anic scholar and teacher at al-Zaytūna; meanwhile, his father, Shaykh Muṣṭafā Meddeb, was a scholar of Islamic jurisprudence and a poet. Meddeb eventually settled in Paris, where he continued to write creative and critical works, predominantly on Islam, Sufism, and critical theory. Al-Masʿadī, on the other hand, returned to Tunisia, where he prolifically penned essays and serialized fiction in literary journals. His political involvement in the Neo-Dustūr party facilitated a series of prominent roles in the postindependence government: he was minister of cultural affairs (1973–1976), Speaker of Parliament (1981–1986), and the mastermind behind Tunisia's educational policy following independence (1958–1968).

Al-Masʿadī frequently stressed the immense influence of an Islamic education on his intellectual formation, noting that his experience was in fact indicative of many from his generation. He said that it was his early *mu'addib* (religious teacher) who taught him to memorize the Qur'an from approximately the ages of five to ten, during which time he was immersed "in the atmosphere of the book" (*fī jaww al-kitāb*) (al-Masʿadī, *Collected Works* 3:340). Of his experience at the "Franco-Arabe" school, al-Masʿadī explains:

> That was an era in which I was influenced by the melodies and musicality of the Qur'an. I used to repeat and recite the parts I had learned in the manner of a chant [*tartīl*]. I memorized the Qur'an as it sounded to my ear—according to its rhythms, the rhythms of the Qur'an—and I realized then that it was not only words but also revelation. Later I began to be influenced by the Qur'an intellectually, although I knew there is nothing within it that invites rational or logical approaches.

> Through this process the reader of the Qur'an arrives finally—if they ponder its meaning logically—at the horizons of free speculation that we call imagination, or everything arising from within the conscience of which *taqwā* [consciousness of God, *or* piety] is comprised. And that is the boundless realm that man finds within the scope of the Qur'an or in God's domain. (ibid.)[57]

At al-Ṣādiqiyya, al-Masʿadī cemented his "Muslimness and Arabness" (*aṣṣalanī fī Islāmiyyatī wa-ʿarūbatī*) (3:341). He continued studying the Qur'an while being introduced to a broader "world of Islamic thought" (*ʿālam al-tafkīr al-Islāmī*) that included Islamic philosophy, *tafsīr* (exegesis), and *fiqh* (jurisprudence)—particularly jurisprudence related to "social life" (ibid.). Even when al-Masʿadī moved to Paris to study at the Sorbonne, where he trained with a range of orientalist (Louis Massignon) and colonialist scholars (Georges Marçais), he continued his Islamic studies.

Despite their common intellectual influences and interlocutors, the divergences between al-Masʿadī and Meddeb's professional paths are echoed in both their critical and literary writings. While Meddeb divested from the Tunisian cultural and political scene, he was active in the French intellectual world. This is reflected in the stylistics of his poetry chapbooks (1987–2001), the Paris-based literary journal *Dédale* that he edited until his passing, and even his monographs against political Islam that aligned with French political debates surrounding *laïcité*.[58] In his first novel, *Talismano*, the imprint of his studies at al-Ṣādiqiyya and al-Zaytūna are perhaps most pronounced.[59]

Meddeb and al-Masʿadī's fiction deftly incorporates the Qur'an, as well as Islamic philosophers such as Ibn ʿArabī, Rumī, Manṣūr al-Ḥallāj, Abū Ḥāmid al-Ghazālī, and Abū al-ʿAlāʾ al-Maʿarrī. Their works also critically engage the corpus of hadith, alongside questions of transmission, verification, and dissemination within Islam. More than simply influences, these texts and figures shape the very formal, grammatical, lexical, and stylistic construction of their respective works. *Mawlid al-nisyān* and *Talismano* echo broader philosophical concerns theorized in al-Masʿadī and Meddeb's critical writings, particularly surrounding the relationship between artistic creation, ethics, and spiritual praxis. I read both novels as articulating and performing a model of literary writing that frames artistic creation as intrinsic to critical Muslim subjectivity. This endeavor is largely expressed through the conceptual language and poetics of Sufism.

Section II opens with a discussion of al-Ṭāhir Waṭṭār's 1974 novel *Al-zilzāl* (*The Earthquake*). Born in eastern Algeria to an indigenous Amazigh family, Waṭṭār attended an Islamic madrasa before he pursued Islamic jurisprudence at the Ben Bādīs Institute in Constantine. He eventually moved to Tunisia to study at al-Zaytūna, where both al-Masʿadī and Meddeb trained. A politically active Marxist deeply invested in Algeria's protracted war for independence (1954–1962), Waṭṭār eventually abandoned his studies at al-Zaytūna to join the National Liberation Front (Front de Libération Nationale, or FLN) as a party controller in 1956. He remained with the FLN until his forced retirement in 1984 due to political divergences from the party. Waṭṭār's leftist political leanings are reflected not only in his short stories, novels, and plays but also in his active role in print media across the 1960s and 1970s.

Waṭṭār is a somewhat controversial figure within the Algerian cultural scene, whose politics fused Marxist ideology with a nationalist ethos reliant upon Islam and the Arabic language as the torchbearers for Algerian national identity. My analysis tempers readings of Waṭṭār as a fervent Islamist and nationalist by examining his subtle engagement with various philosophical and ideological debates within Islam. Chapter 3 focuses in particular on *Al-zilzāl*'s creative rewriting of Qur'anic eschatology in its portrayal of the tortured temporality of postindependence Algeria. As with al-Masʿadī and Meddeb, Waṭṭār's novel mobilizes the Qur'an as a literary framing device and as a formal as well as thematic intertext. The work further draws upon the fourteenth-century polymath Ibn Khaldūn, in addition to major figures within the Islamic reformist movement also referenced in Meddeb's and Djebar's novels.

Al-zilzāl's temporal contortions are echoed in Chapter 4, on Francophone Algerian novelist Assia Djebar's 1985 *L'amour, la fantasia* (Love, fantasia; translated as *Fantasia: An Algerian Cavalcade*). The novel pendulates between the violent expansion of Islam into the Maghreb in the seventh century, the savage occupation of Algiers by French forces in 1830, and the eight-year war for independence between 1954 and 1962. The fourteenth-century North African historiographer and philosopher Ibn Khaldūn is a controversial figure in both Djebar's and Waṭṭār's novels. While *Al-zilzāl*'s misanthropic protagonist takes issue with Ibn Khaldūn's glorification of an Arab culture that he believes to be in decline, *L'amour, la fantasia* recounts the polymath's graphic chronicling of the forced assimilation of Algeria's indigenous population alongside his identitarian affiliation with Arab rather than Amazigh origins. In addition to Djebar's framing of the Arab-Islamic expansion into Algeria as a colonial project, she weaves Qur'anic references to revelation, recitation, and reading into her explicitly feminist historiography. Djebar is undoubtedly one of the most recognized and theorized Algerian novelists of the twentieth century, even being inducted into the illustrious Académie française in 2005. The ease with which she circulates within a postcolonial Francophone cultural sphere signals the ways her work has been critically divested of Islamic (and to a lesser extent, indigenous) valences in order to make her legible as a secular feminist.

Djebar's palimpsestic novel mobilizes a variety of discursive traditions, including the Qurʾan, that reflect the country's fraught colonial history. In the process, it uncouples Muslim ethics from the Arabic language as the privileged site for Qurʾanic knowledge. Moreover, the novel's emphasis on orality and embodiment challenges colonial and national archives with its polyphonic hermeneutics. I read the work in dialogue with Djebar's broader literary and cinematic oeuvre, in which the concept of *ijtihād* is foundational to her revisionist feminist project. *L'amour, la fantasia* delves into Djebar's early studies at a madrasa before her privileged Francophone education: at a French colonial school where her father taught, and as the first Algerian woman to be admitted into the elite *École Normale Supérieure* in Paris.

Moroccan novelist Driss Chraïbi (1926–2007) similarly began his education in a Qurʾanic madrasa at a young age, before attending an elite French school in Casablanca. He completed his studies in France, where he eventually published his first novel, *Le passé simple* (*The Simple Past*) in 1954. It was largely received as an autobiographical work attacking Islam and justifying French cultural imperialism.[60] Chapter 5 instead reads the novel as a complex engagement with the Qurʾan that, like *Talismano*, traces the collusion of religious and state structures under the Protectorate. Manipulating the French language on a grammatical, lexical, and stylistic level, *Le passé simple* goes one step further than *Talismano* or *L'amour, la fantasia*. The novel employs the metaphor of the grammatical tense the *passé simple*, alongside Qurʾanic intertextuality, to stage a double critique against colonial and nationalist teleologies. I read the novel's repeated image of the hallucinatory abstraction *la ligne mince* (the thin line) in relation to both Qurʾanic symbolism and Sufi philosophy.

The closing chapter is on Moroccan novelist, journalist, translator, professor, and literary critic Muḥammad Barrāda (b. 1938). If Chraïbi signals the vanguard of decolonization, and *Le passé simple* as ushering in the modernist Francophone Moroccan novel, then Barrāda exemplifies the postcolonial intellectual, and for most literary critics, his 1987 novel *Luʿbat al-nisyān* (*The Game of Forgetting*) is the paradigmatic Arabic postmodernist novel. Chapter 6 reads Barrāda's literary project in dialogue with his prolific writings on literary criticism, and translations of such theorists as

Mikhail Bakhtin and Roland Barthes. It argues that *Luʿbat al-nisyān* champions polyphonic discourse across literary and theological spheres. This chapter most explicitly applies the Qurʾan as a model for *formal* literary analysis.

Luʿbat al-nisyān is introduced by Barrāda not as a novel per se, but as "*naṣṣ riwāʾī*," or a "novelistic text." Novelization is thus a narrative or discursive mode rather than a fixed generic category—a sentiment echoed across the theoretical writings of Barrāda and his cohort of experimental Moroccan novelists and theorists. The text oscillates between historical, narrative, and metanarrative time, as well as between diegetic and metatextual narrators. I read its authorial decentering and polyphonic narrative structure not as the collapsing of theological discourse as an inherently totalizing force but, rather, as its expansive opening. The chapter's framing of Qurʾanic intertextuality and narratology as commensurable with literary postmodernity unsettles the enmeshment of literary genres within secular epistemes. It instead situates literary experimentation within a nexus of narrative and formal modes, as well as hermeneutical strategies, inflected by the Qurʾan and tradition of hadith.

Maḥmūd al-Masʿadī's *Mawlid al-nisyān*, Abdelwahab Meddeb's *Talismano*, al-Ṭāhir Waṭṭār's *Al-zilzāl*, Assia Djebar's *L'amour, la fantasia*, Driss Chraïbi's *Le passé simple*, and Muḥammad Barrāda's *Luʿbat al-nisyān* problematize conventional generic taxonomies and their attendant historical timelines. Working within and against the grain of a variety of narrative traditions—at once scriptural and literary—they disrupt the ways in which literary modernity is interpellated through false binaries of private/public, ethical/political and sacred/secular. In so doing, they render legible modes of narrativity, embodiment, and reading often deemed epiphenomenal to literary analysis. Reading these novels paratactically with the Qurʾan, *The Literary Qurʾan* models new ways of engaging narrative ethics in literary studies.

PART I

Poetics of Piety

CHAPTER 1

Existential Poiesis in Maḥmud al-Masʿadī's *Mawlid al-nisyān*

نحن نُساقُ بالطبيعة إلى الموت ونُساقُ بالعقل إلى الحياة

We are led by nature towards death and
are led by reason towards life.

Abū Ḥayyān al-Tawḥīdī

This line, from the celebrated polymath Abū Ḥayyān al-Tawḥīdī (930–1023), is the first of three epigraphs that open Maḥmūd al-Masʿadī's 1940s novella *Mawlid al-nisyān* (The genesis of forgetfulness).[1] Al-Tawḥīdī was famously described as "*faylasūf al-udabāʾ wa-adīb al-falāsifah*" (the philosopher of *littérateurs* and the *littérateur* of philosophers) (*ʿAbbasid* 113). When asked about the quote in an interview with the Iraqi journal *Al-aqlām* (The pens), al-Masʿadī said that it captured the relationship of "the concept of death to the tragedy of human existence" (*fikrat al-mawt li-maʾsāt al-wujūd al-insānī*) (al-Masʿadī, *Collected Works* 3:212). His novella, he added, also explores "the problem of death and life, or the tragedy of Man when he confronts the inevitability of death. . . . Put otherwise, in this sense, he suffers from that aspect of his existential tragedy that causes him to be dissatisfied with being ephemeral and transient. He is thus compelled to acquire immortality through means other than those provided by nature" (3:213).[2] Al-Masʿadī follows al-Tawḥīdī with epigraphs from Schopenhauer (1788–1860) and Abu al-ʿAlāʾ al-Maʿarrī (973–1057) that similarly bridge metaphysics and aesthetics.[3] Al-Tawḥīdī and al-Maʿarrī belong to a rich scholarly tradition at the intersection of Islamic theology, philosophy, and literature. Their works interrogate the epistemological dimensions of human existence by emphasizing the ethical valences of reason, imagination, and artistic creation. In opening *Mawlid al-nisyān* with references to al-Tawḥīdī and al-Maʿarrī, al-Masʿadī situates his novella within a distinctly philosophical Islamic intellectual tradition. Moreover, the nearly century-long gulf that separates al-Tawḥīdī and al-Maʿarrī from Schopenhauer suggests an alternative genealogy for European aesthetic philosophy.

Drawing upon a variety of literary, philosophical, and theological influences, al-Masʿadī's fiction traverses genres and historical periodizations. His literary writings build upon the relationship between tragedy and literature in the Sufi poetry of the ascetic Abū al-ʿAtāhiya (748–826), the mystical universalism of the Sufi poet Manṣūr al-Ḥallāj (858–922), the philosopher Abū al-ʿAlāʾ al-Maʿarrī's (973–1058) understanding of rationalist Islam, the poiesis of the self from the theologian Abū Ḥāmid al-Ghazālī (1058–1111), as well as the liminal concept of the *barzakh* (isthmus) from the mystic Ibn al-ʿArabī (1165–1240).[4] His work is also heavily in dialogue with Greek tragedy, and he cites Baudelaire, Camus, Dostoevsky, Gide, Goethe, Ibsen, Malraux, Sartre, Shakespeare, and Valéry among his influences (Omri, *Nationalism, Islam and World Literature* 45; and "Interview" 435).[5] Al-Masʿadī's intertextuality with early Arab and Islamic thought, alongside European philosophy and literature, offers a new vision of literary innovation that moves beyond the reductive binary of cultural authenticity (*aṣāla*) and belated imitation (*taqlīd*). Working within a variety of traditions in a manner that is innovatively novel but also timeless—insofar as most of his fictional works are staged outside of historical time—al-Masʿadī reimagines the Arab/ic literary heritage, or *turāth*, as well as its future potentiality.

The dearth of critical scholarship on al-Masʿadī—easily the most renowned Tunisian public intellectual—within Euro-American Maghrebi studies is rather striking.[6] His name is largely absent from the (predominantly Francophone) Maghrebi canon and is infrequently cited in critical histories of Arabic literature. Moreover, his prolific writings on Arab/ic literature and philosophy are a glaring lacuna within canonical archives of the *nahḍa*.[7] While all of al-Masʿadī's fiction was written in Arabic, much of it has been translated into French, and he wrote some of his literary criticism in French. *Mawlid al-nisyān*, for example, was translated by the Tunisian intellectual Taoufik Baccar (Tawfīq Bakkār) as *La genèse de l'oubli* in a 1993 publication sponsored by the Tunisian Ministry of Culture—a subvention that reiterates al-Masʿadī's status as a national cultural icon.[8]

Across his critical and literary writings, al-Masʿadī explores literature as a creative praxis that speaks to broader existential and humanist concerns.

He theorizes artistic creation as an ethical imperative of human existence: "It is through literature that man achieves some degree of completeness, that he actualizes his humanity and completeness, because he gives his entirety to inquiring into the meaning of existence and the values through which man can be elevated from the level of animals to that of the divine" (*Collected Works* 3:366–67).[9] Expanding upon my discussion of Sufism in the Introduction, this chapter situates al-Masʿadī's aesthetic philosophy within a Sufi-inflected model of ethical Muslim subjectivity.

Maḥmūd al-Masʿadī

Maḥmūd al-Masʿadī (1911–2004) was a prolific writer, educator, editor, trade unionist, and government official. Educated during the French Protectorate, he studied at elite institutions of both French and Islamic thought: the Lycée Carnot and the Sorbonne, as well as al-Ṣādiqiyya and al-Zaytūna University. His commitment to bilingual education carried over into simultaneous teaching appointments at Collège d'Etudes Supérieur in Tunis, where he eventually chaired the Arabic literature department, and at the Centre d'Etudes Islamiques at Paris University. More crucially, al-Masʿadī

> was put in charge of the "Tunisification" and reform of the educational system in the newly-independent country as Secretary of State for Education, Youth and Sports, which led to the conception and implementation of "The Project for Educational Reform of 1958." His goals were universal access to elementary education and the establishment of a modern university system. Among the most prominent aspects of this reform were integration of the Islamic institution al-Zaytūna within the university system as a college for religious studies, and maintaining bilingual education in Arabic and French, two daring moves, which continue to be debated today. (Omri, *Nationalism, Islam and World Literature* 6)

In addition to reforming Tunisia's educational policy following independence, al-Masʿadī was the minister of cultural affairs (1973–1976) and Speaker of Parliament (1981–1986). An active member of the Neo-Dustūr party, his investment in democratizing Tunisia's educational system worked in concert with his direct-action political organization and unionization work around labor and education (7).[10]

Al-Masʿadī also played a prominent role in Tunisian independence, reportedly participating in decolonial negotiations with the French, and contributing to Tunisia's decision to not align with the Axis powers while under

German occupation in 1942 (ibid.). He was a cultural ambassador on behalf of the postindependence government, serving as Tunisia's UNESCO representative (1958–1968), a member of the UNESCO Executive Council (1977–1978; 1980–1985), and an Advisory Board member of the Arab League Educational, Cultural, and Scientific Organization (ALECSO), in addition to advising on Pan-Arab cultural patrimony projects—such as the Syrian *Al-mawsūʿa al-ʿarabiyya al-kubra* (The great Arabic encyclopedia) and the Jordanian Academy of Arabic Language (ibid.).

Cultural journals were a pivotal space for the development of autochthonous print networks that supported national, regional, and global networks of exchange and alliance across the decolonizing world.[11] To that end, al-Masʿadī served as the editor in chief of the literary journal *Al-mabāḥith* (Investigations), which he ran between 1944 and 1947. A remarkable periodical in the history of Tunisia's early print culture, the journal was a "forum for a collective academic project to construct a national culture in Tunisia" that brought together the country's preeminent writers, critics, and public intellectuals (ibid. 6–7). Despite its relatively brief press run, *Al-mabāḥith* (1938–1947) was influential across the Arab world, "reaching a circulation of seven thousand in 1947 at a time when the average circulation of similar periodicals was two thousand" (Omri, "History" 287–88). In addition to embodying the creative zeitgeist of midcentury Tunisia, *Al-mabāḥith* was also the medium through which al-Masʿadī serialized and published his earliest stories, plays, and novels.[12] He was also a frequent contributor to *Al-mabāḥith*'s pseudo-successor *al-Fikr* (Thought, 1955–1986).

Al-Masʿadī wrote during a vibrant period in Tunisia's cultural history when writers, critics, and artists were experimenting with aesthetic styles and theories. He was among such thinkers as Sāliḥ Suwaysī al-Qayrawānī (1871–1941), Zayn al-ʿĀbidīn al-Sanūsī (1901–1965), and the members of the underground group Jamʿat taḥt al-sūr (the below-the-wall gathering)[13]—such as ʿAlī al-Dūʿājī (1909–1949) and Muḥammad Bayram al-Tūnisī (1893–1961)—who ran the avant-garde literary journal *Al-ʿālam al-adabī* (The literary world).[14] Al-Masʿadī inaugurated a generation of Tunisian writers and critics interested in the relationship between aesthetics and ethics in Islam. The critic Maḥjūb bin Mīlād, who wrote the introduction to the first edition of al-Masʿadī's celebrated play *Al-sudd* (*The Dam*), for example, published a treatise on intellectual renewal in Tunisia entitled *Taḥrīk al-sawākin* (Arousing those who are stagnant) in 1955. The text employs the concept of *ijtihād* (individual reasoning independent of precedent) as a basis for collective and individual creativity (Fontaine 185).

Reflecting existentialist themes and motifs, avant-garde Tunisian literature of the 1960s, such as the works of ʿAzz al-Dīn Madanī and al-Ṭāhir al-Hammāmī, sought to generate novel modes of artistic expression (ibid. 186). As Jean Fontaine writes: "Plots were often reduced to backward spirals, in which times were embedded in each other. Heroes deconstructed themselves, and the real was cloaked in dreams. For that matter, members of the Avant-Garde no longer spoke about poetry or prose, but about "ibdâ" (creation)" (187). This emphasis on creativity as an aesthetic—and I would add, ethical—philosophy touches on the heart of al-Masʿadī's theory of literature.

Despite his widespread influence, al-Masʿadī's fiction challenged discourses of the committed intellectual while simultaneously troubling the perceived relationship between cultural innovation and Islamic intellectual traditions. His fictional works and critical contributions to *Al-mabāḥith* and *Al-fikr* were notable for their cerebral philosophical style, esoteric symbolism, and lofty linguistic register. Al-Masʿadī's literary writings are mythical in nature, staged outside of time and space, and devoid of any markers of historical or geographical specificity. As such, Arab literary critics of the time found it challenging to read his aesthetic philosophy in relation to Tunisia's status as a French Protectorate and ongoing efforts at decolonization. They consequently imposed didactic nationalist readings, as the Egyptian novelist and critic Ṭāhā Ḥusayn did with his play *Al-sudd* (*The Dam*), or they dismissed his writing as apolitical artistic navel-gazing, as was the case with the Tunisian critic Tawfiq Bakkār.[15]

Al-Masʿadī is at once a representative and remarkable figure in twentieth-century Maghrebi literature. At first glance, his status as an experimental writer and literary critic seems to contradict his role as a public intellectual and policymaker with prominent positions in the postindependence government. Al-Masʿadī was, in fact, like many Maghrebi intellectuals of his generation—teaching, writing, theorizing, and contributing to the cultural advancement of the postindependence state across a variety of platforms. These figures embodied a holistic model of the engaged public intellectual in ways that disrupt many of the anti-statist assumptions about avant-garde cultural movements. Tunisian intellectuals in particular frequently worked in concert with state institutions and initiatives.[16] They did not see their literary projects as necessarily in conflict with the state; rather, they helped define and shape postindependence cultural trends across their fiction, criticism, teaching, and political platforms. Al-Masʿadī's direct involvement in the development of Tunisia's national education policy and role as minister of cultural affairs, for example, harkens to my discussion of *adab* in the Introduction. Fusing aesthetics and ethics, as well as pedagogy and cultural edification, he illustrates the complex ways in which Tunisian national culture developed in the postindependence period.

Al-Masʿadī's experimental fiction, coupled with his interdisciplinary engagement with a diverse range of intellectual traditions, reflect his broader view of cultural innovation. Speaking in his capacity as the minister of cultural affairs, he stated: "Cultural development must be regarded both as a factor of national identity—or cultural identity—and as an instrument of transformation or change of a society. . . . [D]evelopment and modernization must be pursued under the triple banner of (i) fidelity to oneself, (ii) the profound will to renew, and (iii) the wise and rational selection of borrowing and influences to integrate into the modernization process" (al-Masʿadī qtd. in Davis 2). Al-Masʿadī here outlines the subtle dynamic of authenticity, transformation, and exchange that is crucial to his theory of cultural innovation and literary modernization. Integrating a variety of philosophical, theological, and literary conventions, he challenges their discursive authority in the very act of bringing them together. These subversions play out rhetorically, formally, and thematically across his mythical tales.

Uncanny Worlds

Al-Masʿadī's literary works are characterized by themes deeply embedded within Sufi thought. Plagued by doubt, his protagonists embark on journeys of self-discovery that force them to confront a series of dialectics at the heart of the human condition: reason and faith, self-actualization and annihilation, free will and religious determinism, the transcendental and the phenomenological, as well as the sacred and the profane. Al-Masʿadī's literary works that have garnered the most critical attention include his controversial novel *Ḥadatha Abū Hurayra qāl* (Abū Hurayra spoke, saying . . .) and his play *Al-sudd* (*The Dam*).

Written between the late 1930s and early 1940s, but not published until 1973, *Ḥadatha Abū Hurayra qāl* consists of twenty-two *ḥadīths*, or tales, about Abū Hurayra that are recounted by himself, his friends, and his admirers. The novel's controversy centered on the protagonist, who shares the name, though not the life, of a prominent figure of Islamic history. Abū Hurayra (603–681) was one of the Prophet Muhammad's companions, and a venerable transmitter of hadith often cited in Sunni *isnād*.[17] Staged between the cities of Mecca and Medina, the story appears to take place during the early history of Islam. Al-Masʿadī did not pursue publication until nearly thirty years after the manuscript was written, and even then, it was initially rejected. He was lambasted for the work's perceived parody of the tradition of hadith, as well as his representation of a revered figure of Islamic history as a man who indulged in women, wine, and other prohibited pleasures. Mohamed-Salah Omri argues that the story is a meditation on hadith as a narrative practice that is foundational to Islamic intellectual traditions. He examines its subtle engagement with questions of orality, the chain (*silsila*) of transmission, veracity, and the rhetorical device of concealment (*taqiyya*) that figures heavily within the Qur'an (Omri, *Nationalism, Islam and World Literature* 64–68).[18] Reimagining hadith within the literary form of the novel, *Ḥadatha Abū Hurayra qāl* articulates a mode of narrative ethics that fuses theological and literary traditions.

Al-Masʿadī's play *Al-sudd* (*The Dam*) recounts the mythical story of the steadfast Ghaylān, who enters into a conflict with a powerful goddess, Ṣāhabbā', over the construction of a dam. The leader of a religion replete with a gospel, priests, prophets, rituals, and followers, Ṣāhabbā''s faith is based on the principles of drought and aridity. Driven by the ethical imperative to combat injustice, divine or otherwise, Ghaylān and his reluctant companion Maymūna begin to construct the dam. They are met, however, with a series of natural disasters reminiscent of the Qur'anic foretelling of the Day of Judgment. Ghaylān's fixation on the construction of the dam, despite the innumerable obstacles thrown in his path, reveals the indomitable spirit of human creativity, even against insurmountable forces. The dam is eventually consumed by a storm of apocalyptic proportions in which Ghaylān disappears. The play thus vividly stages an ideological conflict between hegemonic religious authority and the individual, a recurring theme across al-Masʿadī's oeuvre. More crucially, it foregrounds the creative process, in this case, the construction of the dam, as critical to the ethical constitution of the self.

Mawlid al-nisyān (The genesis of forgetfulness) similarly enacts a philosophy of existence that promotes the ethical dimensions of creative endeavors. The novella was written in the early 1940s, serialized in 1945, and published in its entirety in 1974. Like much of al-Masʿadī's fiction, *Mawlid al-nisyān* is written in a dense classical register of Arabic. The story is introduced as *qissa falsafiyya*, or a "philosophical story"—a genre that was promoted in the literary journal *Al-mabāḥith* (48). Although Voltaire popularized the *conte philosophique* in nineteenth-century Europe, the narrative genre has a long history in Arabic literature.[19] Referred to in *Al-mabāḥith* as "symbolic" or "living" literature, the hybrid genre lends itself to the exploration of philosophical or spiritual concerns (ibid.). Structurally, *Mawlid al-nisyān* is relayed as a story within a story. In the brief opening frame narrative, an unnamed man addresses an unnamed woman, recounting a tale about "forgetfulness" from the recesses of time (*fī ghayb al-zamān*). By structuring *Mawlid al-nisyān* as a mythical tale within a mythical frame story, al-Mas'adī displaces the narrative's diegetic temporality, while simultaneously evoking Arabic oral traditions.

The tale traces the physical and spiritual journey of the physician *Madīn al-ḥakīm* (Madīn the wise). After wandering for many years, Madīn and his companion Layla arrive in a new land where they establish a hospice. The facility offers long-term patient care for the terminally ill and dying using a new breed of scientific knowledge. Their medical practices contradict those of the powerful sorceress Ranjahād, who lives in a nearby forest with her followers. Prior to their arrival, the townspeople had relied upon Ranjahād's healing powers, despite the fact that she would often leave them to suffer on the threshold between life and death. Haunted by the passing of his former lover Asmā', Madīn becomes consumed with developing a drug to combat death by allowing for an existence free from the effects of time. When he falls ill with a fever one night, he hallucinates a conversation with Asmā', who describes her inability to move on to the afterlife and desire for an earthly body. Frustrated by the ineffectiveness of conventional science to stop death, Madīn is desperate to relieve Asmā' from her wandering purgatory, and so he appeals to Ranjahād's magic. He asks her to lead him to Salhawā, a magical spring whose waters transform matter into air, and whose plant is rumored to provide *salwa* (consolation) and *sahw* (obliviousness).[20]

Ignoring his companion Layla's warnings, Madīn accompanies Ranjahād on a quest at once experiential and transcendental in nature. Over the course of their journey, Madīn and Ranjahād move through a series of worlds where they experience various supernatural phenomena: disembodied souls stuck in limbo, the cycle of life and death at warp speed, as well as the suspension of time. Inspired by these events, Madīn completes the drug and drinks it in order to "pass from one world into another" (al-Mas'adī, *Mawlid al-nisyān* 104). The drug briefly works, granting him a feeling of eternal permanence, pure existence, and obliterating his sense of memory and self. The transformation is both physical and spiritual, as the drug instills Madīn's eyes with "the light of revelation" (*nūr al-waḥy*), and he believes himself to be embodying the highest form of existence (108). The effects of the elixir are fleeting, however, and Madīn is quickly returned to the material world of the living. Ranjahād reveals herself as a trickster-figure, and Madīn discovers that his quest to exist outside of time was merely a delusion. As the fatal effects of the elixir take over, Ranjahād cautions him: "Being is indeed an eternal curse. Forgetting will not be born. Annihilation will not take place. Time shall not be defeated. The heavens cannot be reached. I am deception!" (*Inna al-wujūd al-laʿnat al-abad. Lan yūlad al-nisyan. Lan yulad al-fanaʾ. Lan yughlab al-zamān. Lan tudrak al-samāʾ. Anā al-buhtān!*) (114). The novella ends somewhat cryptically with Madīn's soul ascending to join the "world of the dead" (*ʿālam al-māwt*) (115).

Journeys of Creation

Madīn's quest to develop a cure for the inevitability of death and the effects of time reaches a pivotal point after he receives a visit from his former lover Asmāʾ. The realization that death is not simply the end but, rather, a perpetual state of limbo induces a psychic break in which Madīn internalizes Asmā's consciousness and experiences in the afterlife. Describing their encounter as a conversation with his *nafs* (self/soul), Madīn explains: "It is as if I am a soul which has disposed of the body and passed from this world into the afterlife, wandering, possessed by time and bewildered by memory, revisited by all that has elapsed of its life . . . for eternity" (*fa-ka'annī bi-l-rūḥ wa-qad takhallaṣat min al-jasad wa-ijtāzat al-dunyā ilā al-ākhira, fa-dhahabat hāʾimatun yaskunuhā al-zamān wa-tuḥayyiruhā al-dhikrā, wa-yazūruhā mā inqaḍā min hayātihā . . . ilā al-abad*) (50). This haunting feeling prompts Madīn to pursue an existence outside of the confines of time, memory, or death.

When his companion Layla questions his conviction that time can be defeated, she does so in a distinctly spiritual register, insisting that time is an "inevitable law, the law of God, the law of the universe, the law of death" (*sunna hatm: sunnat allāh, sunnat al-kiyān, sunnat al-mawt*) (49). Layla's use of the word *sunna* suggests not only law but also the practices and teachings of the Prophet Muhammad upon which sharīʿa is in part founded. Her response reveals the intimacy of the natural and spiritual worlds, where the law of the universe is indeed the law of God. Madīn's description of limbo resonates with the state of *barzakh*, which is referenced in the Qurʾanic suras: "Al-muʾminūn" ("The Believers") 23:99–100, "Al-furqān" ("The Criterion") 25:53, and "Al-raḥmān" ("The Gracious") 55:19–20. While there are various exegetical readings of the concept of the *barzakh*, it essentially describes an intermediate state separating two entities, which can be either immaterial, or physical, as in bodies. Its most common usage derives from the sura "Al-muʾminūn," in which, according to the Qurʾanic translator and commentator Yusuf Ali, it describes "a partition, a bar or barrier; the place or state in which people will be after death and before judgment. . . . Behind them is the barrier of death, and in front of them is the Barzakh, partition, a quiescent state until the judgment comes" (Qurʾan trans. Ali 899).

Islamic philosopher Salman Bashier argues that the concept of the *barzakh* has shifted meaning "from its temporal designation in orthodoxy, signifying a period of time that extends between death and resurrection, to its spatial designation within mysticism" (81)—a dimension we encounter in al-Masʿadī's novella. In the work of the twelfth-century Andalusian Sufi philosopher Ibn al-ʿArabī, for example, the *barzakh* takes on epistemological and even ontological dimensions—allowing meanings to materialize in corporeal form, and both time and space to contract or expand. Building upon the work of Ibn al-ʿArabī, anthropologist Stefania Pandolfo reads the *barzakh* as both a delimiting force and a conceptual framework for theorizing difference. She defines it as "an intermediate imaginal real, an *entre-deux* between absence and presence, spiritual and bodily existence, between self and other, the living and the dead" (Pandolfo, *Impasse of the Angels* 9). In *Mawlid al-nisyān*, the *barzakh* moves between spatial, ontological, and spiritual registers. It signals not only the liminal space between life and death but also the creative possibilities afforded by confronting the very limits of human existence.

Madīn and Layla's journey is staged both physically and metaphysically. Their years of wandering, pilgrimage to this new land (*balad*), in addition to Madīn's subsequent journey with Ranjahād, all harken to the tradition of *riḥla*, or travel writing, in classical Arabic literature. These journeys are framed as both a *hijra*, or pilgrimage, and the ascetic wanderings of a Sufi seeking divine knowledge. Madīn's declaration upon their arrival marks his awakening to the struggle for a higher truth: "These are the lands of death and this is the day of jihad" (*hādhī bilād al-mawt wa-hādhā yawm al-jihād*) (al-Masʿadī, *Mawlid al-nisyān* 62). Al-Masʿadī seems to resignify the physical and spiritual *hijra* of the Prophet Muhammad and his followers from Mecca to Medina in the seventh century. Madīn and Layla are outsiders, and their alterity suggests a prophetic calling. As Layla explains: "When we came to this country he had in him the flame of the prophets (*shuʿlat al-anbiyāʾ*). He wanted to cure illness and bring the dead to life" (35). Madīn's prophetic madness is marked by an unwavering commitment to transgress the boundary between life and death. A common trope within Sufi ecstatic poetry, particularly in the works of Manṣūr al-Ḥallāj, Ḥāfiẓ, and Rumī, prophetic madness is often interpreted as a spiritual experience in the Sufi path toward unification with the divine.

When Madīn embarks on his journey with Ranjahād, he leaves behind the comforts of the hospice and his companion Layla so that he may enter the disorder (*iḍṭirāb*) of nature. Ranjahād occupies a very different cosmological and symbolic world order, in which language, for example, does not exist. Upon entering the dense forest, Madīn is immediately surrounded by a heavy silence (*ṣamt*) and a strange stillness (*sukūn*). He wanders without guidance (*hāʾim ʿalā ghayr hudā*), indicating a spiritual disorientation in addition to a physical one; the term *hudā* appears throughout the Qurʾan to indicate God's guidance for true believers (68).[21] When the distant voice of his deceased lover Asmāʾ beckons Madīn, the trees, which he likens to the columns of a mosque (*ka-sawārī al-masjid*), unravel and a path opens before him (71–72). Akin to the Sufi path of *taṣawwuf*, the clearing marks the beginning of Madīn's spiritual journey. Asmāʾ describes him as *al-musāfir al-rāḥil*—connoting both a wandering traveler as well as someone departed or deceased, as in a wanderer between worlds (70). Her voice warns Madīn that he will always be beholden to time and tethered to memory, walking with his "eyes turned backwards" (71). This prophesy foreshadows Madīn's ultimate inability to conquer the forces of time and death.

In spite of Asmāʾ's warning, Madīn finds himself inextricably drawn to the sorceress Ranjahād because of her ability to invoke the powers of both the natural and supernatural worlds. She embodies the divine qualities that he desires for himself: she can travel without moving, communicate outside of language, exist beyond the laws of time and space, and evolve without changing. Ranjahād's very existence reinforces Madīn's belief in the possibility of achieving a higher state of being; but more crucially, it causes his conviction in scientific knowledge to falter. Madīn frames his relationship to science and reason with the intimacy of piety, describing his *islām* (surrender), *īmān* (faith), and eventually *kufr* (faithlessness) in science and reason. By using faith-based discourse to describe a rational world order, al-Masʿadī troubles the false binary between secular scientific knowledge and spiritual piety. This Sufi conceptual language reveals the interconnectedness of the material and the physical, the phenomenological and the transcendental, the human and the divine, as well as the knowable and the unknown.

While in the forest, Madīn believes he is experiencing union with the universe (*al-ittiḥād bi-l-kawn*) (73). Ranjahād explains that a higher state of being entails not only union but also dissipation (*tatabaddud*), inertia (*jumūd*), and the elimination of sensation (*ḥass*), pain (*ʾalam*), and happiness (*farḥ*). One must also be cleansed of matter (*maʿdin*, literally "mineral" or "metal"), release earthly attachments, and abandon the faculty of reason (ibid.). Ranjahād's description resonates with many accounts of *taṣawwuf*, which includes various stages, also referred to as valleys or stations, on the journey toward divine unification. Throughout *Mawlid al-nisyān*, Madīn experiences and strives for states of consciousness seminal to *taṣawwuf*: *duwār* (vertigo), *ḥayra* (ecstatic wonderment or bewilderment), *ṭahāra* (purity), *sukūn* (stillness), and *fanāʾ* (annihilation). Moreover, the novella consists of seven chapters, a significant number in the Qurʾan and Islam more broadly.[22] Scholars have further commented that the figure of Madīn bears a striking resemblance to the twelfth-century North African Sufi Abū Madīn al-Anṣārī (Omri, *Nationalism, Islam and World Literature* 114). Incorporating *taṣawwuf* into its diegetic narrative, conceptual language, and formal structure, *Mawlid al-nisyān* engages Sufism as both a spiritual philosophy and a literary intertext.

During their journey, Ranjahād warns Madīn that they will encounter many miracles or oddities (*ʿajaban*), adding that he must ask no questions because divine truth is elusive to reason. Just as *Mawlid al-nisyān* unsettles time as a structuring principle of human existence, so too does it call into question language as a system of signification. She cautions Madīn that "There is only the truth that manifests itself to you, which renders language powerless and refutes reason, and which is beyond meaning" (*Wa-innahu laysa min ḥaqq illā mā waqaʿa laka fa-aʿjaza al-lafẓa wa-kadhdhaba al-ʿaqla wa-khalā ʿan maʿnā*) (74). Her antipositivist ethos, which aligns with Sufism's phenomenological orientation, emphasizes the experiential over the transcendental. Divine truth, according to Ranjahād, is not a fixed ontology that one unearths or decodes; rather, it is made manifest to the individual in the course of their spiritual journey. This echoes the principle of *ijtihād*, in which individual perception and experience shape interpretive practices.

A deeply ambivalent figure, Ranjahād nonetheless embodies alternative forms of knowledge and functions as Madīn's Sufi spiritual guide. Despite his tragic end, Madīn's journey expands his epistemological and ontological horizons. The sorceress introduces him to worlds and forces beyond his comprehension, ultimately reinforcing the importance of the symbolic. This tension between language and phenomenological experience is central to Sufi aesthetic philosophy. Dwelling in the space of the ineffable, Sufi poetics interrogate the representational limits "between the human and the divine, the self and the Other, the self and the world" in ways that are intrinsically literary (Elmarsafy, *Sufism in the Contemporary Arabic Novel* 9).

When Madīn encounters Ranjahād in the forest, she mysteriously emerges as if from the *bāṭin* (interior) of the earth, luring him with her command over nature. On both a semantic and conceptual level, al-Masʿadī is invoking the importance of metaphoricity within Qurʾanic exegesis, which emphasizes the dialectic between the text's *ẓāhir* (exoteric) and its *bāṭin* (esoteric) meanings. Invoking one of God's ninety-nine names (al-Bāṭin), the Sufi aspirant cultivates the esoteric dimensions of their *nafs* (soul/self) across their spiritual journey. Throughout *Mawlid al-nisyān*, various "truths" are revealed to Madīn as having emerged from within the *bāṭin* of the earth, the very image mobilized to describe Ranjahād's first appearance. The story's emphasis on the symbolic builds upon the work of the theologian Abū Ḥāmid al-Ghazālī, a key interlocutor across al-Masʿadī's work, who explored the horizons of the imagination through a po/ethical engagement with the Qurʾan. Islamic scholar Ebrahim Moosa writes of al-Ghazālī, "Not only did he acknowledge that figurative or metaphorical discourse is compatible with reason and rationality, but, more importantly, he placed metaphor at the heart of religious discourse" (65).[23] Central to Sufism as both a spiritual praxis and an aesthetic tradition, metaphoricity is at the heart of Madīn's spiritual journey.

Having endured the Sufi stage of *duwār* (vertigo), Madīn is able to enter the "world of forgetting and eternity" (*ʿālam al-nisyān wa-l-khulūd*). In this realm, the forest is still while Ranjahād moves at warp speed; meanwhile, Madīn is weighed down by his memories and earthly attachments. They then enter the "cave of sleepers" (*kahf al-nāʾimīn*), which harbors those whose souls have departed but whose bodies remain in this world—in reference to the story of *ahl al-kahf* (the people of the cave) that appears in the Qurʾan, as well as in Christian theology (77). In the Qurʾanic sura "Al-kahf" (18:7–27), a group of young believers flee religious persecution by taking refuge in a cave. Under God's protection, they sleep for what feels like a day but in actuality is nearly three hundred years. The story has been interpreted as an allegory for spiritual retreat from the material world, steadfastness in one's faith, or as an account of God's protection of his followers. In the context of *Mawlid al-nisyān*, the parable speaks to Madīn's liminal existence. He "followed Asmā's soul and fell asleep to the world" (*fa-nimta ʿan al-dunyā*), becoming neither of the world of the living nor of the dead (79). This *barzakh* space signals the various epistemes between which Madīn shuttles: scientific reason and divine truth, the phenomenological and the transcendental, as well the exoteric and the esoteric.

Across their travels, the spiritual and physical dimensions of Madīn's journey manifest in a melding together of time and space. Ranjahād explains that because time is not a universal phenomenon, it is actually Madīn's perceptual experience of time that has shifted.[24] A subject that has received considerable attention in al-Masʿadī's literary and critical works, time is tied to questions of consciousness, existence, memory, and imagination. According to the concept of *daymūma zamaniyya* (temporal duration), which appears in *Mawlid al-nisyān* and the author's commentary on it, human existence can be experienced only through the individual's understanding of themself in relation to the continuity of time. Eternal existence—*al-wujūd al-muṭlaq* (absolute being) or *wājib al-wujūd* (necessary being) in al-Masʿadī's lexicon—exists only in relation to God's extratemporality. However, since time is experienced through memory, consciousness, and sensory perception, it drives creation and innovation. Al-Masʿadī emphasizes the phenomenological nature of time across *Mawlid al-nisyān*. Madīn, for example, describes a haunting vision of experiencing "the future as cursed by a memory, as if it has passed but cannot be forgotten" (*al-mustaqbilu laʿīnuhu dhikrā, wa-kaʾannamā qad maḍā wa-lam yunsa*) (103). Reading futurity through the lens of memory troubles the idea of temporal or historical linearity. It opens up the horizons of the future across time and space, in a manner that is pivotal to al-Masʿadī's theorization of cultural innovation.

In the next world that Madīn and Ranjahād visit, time is prolonged, and they begin to travel in slow motion, "covering distances as if they were eras long" (*masāfāt kaʾannahā al-ʿuṣūr ṭūlan*) (82). As time and space fuse, Madīn imagines himself "winged and flying through time" (*lahu jināḥān wa-ʾinnahu yaṭīr fī al-zamān*), seeing "time passing beneath him" (*wa-l-zamān min taḥtihi yamurr*) (ibid.). The reference to wings evokes the Prophet Muhammad's winged steed, known as the *burāq*, that carried him upon its back from Mecca to Jerusalem and then to heaven, during the two-part evening journey referred to as the *isrāʾ* and *miʿrāj*. Referenced in hadith literature and the Qurʾan, the Prophet's journey is framed as both spiritual and physical in nature. In the *miʿrāj*, he is said to have ascended through the seven levels of heaven, encountering a different prophet in each. The conjuring of the Prophet Muhammad aligns Madīn's prophetic expedition with a spiritual journey that similarly unfolds in seven stages.

Madīn and Ranjahād then enter a "strange universe" (*kawn gharīb*) called the "world of absolute time" (*ʿālam al-zamān al-muṭlaq*) (83–84). In this world marked by speed, plants and animals grow, wither, and dissipate "in the blink of an eye," highlighting the ephemeral nature of material existence over the perpetuity of spiritual life (83). Time courses through him in this "world of death and eternity" (*'ālam al-mawt wa al-abad*), where all creatures experience the cycle of life in an instant (84). Overcome again by vertigo, Madīn faints; Ranjahād enters his consciousness and "calls out [from] within his self/soul" (*wa-hatafat Ranjahād fī nafsihi*) the story of creation (85). Ranjahād's ability to speak to Madīn from within himself recalls the tempting whispers of Satan and foreshadows that she is a temptress luring the faithful with false truths and demigods.[25] On the other hand, it marks Madīn's internal spiritual struggle and reluctance to accept the impermanence of human existence.

While Ranjahād's creation story resonates with both Qur'anic and biblical accounts, it differs in many crucial ways. She describes the god Salhawā creating (*khalaqa*) the world from nothing in six nights: "He said: 'Oh Worlds, Be'" (*fa-qāl: ayyatuhā al-akwān kūnī*), and they came to be (86). This harkens to the description of creation in the Qur'an from the sura "Al-baqara" ("The Cow"):

بَدِيعُ السَّمَاوَاتِ وَالأَرْضِ وَإِذَا قَضَى أَمْرًا فَإِنَّمَا يَقُولُ لَهُ كُن فَيَكُون

> The Originator is He of the heavens and the earth: and when He wills a thing to be, He but says unto it, 'Be'—and it is. (Qur'an 2:117 trans. Asad)

Al-Masʿadī here cleverly plays on the oral resonance and shared root (*k-w-n*) between the words *kawn*, meaning world or universe, and *kāna*, the verb "to be." He further invokes the image of matter emerging from nothing, as well as the power of divine logos in the act of creation. According to Ranjahād's account of creation, Salhawā is disappointed with the earth, as it is sullied by dirt, oil, tar, excrement, and rot. So, on the seventh day, he creates Man as a creature of "greatness, beauty, and purity" (*al-'aẓama wa-l-jamāl wa-l-ṭahāra*) (al-Masʿadī, *Mawlid al-nisyān* 86). Jealous of Man's purity, the earth confronts Salhawā: "You created me, rendering me from the material of clay. And you created him, rendering him in the image of light. You made me filthy and ugly, and you made him pure and beautiful" (*Khalaqtanī fa-ja'altanī māddatan ṭīnān. Wa-khalaqtahu fa-ja'altahu ṣūratan nūrātan. Wa-khaṣṣaṣtanī bi-l-danas wa-l-qubḥ, wa-khaṣṣaṣtahu bi-l-ṭahāra wa-l-ḥusn*) (87–88). While the earth is composed of matter, Man is made *in the image* of light. The earth's materiality (*māddatan*) contrasts with Man's representational nature (*ṣūratan*). In defiance, the earth explodes and secretes rot, invoking the Qurʾanic account of the Day of Judgment in the sura "Al-zalzāla" ("The Earthquake"):

وَأَخْرَجَتِ الأَرْضُ أَثْقَالَهَا

and [when] the earth yields up her burdens. (Qurʾan 99:2 trans. Asad)

Despite Salhawā's divine power, Ranjahād represents him as a fallible and emotional being, susceptible to disappointment, hopelessness, failure, awe, and even heartbreak (al-Masʿadī, *Mawlid al-nisyān* 86, 87, 89). Moreover, while Ranjahād's rendition of the story of creation bears many similarities to that in the Qurʾan, it more explicitly ascribes to Man divine attributes traditionally reserved for God. Specifically, Salhawā refers to Man as *ʿaẓīm*, or magnificent, one of God's ninety-nine names and attributes (87). He also describes Man as his highest creation: "Be Purity, Magnificence, and Beauty. . . . You are the [great] hope of my creations, the secret of my universes. You are the singular one, [embodying] beauty and consolation. There is no meaning without you" (*Kun ṭahāratun wa-ʿaẓamatun wa-jamālā . . . anta amalī min khalqī, wa-sirrī fī akwānī, wa-anta al-wāḥid al-awḥad, wa-l-jamālu wa-l-salwā, wa-laysa siwāka maʿnā*) (87). This passage resonates with the doctrine of God's oneness or the *tawḥīd*, which affirms that God alone is one (*wāḥid*) and unique (*awḥad*).[26] While some schools of Sunni thought might read this as deification, Sufi poetic discourse frequently uses Qurʾanic language of the divine to describe the path of *taṣawwuf*. In so doing, it embraces the unicity of God's creations and the divine nature of spiritual fulfillment. Al-Masʿadī's tragic heroes embody this ethos, suggesting that humanity approaches the divine through the will to create.

The end of the story of creation bears the most relevance to Madīn's quest, as Ranjahād clarifies why death leads to a state of limbo rather than a moment of deliverance. She explains that Salhawā sent down Adam, followed by Eve, but human beauty was soon marred by "ugliness…clay, fermentation, and death" (89). The first mortal death, of Adam and Eve's progeny, marks earth's victory over humankind. The earth blocks all souls from ascending to heaven after death, compelling them instead to roam eternally, lost in wonderment (*ḥayra*), and burdened by nostalgia (*shawq*) and memory (*al-dhikrā*) (90–91). The explicit use of Sufi conceptual language recalls Madīn's own inability to fully move through the various stages of *taṣawwuf*.

Ranjahād explains that those souls that seek reprieve are briefly granted flesh only to then fall apart and decompose into the earth: "Madīn suddenly saw decomposing skeletons [*ʿiẓām ramīm*] stand up and walk. Then they regained their flesh, color, health, and beauty. Then they aged and fell to the ground where they were consumed by worms [till they] became ashes and returned to being corpses. All in the blink of an eye" (93). The wording of this passage echoes the language and sonic texture of the Qurʾanic description of the Day of Judgment in the sura "Yā Sīn":

وَضَرَبَ لَنَا مَثَلًا وَنَسِيَ خَلْقَهُ قَالَ مَنْ يُحْيِي الْعِظَامَ وَهِيَ رَمِيمٌ

> And [now] he [argues about Us, and] thinks of Us in terms of comparison, and is oblivious of how he himself was created! [And so] he says, "Who could give life to bones that crumbled to dust?" [*al-ʿiẓām wa-hiya ramīm*]. (Qur'an 36:78 trans. Asad)[27]

Ranjahād compares this process to the faculty of memory, whereby nostalgia resembles briefly experiencing the fullness of life, before it fades into oblivion. Memory embodies the ephemeral and fleeting nature of existence, merely tempting humanity with the illusion of temporal permanence.

Before Madīn meets his untimely end, he briefly experiences an existence free from the constraints of the body, memory, or time. Upon consuming the magical elixir that he concocts, Madīn exclaims:

> Now I am Truth in itself. Look, my heart has stopped. Stillness has defeated Time. I neither pass nor change. I am Being. I am eternity. I have not changed since the dawn of time. . . . But who am I? I am born as a new creation every hour. Watch my horizons expand; how vast are my dimensions! Feeling has subsided in me and the beginning has come. I have become great and drunk the heavens. The universes have all dissolved in me [*or* The universes have all been born in me]. (110–11)[28]

In his ecstatic state, Madīn utters words eerily reminiscent of the Sufi Manṣūr al-Ḥallāj's infamous declaration that resulted in his gruesome execution in the eleventh century: *Anā al-ḥaqq*, or "I am Truth." Like al-Ḥallāj, Madīn's self-description is metaphysical in nature. As the embodiment of pure Being, he believes himself to contain the expanse of the universes, existing beyond the laws of time and space. In this moment, Madīn straddles seeming oppositions: he is both ever-evolving and constant, the beginning as well as the end. This incarnation of pure Being evokes not only the power of spiritual transcendence within a Sufi epistemology but also the creative and generative power of the imagination.

Imagining the Unimaginable

Mawlid al-nisyān calls into question the epistemological structures that order and taxonomize the world. Across the novella, Madīn critiques the institutionalization of various forms of knowledge, claiming, "I witnessed gods, the self, religions, thought, and science be erected like barricades, with wisdom and reason as their supposed foundations" (*Ra'aytu al-āliha wa-l-nafsa wa-l-adyāna wa-l-fikra wa-l-ʿilma ka-l-sudūdin tuqāmu wa-tujʿalu lahā al-ḥikmatu wa-l-ʿaqlu asāsan*) (99–100). He argues that such orders bar humanity from actualizing its full potentiality—namely, to "imagine the unimaginable and comprehend the incomprehensible" (*ataṣawwaru mā yastaḥīlu taṣawwuruhu wa-ataʿaqqalu mā lā yuʿqalu*) (106). Madīn rejects the confines of linear time and institutionalized knowledge, moving instead toward a phenomenological vision of the world. He describes this poetic space in Sufi terms as a state of vertigo (*duwār*) that opens up the horizons (*āfāq*) of the imagination. The faculty of imagination is central to al-Masʿadī's conceptualization of Islam as a philosophy of individual self-exploration. This manifests in the structuring of the diegetic narrative as an individual journey through the spiritual experience of existence.

While Madīn eventually learns that his ambitions exceed the boundaries of human existence, the story still functions as a call to individual reflection and innovation. Across his oeuvre, al-Masʿadī shows the labor of the artist to be inextricably linked with the labor of the self. Despite Madīn's ultimate failure to reach immortality, his very ability to imagine its possibility, and his tireless dedication to make it a reality, ultimately signal the expansion of his imaginative and ethical horizons. Before his death, Madīn briefly reaches the heights of the divine in his sublime experience of pure Being. Thus, like many of al-Masʿadī's tragic heroes, Madīn arrives at the finality of human existence not having surpassed but, rather, having pushed its limits. It is precisely this commitment to exceed the very delimitation of human existence that defines the Sufi path for al-Masʿadī: "This for me is the meaning of *taṣawwuf*, namely a haven for the powerless and bounded human who aspires to overcome these boundaries" (*Dhālik huwa ʿindī maʿnā al-taṣawwuf wa-huwa al-malādh bi-l-nisba ilā al-insān al-ʿājiz, al-maḥdūd idhā huwa ṭamaḥa ilā an yataghallaba ʿalā hādhihi al-ḥudūd*) (al-Masʿadī, *Collected Works* 3:301).

In his commentary on the complex heroes that animate his stories, al-Masʿadī writes that death and annihilation (*fanāʾ*) are the inevitable tragedy (*maʾsā*) and fate (*maṣīr*) of every human life (3:130). While his characters' journeys may be tragic, they are not exercises in futility (*ʿabath*) or the absurd (*ʿabathiyya*) (ibid.). Rather, these figures represent the indomitable human spirit in their commitment to challenge and exceed the boundaries that conscript human existence. To be human, then, is to be mortal—or, as al-Masʿadī phrases it, to be "sentenced to annihilation" (*maḥkūm ʿālayhi bi-l-fanāʾ*) (3:131). To enact the existential work of humanity, however, the individual must "work and create as if he were to live forever, all the while knowing that he will die tomorrow" (*yujāhidu wa-lā yazālu yaʿmilu wa-yakhluqu kaʾannahu yaʿīshu abadan fī nafs al-waqt alladhī yaʿlamu fīhi annahu sayamūtu ghadan*) (ibid.). The "human(istic) drive" (*al-nashāṭ al-insāniyya*) to which his characters are committed, often unto death, is the very will to create, build, imagine, and dream. Al-Masʿadī grounds this philosophy within the textual authority of the Qurʾan by citing the sura "Al-raḥmān" ("The Merciful") on the ephemeral nature of humankind in relation to the permanence of the divine (3:130):

يَبْقَى وَجْهُ رَبِّكَ ذُو الْجَلَالِ وَالإِكْرَامِ

> but, forever will abide thy Sustainer's Self, full of majesty and glory. (Qurʾan 55:27 trans. Asad)

By invoking this passage, al-Masʿadī highlights the divine qualities that humanity strives to emulate in spite of their transience. Moreover, in selecting a line that references the "face" (*wajhu*) of God (translated by Asad as "self")—who is nonfigural in the Qurʾan—he subtly calls attention to the Qurʾan's literary use of rhetorical devices.[29]

This dialectic between humanity's aesthetic and existential work is at the very heart of al-Masʿadī's literary as well as critical oeuvre. He posits that artistic creation and innovation begin first and foremost with a thoughtful attentiveness to one's own existence. The creative process, to which al-Masʿadī refers across his oeuvre as *ibdāʿ* (creation, invention, innovation, origination, creativity, or creativeness), entails a commitment to "intellectual openings" (*al-futūḥ al-fikrīyya*) and "existential openings" (*al-futūḥ al-wujūdiyya*) (3:202). *Ibdāʿ*, al-Masʿadī writes, is not a destructive force but rather a (re)generative one: "Revolution for me is the discovery of the new, not destruction . . . , it is the genesis of something that did not exist and the departure of something that did exist [but] whose time has come" (*Al-*

thawra ʿindī hiya iktishāf al-jadīd wa-laysat al-tahdīm . . . hiya an yatawallad shayʾ lam yakun mawjūdan, wa-yadhhab shayʾ kāna mawjūdan wa-inqaḍā dahruhu) (3:203). He adds that artistic creation relies upon cycles of birth and death that are part of the natural world order—a reality that unfolds across the pages of *Mawlid al-nisyān*. Literature then functions as a message, literally a *risāla* in al-Masʿadī's lexicon, to the reader aimed at helping them achieve the highest and most complete form of their humanity (3:199).

In a lecture entitled "The Relationship between the Writer, the Narrative, and the Reader" (*Al-ʿalāqa bayna al-kātib wa-l-naṣṣ wa-l-qāriʾ*), al-Masʿadī describes this dynamic in somewhat otherworldly terms:

> What happens between the literary work and its reader in terms of interaction, impact, and influence—on the affective level and the intellectual, imaginative, or philosophical level—is a secret known only to the reader, because the reader is not subject to laws like those of chemistry. For this reason, we speak of the alchemy beyond chemistry, rather than of chemistry [alone]. This secret is not subject to the laws of nature but is instead a strange matter from which every literary work is born. (al-Masʿadī, *Collected Works* 3:140)[30]

Alchemy is a particularly fitting metaphor in light of Madīn's magical elixir in *Mawlid al-nisyān*. Al-Masʿadī's theory of literature looks beyond science or reason to the sublime heights of the unimaginable. The triad of writer, text, and reader generate singular encounters at once affective, psychic, intellectual, and imaginative that exceed the sum of their constitutive parts. The alchemic nature of artistic creation echoes the mythical worlds that al-Masʿadī's characters inhabit—filled in equal measure with the wonderment and tragedy of human existence. This vision of literature resonates with the concept of *adab*, which encompasses the *adīb*, the corpus of and about *adab*, as well as the readers' engagements with *adab* and its community of producers and readers. Al-Masʿadī frames literature as an intersubjective experience that straddles the individual and the social, the phenomenological and the transcendental, as well as the aesthetic and the ethical. In so doing, he places literature at the heart of Muslim spiritual praxis. This emphasis on the embodied experience of reading signals both the practice of *taṣawwuf*, and a Qurʾanic hermeneutics that moves across imaginative, phenomenological, and esoteric registers.

In this vein, al-Masʿadī's 1958 essay "Islam, nationalisme et communisme" radically reorients Islamic history and discourse by suggesting that the true Islamic conquest was not the geopolitical or ideological proliferation of Islam as a systematic creed, dogma, or religion but, rather, as a philosophy of existence: "If Islam, certainly not as a religion or creed, but as a mode of inquiry and reflection by Man upon himself, were no longer to engender intellectual and spiritual creation in the East, it would definitely be the end of one of humanity's most original, most fertile, and most valuable conquests; the end of the invaluable treasures generated by Islam" (*Collected Works* 4:330).[31] Using as his point of departure this apocalyptic image of civilization, al-Masʿadī theorizes Islam as a mode of questioning and reflection that reinvigorates the past, while simultaneously opening up the horizons of the future.[32] This aesthetic vision of faith as a vehicle for creation rewrites canonical accounts of the expansion of Islam, in addition to reframing the relationship between existence, art, and politics. By exploring Islam as a philosophy of existence intimately connected to the artistic process, it is possible to reimagine the epistemological divide between faith and reason. Al-Masʿadī thus envisions cultural and artistic production as part of the process of individual critical thinking intrinsic not only to being human but to the very practice of Islam.

CHAPTER 2

Carnivals of Heterodoxy in Abdelwahab Meddeb's *Talismano*

> Assaulted from every side by the universalization of the Technological, nomadism and sufism are truths that keep withdrawing from the world. . . . The poet's stance remains the same; in the face of irrevocable absence, the poet remains the guardian of Being, no matter that such a Being would envelop the world completely differently. The incessant revision of the interpretation of the world acts on the bodies and the imaginations. But the principle of the *mise-en-abîme* of the known by the unknown invests existence the same way. The darkness does not dissipate itself, it remains all around, very close, ready to grab the advancing foot, the proffered hand. Similarly, the cosmic coma remains unbreached, despite our lightning-fast breakthroughs that have only shaken the constructions propped up against the pretensions raised by the worry for totality and systems.
>
> Abdelwahab Meddeb, "Wanderer and Polygraphist"

When interviewed days after the 9/11 attacks, Tunisian intellectual Abdelwahab Meddeb bemoaned the "inconsolable . . . destitution" of the "Islamic subject" (Meddeb, "Islam and Its Discontents" 5).[1] He diagnostically charted the peaks and valleys of Islamic civilization in relation to European developments in science, technology, philosophy, and art. Echoing orientalist narratives of decadence and decline, Meddeb noted the flourishing of Islamic thought in the ninth century on the one hand, and the civilizational clefting of the Orient and the West in the eighteenth century on the other.[2] Modern Islam, he argued, is "cut off from its roots," willfully ignoring the diverse permutations of Islamic intellectual traditions (13). Meddeb added that "All that's great in Islamic culture, all that's beautiful, came about not by the application of the Islamic letter of the law but rather through transgression or at least the skirting of that letter, in a will to forget and ignore it" (8). He ascribed these transgressive innovations to "the Sufis and the theosophists who dared to think freely," citing the Andalusian mystic Muḥy al-Dīn Ibn ʿArabī (1165–1240) and the libertine poet Abū Nuwās (756–814) as examples (ibid.). Engaging intertextually with this corpus, Meddeb's literary and critical writings simultaneously channel and champion the "heterodoxical" spirit of early Islamic thinkers.

While Maḥmūd al-Masʿadī and Abdelwahab Meddeb both draw from Sufi aesthetics, politically their projects diverge in crucial ways. *Taṣawwuf* is integral to al-Masʿadī's theory of literary creation as an ethical practice; it shapes both the conceptual language and philosophical underpinnings of his fictional and critical works. There is a dramatic divide, however, between Meddeb's polemical writings against "Islamic fundamentalism" and his poetic meditations on Sufism—a division echoed in critical scholarship on the author.[3] His monographs *La maladie de l'Islam* (*The Malady of Islam*, 2002), *Sortir de la malédiction: L'Islam entre civilisation et barbarie* (Breaking the curse: Islam between civilization and barbarism, 2008), and *Pari de civilisation* (translated as *Islam and the Challenge of Civilization*, 2009) toe the line of contemporary French rhetoric on *laïcité* in their reliance on a clash-of-civilizations model of cultural incommensurability. Meddeb's romanticization of Sufism lends itself to the false binary between peaceful/moderate and violent/extreme Islam that animates contemporary political rhetoric and has fueled an industry of apologist writings. Across his fiction and criticism, Meddeb explicitly pits Sufism against the straw man of Sunni Islamic orthodoxy, whose hermeneutic rigidity he directly links with Islamic extremism and violence.

Meddeb's narrative writings on Sufism bookend his literary career—from his two novels *Talismano* (1979) and *Phantasia* (1986), to his last works: *Instants soufis* (Sufi moments, 2015) on the celebrated Sufi figures Ibn ʿArabī, Rumī, and Rābʿia, and the more autobiographical *Portrait du poète en soufi* (Portrait of the poet as Sufi, 2014). His poetry collection *Tombeau d'Ibn Arabi* (1987) and poetry chapbooks similarly invoke Sufi aesthetics and imagery. Meddeb's literary turn to poetry over prose in the mid-1980s reiterates his reading of Sufism as a *poetic* tradition associated with Islam's past and distinct from contemporary modes of Islamic praxis. This chapter analyzes his first novel, *Talismano,* within the context of Meddeb's distinction between orthodox Sunni Islam and heterodox Sufism. Its parallel reading alongside Maḥmūd al-Masʿadī, however, renders legible the ways in which the novel offers a metameditation on the relationship between ethics and aesthetics in Islam.

Literary (R)evolutions

Born into a long line of Islamic scholars in Protectorate Tunisia, Abdelwahab Meddeb (1946–2014) was a poet, novelist, translator, essayist, Islamic scholar, art historian, cultural and political critic, as well as a professor of comparative literature at the University of Paris X-Nanterre. A celebrated figure in the French cultural scene, he hosted a weekly radio program titled *Cultures d'islam* on *France Culture* and directed the experimental French journal *Dédale* (1995–2000). Meddeb's editorial statement for the journal tellingly describes its mission along the binary of tradition/modernity: "taking references beyond their borders so that they may participate in the foundation of an expanded communal understanding, established through the confrontation of traditions, with the knowledge and methods proposed by the continent of modernity" (*sortir les références hors de leurs frontières afin qu'elles participent à la fondation d'un sens commun élargi, établi dans la confrontation des traditions avec le savoir et les méthodes que propose le continent de la modernité*) (http://ededale.free.fr/). Dedicated to "creation" and "thought," this Francophone "multiculturalism in action" traverses geographies and histories "from Greece to Rome, from Egypt to Morocco, from Andalusia to Africa" (ibid.).

Meddeb's labyrinthine novel *Talismano* is a fictional, at times hallucinatory, journey through this very Mediterranean imaginary that crosses languages, temporalities, mythologies, and religious discourses. It follows an unnamed narrator-author in two rather ambiguous moments in time and space: participating in an impromptu revolution in Bourguiba-era Tunisia and writing a novel while living in exile in Paris. Interspersed throughout the narrative, which moves almost indiscriminately between Tunisia and France, are a series of spatial, temporal, and textual detours. These digressions take us into the recesses of our narrator's psyche, the archives of Arab, Islamic, and European intellectual traditions, and traipsing across the Mediterranean. As it meanders through the Maghreb, Mediterranean basin, and Europe, *Talismano* simultaneously performs and theorizes the region's unique ethnolinguistic and religious heterogeneity. Its literal and figurative cartographies of the Mediterranean—as an imagined and geopolitical site—problematize totalizing discourses of Arab-Islamic identities mobilized in Tunisian nationalist rhetoric.

The diegetic narrative recounted by *Talismano*'s narrator-author presciently traces the evolution of a popular rebellion as it winds its way through the cityscape of Tunis's *medina*, or old city, bearing a motley retinue of prophets, artisans, guildsmen, musicians, sorceresses, alchemists, magicians, tattoo artists, calligraphers, and prostitutes. The leaderless popular revolution takes shape after a doomsday prophet foretells the coming end of times to a listless crowd. The group eventually fall prey to his eschatological sermon as they descend into a Sufi-like *dhikr*, or devotional trance. Emboldened by this hypnotic collective energy, the city dwellers embark on an anarchistic journey across Tunis's *medina* in the compressed narrative time of one day. Ransacking and occupying much of the city along the way, the revolutionaries organize by profession and guild as they seize and redistribute land, weapons, food, and water. The capitalist foundations of postindependence Tunisia are promptly reimagined as the dinar is replaced by a barter economy, and masses of the rural poor descend upon the city to join the revolution. Meanwhile, the police, landed gentry, bureaucrats, as well as the political and religious elite, are all ousted or imprisoned as the country's socially, politically, and economically marginalized populations take over the capital.

The group quickly molds an antistatist ethos that largely takes aim at the notoriously authoritarian rule of Habib Bourguiba, the former EC member of the Neo-Dustūr party who took presidency on the coattails of independence in 1957. As prime minister of the newly established republic, he led a two-decade one-party state and was infamously voted "President for Life" by the Tunisian National Assembly in March 1975. After being declared mentally unfit to rule, Bourguiba was eventually unseated from power in 1987 by Zayn al-ʿĀbidīn bin ʿAlī, who was himself dethroned during the Tunisian uprisings in 2011. While Bourguiba's long shadow and infamous cult of personality certainly loom within the pages of *Talismano*, Meddeb directs his ire at the institutions and rhetoric of both state and religious power. To that end, the crowd makes its way to al-Zaytūna Mosque, one of the oldest and most venerated institutions of higher learning in the region, particularly for the Islamic sciences.[4] With the technical assistance of a gifted sorceress and a Jewish alchemist versed in the ancient Egyptian art of mummification, they stitch together, or literally re-member, the unearthed remains of corpses to assemble a three-eyed and four-breasted female idol that becomes the literal and symbolic locus of their new movement.

The narrative follows the crowd, along with our narrator and his travel companion Fatima, as they journey through Tunis's winding *medina*. After a night of revelry and idol worship at al-Zaytūna, the cortege of misfits makes its way through the Halfawīne quarter bearing the idol on a palanquin so that it may be burned in a ritual effigy. The uprising is brought to an abrupt halt when the city is surrounded and attacked by a series of foreign invaders: Spanish, French, and eventually Turkish janissaries, along with their hired thugs. As the revolutionaries are hemmed in by an uncanny reenactment of the Maghreb's various colonial occupations, the keys of the city are returned by the first to surrender: the "learned men," a jab no doubt at the privileged elite who served as the architects and financial beneficiaries of the newly formed state. Tunis is raided, pillaged, and plundered, while al-Zaytūna is converted into an army base, suggesting the collusion of military power with religious authority. In the novel's epilogue, we learn that nearly one thousand rebels flee the city and divide into two: half continue their pagan *hijra*, or journey, into the desert, while the rest migrate westward.

The winding diegetic narrative echoes the book's formal and rhetorical innovations. Structured loosely around sections both thematic and spatiotemporal in nature, the novel moves from a rather elliptical prologue, through "Retour prostitution" (Return prostitution), "Idole ghetto" (Idol ghetto), "Procession outre-monde" (Otherworld procession), and closes with a brief epilogue. The pseudo-chapters, like the work as a whole, signal an attempt to reimagine the genre of the novel. Blurring the line between the temporality of the events (the *histoire* or *fabula*) and that of the narrative (the *récit* or *syukhet*), *Talismano* metacritically interrogates the relationship between textual representation, consciousness, and history. This occurs not only in its formal composition but at the level of sentence structure, syntax, and grammar.

In the tradition of experimental Francophone Maghrebi writers such as Driss Chraïbi, Rachid Boudjedra, Assia Djebar, and Abdelkébir Khatibi, Meddeb expertly erodes the lexical foundations of the French language. The novel defies nearly every grammatical rule, with many of the lengthy sentences lacking a verb, subject, article, or preposition.[5] Moreover, this linguistic play operates translinguistically; for example, in the anastrophic manipulation of word order to apply Arabic sentence structure to French. This generates a disorienting reading experience where it is often challenging to pin down the narrative's "unruly I," or even to distinguish between unfolding, remembered, or imagined events (Meddeb, *Talismano* 54). The novel lives up to its namesake, the talisman—rendered in Italian as *Talismano* in a nod to pan-Mediterraneanism—inviting the ambitious reader to decipher its various signs and symbols. Despite the frequent bouts of self-reflective metacommentary, the work actively resists interpretation. Like the talisman, its structural recalcitrance fosters a very particular mode of reading that I argue is seminal to Meddeb's theorization of Islam as an inherently critical hermeneutical practice.

Consequently, the handful of Anglophone scholars who have analyzed *Talismano* have each theorized how one should read the text. The novel's translator, Jane Kuntz, for example, cautions that Meddeb's "ideal reader would almost have to be his intellectual match" but ultimately suggests that readers "surrender" to the text—an apt turn of phrase given the novel's engagement with Islam (Kuntz vi).[6] Ronnie Scharfman, on the other hand, frames Meddeb's corpus of writing as *textual nomadism* that should be read *nomadically*, namely, with a wandering eye toward form and meaning. Meanwhile, Dina Al-Kassim coins the neologism *calligraphesis* to theorize *Talismano*'s "practice of a figural rendering that contains within it both the specificity of meaning and the excess of its own staging," basing the term on the novel's "use of calligraphy as a figure for the relation of egoic self-knowledge to the unconscious, and the formal technique of manipulating French grammatical and syntactic forms to the point of incomprehensibility" (115). Finally, David Fieni theorizes Meddeb's "iconoclasm" in *Talismano* and *Phantasia* as *virtual secularization*, or "a translation of Islamic cultural practices from Arabic into French" (138). The difficulties of the text on both a structural and symbolic level are clearly echoed across the critical reactions within the field, which rely on the creation of a new conceptual vocabulary to approach the work. Working from within the novel's thematic and formal lexicon, my analysis interrogates how *Talismano* invites and theorizes decentralized and nonhierarchical practices of reading, writing, and interpretation that are pivotal to Meddeb's engagement with Sufism.

Exorcising Orthodoxy

In addition to the novel doubling as a metaphor for revealed texts, *Talismano* launches its theological critiques from within Qurʾanic discourse. It targets the hegemonic institutions and exegetical practices that have codified certain forms of religious orthodoxy, while affiliating with Sufi thinkers and practices. True to Meddeb's veneration of transgression, the novel celebrates various persecuted figures: from the tenth-century Iranian mystic Manṣūr al-Ḥallāj,[7] who was brutally tortured and executed for heresy in Baghdad, to the eleventh-century Iranian Sufi Shihāb al-Dīn Suḥrawardī, also tried and executed for heresy.[8] Like Maḥmūd al-Masʿadī, Meddeb also draws upon esoteric literature from the Andalusian philosopher Muḥy al-Dīn Ibn ʿArabī,[9] the twelfth-century theologian Abū Ḥāmid al-Ghazālī, the mystic poet Jalāl al-Dīn Muḥammad Rūmī, and the enigmatic organization Ikhwān al-ṣafāʾ (The brethren of purity).[10]

The revolutionaries resignify codified Islam through their literal occupation of its institutions. The epicenter of the revolutionary movement, al-Zaytūna becomes a site of idol worship, revolutionary manifestos, drinking, singing, dancing, and even group sex. The venerable mosque emerges as an egalitarian space of social mobilization beyond the reach of politically or religiously sanctioned power. Once the home to "long-winded theological harangue," it is converted into a space for radical discourse: "these words heretofore unheard, words shunned and cast out by officially sanctioned wisdom for fear of its casting a coarse shadow upon the city. Living words of experience, officialdom laid bare" (Meddeb, *Talismano* 75). Meddeb aligns al-Zaytūna with other such institutions of religious learning across North Africa, particularly al-Azhar in Cairo[11] and al-Qarawiyyin in Fès.[12] These institutions propagate what he refers to as "hegemonic Islam, a reductive monotheism, bordering on Christendom, both masters of a civilization claiming to be unique and universal, believing in progress and taking comfort where natural instinct is suppressed" (157). Meddeb mocks the doctrinal rigidity of al-Azhar and its "totalitarian sheikhs," citing their "centuries-old submission to the Word . . . backed by a plethora of powers: Fātimid, Ayyūbid, Circassian, Bahri, Mamlūks" (105). Al-Qarawiyyin is similarly attacked for being a "pedantic gem, archaic presence, gangrene of the just . . . [where] education is subjected to ritual, designed to garner protection from the powerful, keeping them at bay through imitation; a corpus of fetwas is deposited there, all questioning in vain" (106). Targeting the collusion of these religious institutions with various state powers, Meddeb calls attention to their manipulation of pedagogical and juridical tools for financial, social, or political gain.

Talismano's parody of institutional doctrine seems to echo Meddeb's own experience studying at al-Zaytūna under the tutelage of his father, Shaykh Muṣṭafā Meddeb, a scholar of Islamic jurisprudence. The novel recounts the challenge of learning within a structure of rote recitation that relied upon the precision of transmission, the compartmentalization of knowledge, as well as the acceptance of canonized interpretations of the Qur'an and hadith (107–8). *Talismano* contrastingly performs a poetics of writing and reading that sees texts as perpetually moving targets. The narrator-author states of his own writing that "a text is not immutable, but open, carrying events and words along in its stream picked up from both lived experience and fiction" (205). This understanding of texts as interpretive invitations or openings ("ouverture," likely a translation of the Arabic *futūḥāt*) permeates not only Meddeb's conceptualization of fiction but more crucially his approach to scripture.

Meddeb invokes the principle of *ijtihād* (individual reasoning independent of precedent) in *Talismano*'s metacommentary on its intentional opacity and infinite interpretative possibilities. The novel critiques religious institutions that stifle the creative or phenomenological dimensions of spirituality in their exclusive reliance on genealogical structures of transmission, such as the chains of transmission employed to verify hadith. Whether mockingly invoking his own elite family bloodline of "theologians, wealthy merchants, feudal lords, bureaucrats, doctors, notaries, lawyers, judges, and other notables," criticizing the self-legitimizing power of the Moroccan monarchy in its claims to Sherifian lineage or taking aim at the thuggery of Tunisia's feudal lords and landed gentry, Meddeb's disdain for the concentration of wealth, power, and knowledge across religious and state institutions echoes loudly (9).[13]

Al-Zaytūna's renegade occupation is imbued with the kinds of religious practices (spirit possession, exorcism, ritual sacrifice, ecstatic dance, and spiritual music) that dominate *zāwiyas*, Muslim temples that often function as pilgrimage sites and shrines devoted to venerated patron saints or leaders of Sufi orders. These forms of ritual religious observance are central to many Muslim communities, particularly in the Maghreb. Historically, *zāwiyas* have served a number of community functions, such as offering educational facilities and serving as political centers for anticolonial mobilization—particularly for rural, tribal, and ethnic minority groups.[14] Historian Julia Clancy-Smith writes on *zāwiyas* in Algeria and Tunisia: "Saints' cults created networks of political and cultural control, and, since oasis shrines attracted agriculturalists and tribespeople, they reinforced rural-urban independence. Expressing the cultural specificity of a community, organized cults and shrines did, at times, form the locus for collective opposition to the intrusions of outside powers" (36).

Zāwiyas are structured around complex lineages that run against the grain of official forms of monarchical or state power, and their holy personages often bear a kind of anarchic outsider energy (36–37). *Talismano* resignifies Sufi symbolic language in order to democratize state and religious forms of power: "Our era is based upon the abolition of the saint. . . . Let us eliminate the saints, but divide up the spoils of sainthood: that each shall wear around his head a ray of the halo that one saint alone used to monopolize" (Meddeb, *Talismano* 172). The revolutionary social order redistributes not only material wealth and its attendant structures of power but the very genealogical orders of religious authority as such. Meddeb's call to redistribute saintly power further speaks to his investment in the spiritual autonomy of the individual, who he suggests should not be beholden to official forms of religious mediation.

Meddeb's critique of Islam's political mobilization extends into the archives of the *nahḍa*, or Arab cultural "renaissance," and particularly to figures of the Islamic modernist or reformist movement.[15] The novel recounts an imagined politico-theological debate between the revolutionaries and various reformers: the Egyptian Muḥammad ʿAbduh (1849–1905),[16] the Tunisian al-Ṭāhir al-Ḥaddād (1899–1935),[17] the Algerian al-Bashīr al-Ibrahīmī (1889–1965),[18] and the Moroccan Muḥammad ʿAllāl al-Fāsī (1910–1974).[19] Within each of their respective national contexts, these figures sought to initiate social and political reforms in dialogue with Islam. In keeping with the discourse of cultural rebirth associated with the *nahḍa* movement, they called for a return to the fundamental principles of Islam, which they argued held the keys to cultural and national modernization. Much of the critical scholarship on the *nahḍa* emphasizes its privileging of the West as the agent of Arab cultural (re)birth, or the retrofitting of Arab and Muslim cultural history into a model of Western technological and scientific modernity.[20]

In the novel's imagined exchange, the Egyptian reformer Muḥammad ʿAbduh lambasts the carnivalesque revolution as "The worst debauchery, the most disgraceful disarray, the mortifying spectacle of Arabs in all-out attack on civil reason" (247). Maître (Master) Mahmud, "a goldsmith in the service of the revolution," retorts that the movement is driven not by a Janus-faced concept of progress that looks to the past in order to keep apace with Europe but rather by a radical reconceptualization of civil society as such (84). He adds: "This hasn't been an attack but an exorcism; we are haunted by history that spirals ad infinitum, carrying us toward apostasy. . . . Our incursions and deeds will not go down in history as a revolt against the rational side of the State; we represent neither its reverse nor its double. Understand that we are other: generous and long-suffering. Those of your ilk, people of god and of reforms, are to be crushed" (247).[21] David Fieni reads this exchange as a "double critique" in which Meddeb "exploits the premises of the *nahḍa* to intervene into the legacy of colonialism and what he sees as the decadent condition of the postcolonial Arab Islamic nation-state," in addition to mobilizing a "Nietzschean critique of the nihilism of Western scientific progress to intervene in the rise of the imbricated fundamentalisms of globalization and religious reform movements" (146). He argues that Meddeb seeks to uncouple Arab reformist discourse from a modernization narrative that privileges Western technological modernity—even when it culls Arab and Muslim cultural archives.

In staging this transtemporal encounter between ʿAbduh and *Talismano*'s revolutionaries, Meddeb brings to light the fraught stakes of reformist ideology within the Neo-Dustūr party's state-building project.[22] Under the leadership of the militantly anticolonial Habib Bourguiba, the party rejected the pan-Arabist and pan-Islamist inclinations of prominent former party members such as General Ṣāliḥ bin Yūsuf (Perkins 122). Bourguiba's nationalist platform neutered the political power of Islamic institutions—for example, by absorbing the two sharīʿa courts into the state and instituting a progressive Personal Status Code (Salem). Written twenty-five years after Tunisian independence, *Talismano* suggests that the Bourguibian-led government relied upon Western epistemes and teleological discourses of modernity. Master Mahmud's battle cry to destroy the "people of god and of reforms" fueling Tunisia's recursive history is ultimately a call to radically reimagine the state as such.

Talismano's disavowal of reformist rhetoric materializes in the figure of the idol created by the revolutionaries during their encampment in al-Zaytūna. The novel describes the construction of the idol as an orgiastic carnival that taps into "the insatiable cannibalism that slumbers in all mankind," leaving its participants and witnesses "both fascinated and baffled by the disgusting, frightening spectacle being inflicted upon them" (81). The idol is constructed from the unearthed remains of corpses, with each body part selected by the sorceress Saïda based on the deceased's name and crime. The act of desecrating the dead, already a sin in Islam, is coupled with the grotesque assembly of the idol from the disembodied parts of buried criminals. Despite its manipulation of normative anatomical correctness, the idol is clearly gendered as female. It is endowed with "four mothering breasts," a "slightly rounded belly," and "a vagina now enlarged into flower or wound [*blessure*]" (82). The maternal overtones of the idol's physiognomy suggest that the revolution is both an exorcism and a self-generating (re)birth—in line with the novel's critique of the reformist rhetoric of the *nahḍa*. It can also be read as a perversion of the nation-as-mother metaphor. By functioning as an embodied assemblage of criminality, the idol signals the very illicit acts upon which the nation-state as both a geopolitical reality and an ideological entity is founded.

With respects to its religious symbology, the idol operates as an "anthropomorphic reconstitution of myth" rather than the substitution of one institutionalized form of religious authority with another (83). The revolutionaries hail it as

> a simulacrum that shall rid us forever of archaic resonance, and celebrate our outmaneuvering of power. In order that power might pass irreconcil-

> ably into our hands, we must destroy said power with violent eloquence, besieging the city with cathartic spectacle. The idol produced in such a way is nothing in itself, does not feed a new fiction to furbish faith and belief; rather, it puts an end to a kind of power, a cult of submission. It exorcises not a reputedly tyrannical, often bloody past, but the bewildering instincts that bristle atavistic with each new spilling of blood. (112, translation modified)[23]

This exorcism—both symbolic and literal—brings together pre-Islamic rituals, ancient Egyptian cosmology, Greek mythology, and Sufism. That these threads should stitch together a rag-doll idol exalted within al-Zaytūna, the very epicenter of sharīʿa in Tunisia, speaks to a more deeply embedded critique within the novel's pages.

In its use of irreverence, vulgarity, and the carnivalesque to upend political, religious, and discursive authority, *Talismano* invokes Arabic literary genres such as *mujūn* poetry[24] and the picaresque *maqāma*,[25] as well as the irreverent prose of the ninth-century writer al-Jāḥiẓ.[26] In the Francophone tradition, it calls to mind François Rabelais's sixteenth-century epic pentalogy *Gargantua and Pantagruel*, whose risqué content and graphic imagery targeted the conservative religious and political establishment.[27] Carnivalesque works undermine state and religious institutions through the very taboos that they police: sex, death, crime, the body, mysticism, the occult, madness, and dreams. On a formal level, they disrupt narrative, linguistic, and semantic rules as a means of "social and political protest," thereby exposing the "identity between challenging official linguistic codes and challenging official law" (Kristeva 36). More than a momentary purging of the systemic power it seeks to destroy, the carnival play-space seeps beyond the pages of the text to bear upon our very ability to read and interpret it. This lingering textual, thematic, and formal disorientation impacts not only the hierarchies of power overthrown within the novel's diegetic narrative, but it unsettles our own thought patterns as readers and critics. *Talismano*'s ambivalent movement between high and low registers of speech, languages, and discourses rearranges the psychic universe of the self, as well as the very corporeality of lived and bodily spaces.

Achille Mbembe's work on the aesthetics of vulgarity is generative for thinking through *Talismano*'s mobilization of Qur'anic and Sufi discourse to critique the Tunisian postcolonial state. He writes that the postcolony "*creates*, through administrative and bureaucratic practices, its own world of meanings—a master code" that enforces the state's "regime of violence" (102–3). Carnivalesque (ludic, satirical, and grotesque) forms of unofficial culture reappropriate these codes in order to expose the state's structural dependence on institutional and discursive modes of violence. The vulgarity of state power is most prominently embodied in the archetype of the postcolonial despot and his agents of enforcement: security, military, education, and state institutions. A cliché of the benevolent dictator, Bourguiba was known as *al-mujāhid al-akbar* (the Supreme Leader) and subscribed to the storied accoutrement of autocratic power. His self-veneration with statues and accolades, alongside his political fanfare, read to his many opponents as a kind of ecstatic demagoguery. The inscription on his mausoleum, for example—which was built under his presidential supervision in 1963 to resemble a sacred tomb—reads: *al-mujāhid al-akbar, bānī tūnis al-jadīda, muḥarrir al-mar'a* (the supreme leader, the builder of the new Tunisia, the liberator of women). Official forms of power, Mbembe reminds us, self-fashion as a fetish object "that aspires to be made sacred" (111).

Talismano's revolutionary procession meanders between sites of state power (prisons, hospitals, universities, schools) and heterotopic spaces of otherness (cemeteries, hammams, brothels, the Jewish quarter). Al-Zaytūna's selection as the revolutionary center in which to erect the idol signals the novel's remythologization of official forms of power through the manipulation of its discursive signs and symbols. The idol's grotesque corporeality functions as both the reification and subversion of obscene forms of power, while its effigy reveals the ways in which the carnivalesque can drain the fetish object of its aura. For Mbembe, this ludic ambivalence has the power to demystify "the official fictions that underwrite the apparatus of domination" (111). Because of its engagement with Sufism, *Talismano*'s use of the carnivalesque reclaims the power of imaginative spaces in a more subversive fashion than Mbembe accounts for.

Talismano radically disrupts the various sites within which state power is flexed: from the intimacy of private bodies to the public squares and streets of the cityscape. The revolutionaries' undisciplined bodies and creative toppling of state power through the material destruction of Tunis expose the false genealogies on which this power is erected and enforced. By hyperbolizing the collusion of state and religious structures in Tunisia, *Talismano* reveals the sacred profanity at the heart of state power. This pseudo-sacrilege underscores the manner in which official structures of power rely upon sacred mythologies. The novel's creation and subsequent destruction of effigies of power—in the figure of the idol, as well as the rhetorical and material sites of officialdom—is a form of "theography," in which the state qua god "is devoured by the worshipers" (112). This is complicated by the official spaces of theological discourse, such as al-Zaytūna, that are resignified by the revolutionaries for effigies and orgies at once sacred and profane. As with al-Masʿadī, Meddeb's characters seek to generate a new cosmological order that relies upon on the imaginative spaces afforded by Sufism as both an aesthetic and ethical praxis.

Textual Talismans

Talismano's parody of the rituals of power occurs not only in the diegetic narrative but also in the relationship between the author, the reader, and the text. Employing an authorial voice that is at once self-consciously neurotic and blatantly antitheological, *Talismano* extends its critique of mythologies of origin to the novel itself. The polyphonic work frequently engages in extratextual references to the novel as a fiction and the author as a literary trope. It is replete with signs that refer back to Meddeb as the narrator-author, a figure along the margins of the text that exists within a complex assemblage of (super)egos. Meddeb's metacommentary on the process of writing, the relationship between memory and consciousness, as well as the fragility of the figure of the author, call attention to the fictitiousness of the novel as well as the reality that it parodies. His determination to keep the reader at all moments simultaneously inside and outside the diegetic narrative desacralizes both the text and the figure of the author. The demystification of the author as the progenitor of the text, and the novel as a self-contained work, has critical repercussions for *Talismano*'s relationship to Qurʾanic textual and hermeneutical practices. As a metaphor for revealed texts such as the Qurʾan, the novel calls into question the literary mythology of author as god. By democratizing the acts of writing and reading, the work opens up literary and theological texts to a proliferation of meanings and interpretations, as the concepts of *ijtihād* and *taʾwīl* (esoteric hermeneutics) promise.

Talismano's transference between fiction and revealed scripture materializes in the text drafted by the revolutionaries as a substitute for the hegemony of the Qurʾan. Much like the idol, the revolutionary text is an assemblage of various textual and religious traditions. Alternatively referred to as "the text of the future," "the new Book," "the bold and disconcerting new text of the revolution," or simply "the text," it is a Qurʾanic pastiche that allows the revolutionaries "to exorcise themselves by this ritual of allegiance" (Meddeb, *Talismano* 103, 171, 188, 173, 174). This is reflected not only in the content of the pseudo-sacred text, to which Meddeb pays little attention, but in its performative function: "I discover a black man dressed in white standing at the rostrum before a large lectern, reciting the text of the future, rejuvenated revelation, a new craving for reiteration of the word, no longer immutable but transformed into a call for an uncommon spirit ceasing to respect official law, the signature that standardizes behaviour. But the swaying of the upper body remains at root Qur'anic" (103, translation modified).[28] This new book is a reimagined emblem of existing forms of religious discourse and ritual that invites comparison with the Qur'an. It mimics various embodied modes of religious praxis within Islam: from the act of revelation itself, to dictates of Qur'anic recitation such as *tartīl* (hymnody) and *tajwīd* (elocution). Moreover, the recitation of the new book occurs at the very hearth of sanctioned Islamic authority—the minbar, "staircase and scepter of the commander of the faithful"—signaling its supplanting of official sites within Islam, both textual and spatial (102).

The resignification of religious texts and practices is perhaps best illustrated in the titular talisman—a revelatory object imbued with textual, symbolic, and fetishistic power. At once a metaphor and a fetish object, an illustration of a talisman adorns the text just before the final section. During a visit to Egypt, the narrator encounters a Nubian café owner in Aswan who asks the spiritually skeptical narrator to write a talisman that will rid the café of the "occult powers" that haunt it (142). Miraculously, his intuition proves prophetic as the narrator awakens from a fitful night's sleep to write the enclosed talisman: "with the force of prophecy, believe it or not, the talisman was revealed [*révélée*] in its entirety, words, figures, and all, to fulfill the Nubian's request, though I myself did not fully understand its content" (143/136). As with the revolutionary new text and the novel itself, the talisman is a pastiche that combines stock praises of God and Qur'anic invocations with more unorthodox elements such as the inclusion of the Taoist (also Daoist) compound ideogram 道 ("Tao" or "Dao"), meaning "passage" or "the way."[29]

The images that adorn the talisman—described in the text as "male circles and crescents doubled female [*croissants dédoublés féminins*], assembled, eye gazing upon floating sword, measure of history, qalam reed pen [*calame*] reassuring the will to write in emulation of the fiat, equivalence between the huwa, itselfness [*ipséité*] of the Sūfi and the Tao ideogram"—demonstrate a close affinity between the textual and the visual (ibid.). They borrow from iconography common to Islamic talismans and amulets: the sword, pen, eye, and crescent. In this context, however, they indicate the divine command to write and read. The use of the French word *calame* (reed pen, quill, or stylus, from the Greek *calamus*), rather than the Arabic term *qalam* (reed pen), calls attention to their homophonic qualities while also marking their differentiation. The soft "c" in *calame* as opposed to the hard "qāf" of *qalam* further plays on the phonetic resonance with another Arabic word: *kalima*, or word.

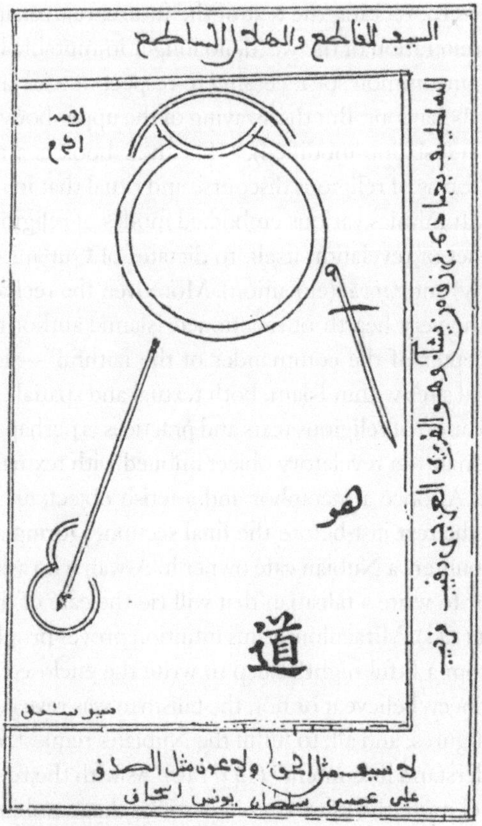

Figure 1. Meddeb's Talisman.

While they are etymologically divergent in Arabic—*k-l-m* versus *q-l-m*—the use of the French word rather than Arabic in a text that is rife with transliterated Arabic terms suggests a very intentional play on words.[30] Although *calame* is recognizable to a French reader, the Arabic listener encounters an entirely different series of oral and literary associations.

In this regard, the talisman calls to mind two Qurʾanic suras: "Al-ʿalaq" ("The Germ-Cell" or "The Clot"; 96) and "Al-qalam" ("The Pen"; 68).[31] The *qalam* in the sura is an instrument of divine revelation and knowledge, particularly since Muhammad was said to be illiterate at the time of the first revelation. By qualifying the talisman with the word "emulation" (*émulation*), the narrator suggests that although he is inspired by the Prophet's own revelations and Gabriel's divine command of *iqraʾ*—meaning both read and recite—he merely partakes in "the archetype of revelation" (*l'archétype de la révélation*) (Meddeb, *Talismano* 143/136).

In his commentary on the sura, Muhammad Asad writes of the pen's significance:

> "The Pen" is used here as a symbol for the art of writing or, more specifically, for all knowledge recorded by means of writing: and this explains the symbolic summons 'Read!' . . . Man's unique ability to transmit, by means of written records, his thoughts, experiences and insights from individual to individual, from generation to generation, and from one cultural environment to another endows all human knowledge with a cumulative character; and since, thanks to this God-given ability, every human being partakes, in one way or another, in mankind's continuous accumulation of knowledge, man is spoken of as being "taught by God" things which the single individual does not—and indeed, cannot—know by himself. (Qur'an trans. Asad 1099)

According to Asad, the references to "al-ʿalaq"—meaning either germ-cell or blood clot—indicate that as a product of divine creation, man is imbued with "the will and ability to acquire knowledge" on a cellular level (ibid.). Framing intellectual pursuits as a biological imperative, the sura combines the act of biological creation with the quest for knowledge, as well as spiritual pedagogy with revelation.

Asad further argues that the reference to *al-qalam* in sura 68 of the same title alludes to the foundational act of revelation in "Al-ʿalaq." It opens with a divine oath sworn on the instrument of the *qalam*: "CONSIDER the pen, and that they write [therewith]!" (Qur'an 68:1 trans. Asad). Qur'anic commentator Yusuf Ali writes that "the mystical Pen and the mystical Record are the symbolic foundation of the Revelation to man" (Qur'an trans. Ali 1585n5593). This reading reiterates the divine genealogy of knowledge, beginning with the Prophet Muhammad's miraculous revelation, which lies at the very heart of being both human and Muslim. *Talismano*'s reference to divine revelation and the *qalam/calame* situates the novel within an exegetical model that privileges the sacred pursuit of knowledge through the acts of writing, reading, and interpretation.

The talisman invites interpretation, all the while resisting being fully legible, even to those able to decipher Chinese and Arabic text in a French Tunisian novel. *Talismano* thus champions nonheteronomous modes of reading and interpretation while teasing the reader with illegibility. Moreover, "simply by infiltrating the French book with Arabic and Chinese writing that demands a physical motion for reading (the book must be turned to decipher the sideways text), *Talismano* reshuffles the dominant hierarchy of value by redrawing the map of reading" (Al-Kassim 118). The insertion of the talisman in the novel unseats the French language by compelling it to share the stage with Arabic and Chinese. It further imposes an embodied act of reading, in the literal turning of the book to decipher the text, as an act of textual disruption.

The Taoist ideogram is placed next to the Arabic word *huwa*, a term frequently employed in Sufi iconography and intoned in *dhikr* as a symbolic placeholder for Allah. In Arabic, *huwa* is the masculine third-person singular nominative pronoun that most commonly translates to "he." It is also a contraction derived from the end of the phrase *lā ilāha illā huwa* (there is no God but he), which serves as an intimate alternative to the more conventional saying *lā ilāha illā allāh* (there is no God but Allah). As spiritual philosophies, both Taoism and Sufism rely upon the symbology of the path or way.[32] This individual journey of spiritual awareness often entails relinquishing worldly desire, ego-centered notions of the self, and language as a significatory order—as I discussed in Chapter 1 in relation to Maḥmūd al-Masʿadī's *Mawlid al-nisyān*.

The Arabic text written along the top and bottom edges of the talisman reads: "*al-sayf al-qāṭiʿ wa-l-hilāl al-sāṭiʿ / lā sayf mithla al-haqq wa-lā ʿawn mithla al-sidq*," and is rendered in the original French as: "*L'épée qui tranche / Le croissant qui scintille / Pas d'épée comme la vérité / Pas d'aide comme la sincérité*" (The slashing sword and the shining crescent / There is no sword like truth, and no succor like sincerity) (Meddeb, *Talismano* 143/136, translation modified). Meddeb does not translate much of the remaining text, particularly the writing along the right side of the talisman, which requires physically turning the book to be read: "*Allāh laṭīf bi-ʿibādihi yarzuqu man yashāʾ wa-huwa al-qawwī al-ʿazīz raqīb qarīb*" (Allah is gracious/gentle to his servants; He blesses those He wills; and He is the powerful, the mighty, the exalted, the near). The lack of a translation makes portions of the text inaccessible to the French reader unfamiliar with Arabic, as with much of the wordplay throughout the novel.

The talisman contains various invocations of God's divine attributes embodied within his ninety-nine holy names. In this context, the omission imbues the incantation with a symbolic power that exceeds semiotic or translational parsing—as with the Taoist ideogram or the word *huwa*. Along the bottom of the talisman are the names of the Abrahamic prophets ʿĪsā (Jesus), Yūnis (Jonah), and Isḥāq (Isaac), as well as ʿAlī (ʿAlī ibn Abī Ṭālib, the cousin and son-in-law of the Prophet Muhammad) and the title Sulṭān.[33] In the upper left-hand corner is the word Allāh, with Ādam (Adam) written below it. Notably, the text along the sides is written in *maghribī* script, and specifically, the *mabsūṭ* style generally reserved for the Qurʾan. By contrast, the word *huwa* is rendered in *ruqʿa*, a more formal script of the Ottoman period commonly used for seals and official documents.[34] Meddeb thus modulates the meaning and significance of the text with the use of different scripts from the archives of Arabic calligraphy.

The talisman's polyphony is further complicated by Meddeb's own presence within the imagistic text. As Dina Al-Kassim astutely observes, within the "series of conventional lines praising god, the author has cleverly encrypted his own name, Abdel-Wahab-Me deb [*sic*], in a series of synonyms" (Al-Kassim 117). By graphically imprinting his name within the narrator's talisman, Meddeb literally inscribes himself within the (pseudo) religious text. We must recall, however, that the narrator insists that the talisman, despite his initial reservations, was beyond his own comprehension. It is thus a palimpsest not only of texts but also of authors, readers, and interpreters.

The talisman functions not only as a metaphor for revelation but also as a visual-textual object with a material presence in the book. On the threshold of the legible and the illegible, it moves between languages, scripts, words, images, icons, and symbols. As an object, it compels the reader to engage in embodied acts of reading by disrupting the orientation of the book's pages. As a text, it is in a state of perpetual self-translation, as if in coded dialogue with itself. As a talisman, however, it offers protection and good fortune only to its intended—in this case, the Nubian café owner. As readers, we are left puzzling over an enigmatic object drained of its divine aura. We approach it forensically, picking apart its words and images. We bring ourselves physically and psychically into the analytic space. It is what the talisman, and Meddeb, demand of us. A microcosm for the novel as a whole, the talisman/novel hover on the edge of intelligibility, fostering reading practices that align with Meddeb's phenomenological hermeneutics. Relying upon a mode of symbolization that mirrors the Sufi dialectic between the human and the divine, the transcendental and the phenomenological, the exoteric and the esoteric, *Talismano* mobilizes textual excess/absence to generate ethical and imaginative openings. It builds upon the tradition of apophasis by exalting the ineffable dimensions of spiritual experience against the theological logocentrism that Meddeb aligns with orthodox Sunni Islam. In so doing, the novel enacts a model of writing, reading, and interpretation as an ethical praxis bound to the spiritual cultivation of the self.

Arabesques of Selfhood

Talismano's semiotic economy of excess is further inscribed in Meddeb's extensive meditations on the praxis of writing. The narrator-author frequently likens the novel's nonlinear narrative style to Arabic calligraphy and the arabesque. Both forms reside between the symbolic and the mimetic, simultaneously embodying an aesthetics of textual excess and "a metaphysics of absence" (Elhariry 257). In his ruminations on writing, Meddeb invokes the ancient Egyptian god Thoth, a mediating force associated with divine arbitration, the judgment of the dead, science, and magic, who is also the creator of the alphabetic system of writing and scribe of the underworld. After he begs Thoth to teach him the secrets of writing, the narrator strikes up a series of conversations with various philosophers, theologians, and novelists on how and why they write. Hailing largely from Mediterranean countries, they range from canonical European thinkers such as Cervantes, Jean Genet, Cavafy, to polymaths of the Arab world such as Ibn Baṭūṭa[35] and Ibn Khaldūn,[36] the philosophers Ibn ʿArabī and al-Ghazālī, the Persian poet Rūmī, and the Turkish mystic and poet Yunus Emre.[37] For these thinkers, writing is a form of spiritual praxis inextricably linked to subject formation. Sharing many of the same philosophical interlocuters, Meddeb's Sufi-inflected approach to literary creation echoes Maḥmūd al-Masʿadī's aesthetic philosophy.

In an imagined conversation with the narrator-author, Ibn ʿArabi discusses the commentary he wrote in defense of his poetry collection *Tarjumān al-ashwāq* (Interpreter/translator of desires), which was criticized for its intimate representation of divine love.[38] Ibn ʿArabī's notoriously cryptic analysis applies the Qurʾanic dialectic between the *ẓāhir* (exoteric) and *bāṭin* (esoteric) to his poetry collection. The process of unearthing the latter entails an interpretative act of revealing that Ibn ʿArabī describes as *kashf*, unveiling or uncovering. A concept with revelatory overtones, *kashf* references gnostic knowledge acquired by Sufis in their personal communion with the divine.[39]

Ibn ʿArabī describes the intensely phenomenological nature of interpretation as providing one with "the satisfaction and nourishment [*la nourriture*] of their intelligence" (231/215). Writing, he elaborates, resembles the Sufi stages of *tafātuḥ*, or opening up, and *fanāʾ*, or annihilation of the self into the divine. It entails "the death of the self [*mourir à soi-même*]. . . . To write is to reflect energy as it opens up to you [*Écrire c'est refléter l'énergie telle qu'elle s'ouvre à toi*]. Arouse it. Contemplate it. Delight in its richness. Renew your vigor. Inscribe your experience upon the mirror of the world. Project yourself as fragment of the archetype [*Projette-toi fragment de l'archétype*]. Reside at limit's edge [*Sois au bord de la limite*]" (230–31/215). Criticizing the Arab Peripatetics, al-Ghazalī similarly experiences writing as both transcendental and embodied: "There is knowledge that is incommunicable [*des connaissances incommunicables*], there is a knowing [*un savoir*] that requires experience, a bodily initiation. . . . . I contest any writing restricted to describing things as they are observed, as nothing but fixedness, without grasping the implications that transfigure them" (234–35/218–19, trans. modified).[40] Meddeb's narrator-author teases out in both Ibn ʿArabī and al-Ghazalī a model of writing that, true to the concept of *adab*, nourishes the intellectual and spiritual faculties of the writer, just as it cultivates those of the reader.

Talismano's approach to writing is intimately connected to its understanding of the self, insofar as writing in the novel is analogous to the analytic space.[41] The narrator-author's preoccupation with theorizing the self echoes the novel's concern with the complexities of textual representation. He writes that the analytic process centers on the self as "an enigma irreducible to meaning, to law, to all standards" (*énigme irréductible au sens, à la loi, à la mesure*) (55/57). Sufism, however, offers an alternative model of subjectivity, one that is "in thought and practice, devoted to the glory of extinguishing the I, rendered wholly material and only very secondarily ascetic" (*la gloire de l'extinction du je, matérialisé corps très subsidiairement ascétique*) (56/58). Meddeb likens this embodied experience to the moth drawn to the eternal flame—a frequent motif in Sufi literature, including in Manṣūr al-Ḥallāj's *Kitāb al-Ṭawāsīn*.[42]

During their encampment in al-Zaytūna, the revolutionaries organize themselves by guild, with each group convening around their respective symbol. The calligraphers reinvigorate al-Ḥallāj's *Kitāb al-ṭawāsīn*, which he wrote while in prison. The infamous text includes two chapters of dialogue between Iblīs (the devil) and God about his refusal to bow down to Adam. Respecting the revolutionaries' new convention of *suppression of the Name*, by which the name of God is to be absent from all texts and iconography, the calligraphers substitute each instance of Allah with a void. Al-Ḥallāj's revised text reads as follows:

> *The point is the principle of any line, and the line is but an assemblage of points. And all lines, straight or curved, spring from this same point. And anything that falls under our gaze is a point between two others. Here is the evidence that* [the void] *is apparent through each act of contemplation. This is why I declare: there is nothing in which I do not see nothingness* [the void!]. (113)[43]

Al-Ḥallāj uses the geometric concepts of the point and line to illustrate the omnipresence of the divine within all things sensible or imaginable. By stating that everything originates "*de ce même point*," he articulates the divine interconnectedness of all acts and objects of creation. Substituting Allah with a void—or that which refuses to be named—the calligraphers' new text replaces what Mohammed Arkoun calls "Islamic logocentrism" with a literal spatial opening.[44] In re/un-writing al- Ḥallāj's notorious text, Meddeb further radicalizes an already controversial figure within Islamic history. *Talismano*'s heresiology invokes and celebrates liminal figures in order to craft an alternative Islamic intellectual genealogy.

Meddeb mobilizes the visual-textual metaphors of calligraphy and the arabesque to stage graphic interventions into theological logocentrism through the Sufi conceptual language of the ineffable. In contrast to the representational nature of painting in Christianity, Meddeb writes that Islamic calligraphy's graphic ornamentation "dissolved the meaning of the written word in the calligrapher's sweeping, jubilant gesture" (*ou plutôt dissolvent le sens de l'écrit par le geste ample et jubilant*) (113/110). Because it "overruns the bare space of representation to flourish and ferret about, arabesque-like" (*envahit l'espace nu de la represéntation pour y fleurir et s'y farfouiller arabesque*), writing encapsulates both an excess and a loss of meaning (Meddeb 114/111). The disruptive yet generative power of *Talismano*'s itinerant textual trajectories reaches a climax in the novel's closing section.

Nomadic Cartographies of Resistance

As the revolutionary retinue make their way across the city toward the vast expanse of desert that covers much of southern Tunisia, they debate their fate. One group of sorceresses suggest that after the ritual exorcism they must leave Tunis in order to attain the ineffable and inconceivable. Describing the city as a "tomb," they count down the hours until their burial. The sorceresses warn: "Our turning toward timeworn values and the reemergence of the dying craft guilds do not constitute a return to the way things were, nor the fantasy of a weak imagination . . . no, we are neither backsliding nor simplemindedly well-intentioned when it comes to tradition. We are more modern than you may think. We are readying ourselves to galvanize the as-yet unthought" (201).[45] The group's carnivalesque activities are described as heralding a new age, that of "the unthought" (*l'impensé*)—recalling Madīn's desire to "imagine the unimaginable" in al-Masʿadī's *Mawlid al-nisyān. Talismano*'s resuscitation of seemingly anachronistic modes of social, economic, and religious organization—such as the craft guilds or practices like mummification, alchemy, and sorcery—signal a ritual exorcism of the Maghreb's past in an attempt to facilitate *that which has yet to be imagined.* Suggesting that they move from the "despair and ruin" of the city toward the mountains and desert, the sorceresses prophesize "a retreat outside this history whose final cataclysm is still liable to take us unawares" (*le retrait hors cette histoire dont le cataclysme final risque de nous surprendre*) (201–2/189). The desert, with its mythic "nomadic ancestry" (*aïeux nomades*) offers a reprieve from the concentration of state and religious power rooted in the very architectonics of Tunis as a postcolonial metropolis (11/17).

In the novel's brief epilogue, we learn of the group's divided fate: on the coattails of the besieging of the city by the neocolonial forces of the Spanish, French, and Turkish, as well as their local thugs, the revolutionaries take leave of the city: "*Hijra, voluntary migration, in the footsteps of Hājir, Hagar, beyond defeat, into retreat: orphans all*" (*Hijra migration voluntaire, à suivre le chemin de Hâjir, Agar, hors défaite, vers le retrait: orphelins*) (259/241). Spending months in limbo, the group eventually divides into two; half continue their pagan revival in the tradition of the Banī Murra desert nomads. Our narrator's choice to migrate west, but not in exile, mirrors his interspersed references throughout the story to Paris as his chosen city of exile and likely reflects Meddeb's own proclivities. This westward migration is imbued with the nomadic spirit of the region's desert-dwellers, the Sahrawis and Touaregs, and entails the metaphoric extension of the desert's imaginative possibilities: "*As for myself, I join those bound westward* [*au chemin de l'occident*], *taghrīb and not ghurba* [taghrîb *et non* ghurba], *to gather the scattered forces of nomads, Sahrāwis and Touāregs, to deepen the capacities of the desert* [*à approfondir les capacités du désert*]" (260/242, translation modified).

The stream-of-consciousness passage that closes the novel brings together the various narrative and thematic threads running through *Talismano*; I quote at length:

> *We have confided through writing, but without giving you a foothold, have strained your eyes with our arabesque of words, have recommended the circuits of our journey, have warned you of the fissure in all that meets the eye, have unsettled you on high moral grounds, have ruined among you the most robust constitutions, have dusted myself off, vanished into thin air, have found my way inside you through the least perceptible slit; text like dust to be read as the Book in reverse, a text replete, where four or five ideas repeat, in the tawdry play on difference, having despaired of any law, interleaving experience where, through my I, the living might find mutual recognition: put down in writing, dreamed in reverse in the Book, dearly departed allograph that disoriginates a sated sensibility, transcribed left to right while body and eyes follow their meditative course in the text from right to left, in the same horizontal continuity the inverse direction becomes clear: words of exile, sun concealed, man disappearing, from the here to the there we wander between concealed and revealed, sunset to sunrise, favoring blood-red fall over luminous rebirth, genesis of the ephemeral, stealthy sundown: maghreb; beyond veils, reappear to the pagan yes through the text as long as the days are shortening, to affirm its presence on the trail of abandonment, by antithesis and physically inverted graphic, by return to themes that withstand no words: body, pleasure, death, desert; all unutterable and transformed into moments of uttering by way of the language of metaphor, rendered archaic even to oneself, old as the world, to repeat that the light to brighten our lands shall come from women: by the planet Jupiter, by chrysolite, by Venus, by hematite, the female will make*

> *fertile the beds tread upon by male readiness; and by this new suffusion may the divided body recover its orphaned other.* (261–62/243–44)[46]

This passage is a meditation on the reader's journey that mirrors the narrator's wanderings on foot. More than a mere dazzling "*arabesque des mots*," *Talismano* disrupts hegemonic and heteronomous epistemologies. By virtue of its use of French, however, the text writes against itself: from left to right, while the body and eye instinctively move from right to left. Meddeb plays with various images of concealment and revealing by translating the Qur'anic concepts of *ẓāhir* and *bāṭin*. Meddeb's neologism *allographie* signals the itinerant textual steps that comprise a rhizomatic network of writing and signification that evades the imposition of fixed meanings. This process relies upon a semantic as well as graphic logic of inversion and antithesis that calls to mind the novel's metaphors of calligraphy and the arabesque as symbolic placeholders for the divine. It is through the body as an instrument of writing and reading that one may approach spiritual completion, or recover "*sa parcelle orpheline*."

Al-Masʿadī's *Mawlid al-nisyān* and Meddeb's *Talismano* both engage with the conceptual language of *taṣawwuf* as an aesthetic and ethical philosophy. They mobilize Sufi figures, texts, and practices in order to stage alternative epistemologies and ontologies of Being. For al-Masʿadī, the ethical cultivation of the Muslim subject begins with attentiveness to the condition of human existence as the foundation for creative pursuits. Meddeb similarly imbues the creative process—particularly the acts of writing, reading, and interpretation—with Sufi poetic language. Despite their respective aesthetic stylizations—the dense symbolism of al-Masʿadī's formal prose and the textual excess of Meddeb's meandering novel—both works rely upon a conceptual and textual performance of the ineffable dimensions of spiritual praxis.

Like *Talismano*, al-Ṭāhir Waṭṭār's 1974 novel *Al-zilzāl* (*The Earthquake*) mobilizes Qur'anic discourse in order to critique the failures of the postindependence regime. Whereas Meddeb draws upon Sufi and Qur'anic intertextuality, Waṭṭār explicitly maps apocalyptic Qur'anic rhetoric onto his novel. Mobilizing decadent, carnivalesque, and mythic imagery in order to upend various structures of power, both novels critically examine the ethics of reading and interpretation.

PART II

Ethics of Embodiment

CHAPTER 3

Apocalyptic Aftershocks in al-Ṭāhir Waṭṭār's *Al-zilzāl*

> The nursing female will be distracted from her nursling. Every pregnant female will abort her pregnancy. And people will be drunk but not in intoxication. No. More likely, every hoarder of oil, sugar, and semolina will abandon what he's hoarded. Everyone carrying a basket or shopping cart will drop it and everyone will stop talking for a moment. This is the description of the earthquake in Constantine. The nursing female will be distracted from her nursling only after she runs through the streets chasing after food. All the fetuses in the stomachs of these cows of Satan are less valuable than five gallons of oil, or five pounds of sugar. And could these people possibly be drunker than they are now? They've been showing signs of drunkenness for a long time.
>
> AL-ṬĀHIR WAṬṬĀR, *The Earthquake* (88/83–84, TRANSLATION MODIFIED)

Seamlessly integrating the Qurʾanic sura "Al-ḥajj" ("The Pilgrimage"), which warns of the major signs of the apocalypse, al-Ṭāhir Waṭṭār's 1974 novel *Al-zilzāl* (*The Earthquake*) resignifies Islamic eschatology in its portrayal of postrevolutionary Algeria.[1] By removing Qurʾanic voweling, verse marks, and quotation marks, Waṭṭār blends the sura both formally and thematically into the diegetic narrative—rendering them nearly indistinguishable.[2] Moreover, he modulates the sura's tone by excluding its cautionary opening: "One day you will see" (*yawma tarawnahā*) in order to shift its apocalyptic temporality. Waṭṭār removes the sura from its moral context of spiritual accountability, inserting it instead within a material economy of consumption and greed. He further infuses the sura's symbolic representation of the apocalyptic end of life, which is invoked through its references to aborted fetuses and abandoned infants, with a markedly gendered critique of Algerian society. Recalling Constantine's 1947 earthquake, as well as the Qurʾanic foretelling of the earthquake of the Day of Resurrection (Yawm al-Qiyāma), Waṭṭār represents the apocalypse through both prolepsis and analepsis. Such subtle manipulations of Qurʾanic text are performed throughout *Al-zilzāl* and contribute to Waṭṭār's attempt to turn the Qurʾan into a living literary repository, as well as a vehicle for social, political, and moral critique.

Satirically narrated through the perspective of the misanthropic Shaykh ʿAbd al-Majīd Bū al-Arwāḥ, *Al-zilzāl* traces his return to the city of Constantine after an absence of sixteen years. Bū al-Arwāḥ seeks to evade the nationalization of private property planned under the 1970s agrarian revolution by registering his extensive landholdings with distant relatives. His plans are thwarted, however, when he is confronted with Constantine's transformation under Algerian socialism. Disturbed by the seeming dissolution of social hierarchies, Bū al-Arwāḥ is haunted by increasingly prescient images of the earthquake of the Day of Resurrection. A caricature of the religious elite who prospered under French imperialism, Bū al-Arwāḥ manipulates Qurʾanic discourse to suit his personal interests. Even his name—*Bū*, a contraction of *Abū*, meaning father, and *al-arwāḥ*, meaning "the souls"—speaks to his self-appointed role as a patriarchal spiritual savior. Similar to Abdelwahab Meddeb's *Talismano*, *Al-zilzāl* upends various teleologies by cutting across narrative, historical, and theological time. Constantly blurring the line between reality and fiction, past and present, as well as history and mythology, the diegesis also moves in and out of the consciousness of a single narrator as they traverse the city in the contracted narrative time of a single day.

This chapter investigates *Al-zilzāl*'s mobilization of Qurʾanic eschatology to unsettle Algerian nationalist discourse. In its broader theological sense, eschatology generally denotes an apocalyptic end of time, history, or humanity. Islamic eschatology encompasses a complete reordering of the world through the foretold major and minor signs of the apocalypse, the Day of Resurrection, as well as the final judgment. Islamic theologians offer a diverse range of exegetical interpretations of Islamic eschatology.[3] While many emphasize the literal end of the world, some theologians interpret eschatology as a metaphysical end to reality and unification with the divine—as we saw in Maḥmūd al-Masʿadī's *Mawlid al-nisyān*.[4] *Al-zilzāl* integrates Islamic eschatology into both its thematic and narrative structure by translating its central concepts—moral disquietude, social chaos, temporal disorientation, planetary disruption, states of limbo, and resurrection—into an aesthetic lexicon that shapes the novel's construction of narrative time and space.

Al-zilzāl's apocalyptic rhetoric, however, does not simply expose a totalizing end in itself. Rather than ordering history as a series of colonial ruptures, the novel's eschatological structure transforms the present into a suspended state of destruction, chaos, and trauma bound to an emptied future—as in Mikhail Bakhtin's eschatological chronotope.[5] By reworking Islamic eschatological symbolism and mythology, *Al-zilzāl* stages a political, aesthetic, and historiographic intervention into the very foundations of Algerian nationalist discourse. Reading Algerian nationalist rhetoric through "mythological themes of quest, voyage, descent into the underworld, rites of passage[,] . . . death and resurrection, hero-births, withdrawal and apotheosis," Waṭṭār resignifies the apocalyptic concept of the end to illustrate the untenability of teleologically staged historical narratives (Granara, "Mythologising" 1–2). The novel critically investigates discourses of Algerian national identity in the projects of Arab socialism, economic nationalization, agrarian reform, Arabism (*ʿurūba*), and Islamism.[6] Through literary manipulations of Qurʾanic eschatology, *Al-zilzāl* renarrativizes postindependence Algeria in relation to early Islamic history, the Arab invasion of North Africa, French colonialism, and capitalist globalization.

"Islam Is My Religion, Arabic Is My Language, Algeria Is My Homeland"

Born to an indigenous Amazigh family in eastern Algeria, al-Ṭāhir Waṭṭār (1936–2010) was a prominent journalist, critic, and writer, as well as an active member of the National Liberation Front (Front de Libération Nationale, or FLN).[7] While his primary spoken language was Tamazight and politically Waṭṭār was a notable defender of Berberophone languages, his formal education was almost exclusively in Arabic. He began his education at an Islamic madrasa and eventually moved to Constantine in 1952 to study Islamic jurisprudence at the Ben Bādīs Institute. Waṭṭār continued his religious education at Zaytūna University in Tunis between 1954 and 1956, eventually leaving to join the ranks of the FLN. Though initially formed as a revolutionary body that led the resistance movement in Algeria's war of independence (1954–1962), the FLN controversially emerged as the dominant and only constitutionally acknowledged party in Algeria's postindependence government. The party fused together three primary ideological tenets: Algerian nationalism, socialism, and Islamism. Following independence, Waṭṭār moved back to Algeria, where he assumed the position of FLN party controller. While he held his post until 1984, Waṭṭār's political leanings diverged from the FLN's official party line, and he was increasingly marginalized for his Marxist views, a conflict that is played out in Waṭṭār's 1974 novel *Al-lāz* (The ace).[8]

Waṭṭār's complex relationship with Algeria's leading party can be read across his literary and critical writings. Contributing to and founding various Arabic periodicals—including: *Al-aḥrār* (The liberals), *Al-jamāhīr* (The masses), and *Al-sha'b* (The people)—Waṭṭār was frequently subject to censorship under the regime of Houari Boumédiène (1965–1978). Debbie Cox argues that the anticipation of government censorship shaped the structural and thematic motifs of his fiction. She reads the political ambivalence of Waṭṭār's writing as simultaneously symptomatic of, and in opposition to, the state ideologies of 1970s Algeria—a time he would come to revisit in *Al-zilzāl*. In her reading of *Al-lāz*, for example, Cox highlights the novel's representation of the conflicts and contradictions that plagued the FLN surrounding questions of "unity, identity, the role of religion, and history itself," a theme continued in both *Al-zilzāl* and Waṭṭār's 1975 novel *'Urs baghl* (A mule's wedding) (Cox, "The Novels" 99).

Deeply invested in Algerian Arabism, Waṭṭār infamously stated when asked by an interviewer whether the murder of the Francophone novelist Tahar Djaout in 1993 was a loss for Algeria, that it was "a loss for his children, a loss for his wife, and a loss for France."[9] Djaout's murder was among the first of a wave of violent killings targeting Algerian journalists and intellectuals, most of whom were Francophone, that took place during the 1990s.[10] While the exact details of his murder remain unknown, many believe it to be the work of the militant organization Groupe Islamique Armé (GIA). Due to his controversial statement, Waṭṭār's works have often been read as promoting an Arabist or Islamist agenda.[11] While I argue that *Al-zilzāl* reveals the ambivalent and complex position that Arabism and Islamism occupy in Algerian history, it is necessary to contextualize this within Waṭṭār's broader views on Francophonie. Waṭṭār explained in the interview that it was precisely over "the issue of the Arabic language and national identity" (*qaḍiyyat al-lugha al-'arabiyya wa-l-huwiyya al-'arabiyya*) that he and Djaout had a falling out. He continued: "Tahar Djaout was mistaken when he considered the French language to be an Algerian and national language. French, in Algeria, is the language of the administration, the language of the elite. . . . This is one form through which French colonialism continues and it is our right to refuse this. It is [in fact] our responsibility to refuse it" (Waṭṭār, Interview). Although *Al-zilzāl* contests the unilateral institutionalization of Arabism and Islamism as statist policies, Waṭṭār's denial of Tahar Djaout as a *legitimate* Algerian national voice renders legible his refusal of a Francophone legacy for postrevolutionary Algeria.

Waṭṭār's comments on Tahar Djaout's death need to be contextualized within the complex history of Algerian nationalist discourse. As historian James McDougall argues, the modernist discourse of Algerian national identity borrowed, in large part, from the Algerian Salafi reformers who promoted a "unitary, undifferentiated and exalted model of community upon which the revolutionary order would come to rest" (McDougall, *History and the Culture of Nationalism* 3).[12] *Al-zilzāl*'s eschatological motifs and structure unsettle this purist ideology in ways that attenuate Waṭṭār's staunch Arabism nearly twenty years later. The novel's engagement with colonial-era pedagogy and language policy, the Islamic reformist movement, anticolonial and nationalist rhetoric, as well as postrevolutionary policies around educational, religious, agricultural, and economic reform, play out against the heterogeneous history of Islam in Algeria.

While the majority of Algeria's Muslim population is Sunni of the Mālikī school, there remain small Ḥanafī and Ibāḍī contingencies, as well as a minority community of schismatic Khawārij.[13] Algeria also has a long tradition of Sufi brotherhoods, to which a number of the ʿulamāʾ themselves belonged during the medieval period (L. C. Brown 56).[14] Even more dramatically than in Morocco and Tunisia, French colonial policies fueled inter- and intrareligious tensions by differentially governing Arab Muslims, Arab Jews, and indigenous Berberophone/Kabyle populations. A major figure signaling this history in Waṭṭār's novel is the Algerian reformer Shaykh ʿAbd al-Ḥāmid Bin Bādīs (1889–1940). One of the prominent reformers of the early twentieth century, Bin Bādīs founded the Algerian Association of Muslim ʿUlamāʾ in 1931. He was also largely influenced by Egyptian Muslim reformist thought—particularly the writings of Muḥammad ʿAbduh (1849–1905) and Jamāl al-Dīn al-Afghānī (1838–97)—to which he was exposed during his studies at Zaytūna University in Tunis.[15] As Islamic sociologist Charles Kurzman explains: "Ibn Badis formulated a program that asserted the Arab and Islamic identity of Algerians, stressed Arabic and Islamic education, and prepared Algerians for independence from the French. In addition, he proposed a modernist interpretation of the Qurʾan that attributed the decline of Islamic society to mystical practices, intellectual stagnation, disunity, and political despotism" (93). This rhetoric was largely spread through the reformist journals *Al-muntaqid* (The critic) and *Al-shahāb* (The meteor). It also informed the pedagogical practices of the network of free Islamic and Qurʾanic schools established by the association in order to provide an Arab/ic alternative to the French educational infrastructure.[16]

Algeria's first independent president, Ahmed Ben Bella (1962–1965), inaugurated the country's aggressive Arabization (*taʿrīb*) policy, primarily through the implementation of mandatory hours of Arabic study (Ait-siselmi and Marley 197). He also instituted a number of Soviet-influenced economic policies, such as the nationalization of private industry and an agrarian reform policy (Naylor 56). Additional reforms emerged under President Houari Boumédiène (1965–1978), who shifted attention to urbanization and the industrial sectors of Algeria's economy, funded in large part through the nationalization of Algeria's oil industry. Boumédiène's cultural revolution continued to emphasize Arabic and Islam as the primary vehicles of Algeria's modernization and its reinstatement to precolonial glory—a very different approach than Bourguiba's in Tunisia. While these reforms carried on the political projects initiated by the Front de Libération Nationale (FLN) during the battle for independence, they privileged "an Algeria founded on ('pure') Arabic and ('pure') Islam [that] left little room for other languages—the Berber and Arabic dialects of the population—and cultural expression, including the everyday, lived Islam of both berberophones and arabophones" (McDougall, "Myth and Counter-Myth" 68).

Algerian reformist rhetoric was mobilized under both Ben Bella and Boumédiène in the state's self-fashioning as a "technocratic orthodoxy" that fused together religious authority and the promise of modernization (Vatin 233). *Al-zilzāl*'s eschatological register reconfigures precisely this double invocation of a glorious Islamic past with the future of modernity—similar to Meddeb's attack on Muḥammad ʿAbduh in *Talismano*. The novel critiques the regime's *double ideologization*, to borrow Moroccan historian Abdallah Laroui's turn of phrase to describe the manner in which Marxist ideologies were simultaneously assimilated, "Arabized," and prone to dogmatism (Laroui 106–7). The postrevolutionary government "made itself legitimate by claiming that it alone could do both in upholding religion and in modernizing the country. The intercessor between God and development is no longer a saint, a prophet, or a muftī, but rather, the state apparatus" (Vatin 233). Waṭṭār's novel challenges the liberatory rhetoric of Algerian socialism by paralleling it with both the Arab-Islamic expansion into North Africa and French colonial modernizing discourse. In so doing, it unravels their mutual reliance upon a teleological model of historical time and the mythic promise of future progress.

Narrative Apocalypse

Al-zilzāl's eschatological register manifests in both the apocalyptic representation of Constantine as a site of ruin, decay, and death, as well as in the tormented temporality through which Bū al-Arwāḥ navigates this dystopic space in the compressed span of one afternoon. The city of Constantine, like Bū al-Arwāḥ's consciousness, occupies a threshold past-future temporality. It is both a relic of an atavistically imagined precolonial past, and a haunting reminder of utopian colonial modernity gone awry. Due to the interconnected nature of narrative time and space, the threshold, as Bakhtin reminds us, is linked to our very understanding of consciousness within the novel (Bakhtin, *Problems* 167–72). *Al-zilzāl*'s spatial and temporal liminality reflect a state of moral and psychological limbo that is also a potential site of transgression—as we saw in both *Mawlid al-nisyān* and *Talismano*.

Shuttling between various discursive modes, *Al-zilzāl* distorts the boundaries between various kinds of speech. It undermines authoritative historical narratives, state-endorsed social and political configurations, as well as narrative genres and structures. Like that of *Talismano*'s narrator-author, Bū al-Arwāḥ's account is highly fragmented and alternates between dialogue, stream of consciousness, memories, dreams, and hallucinations. This is further interrupted by the frequent intrusion of voices representing the masses of Algerian society. The novel's constant shifts between speakers, genres of speech, past and present, as well as reality and fantasy, generate a disorienting narrative topography. In this sense it recalls the Qur'an's formal qualities of multivocality, nonlinearity, asynchronicity, and grammatical or rhetorical code-switching.

Al-zilzāl's use of different registers of Arabic challenges the institutionalization of Arabism and Islamism as discursive orthodoxies that exclude other possible iterations of Algerian national identity. Bū al-Arwāḥ's thoughts and speech are almost exclusively delivered in Qur'anic and classical Arabic, standing in marked contrast with the masses that drown out his Qur'anic recitations with their discussions of poverty, corruption, and globalization. Their dialogue is rendered in a modified Modern Standard Arabic that is infused with the rhythm, cadence, and inflection of colloquial Algerian Arabic. This distances Bū al-Arwāḥ's Qur'anic Arabic from the everyday lived discourse of the Algerian social body, a distance the novel compels its readers to navigate and mediate. In so doing, *Al-zilzāl* highlights Arabic's internal diversity as a heteroglossic language that encompasses multiple registers of speech. Bū al-Arwāḥ's self-interested use of the Qur'an and hadith to justify his abusive relationships with women and expand his landholdings further demonstrates the ability of religious discourse to be manipulated for personal ends.[17] The Arabic language is thus the medium of official discourse, as well as the very currency of its undoing.[18] Waṭṭār's novel lays out these contradictions most explicitly in Bū al-Arwāḥ's simultaneous externalization and internalization of the Qur'anic vision of the end of times.

Engaging with the long history of travel writing in the Arabic literary tradition, *Al-zilzāl* uses geography and time to reorient social, historical, and political mythologies.[19] In this regard, the novel integrates a variety of tropes from the classical Arabic tradition that range from the *riḥla* genre of travel writing, to the archetype of the corrupt shaykh.[20] In addition to Shaykh Bū al-Arwāḥ's journey from Algiers to Constantine being a *riḥla*, or voyage, it also figures as a *hijra*. The Qur'anic sura "Al-ḥajj," which is intertextually woven across the novel, references the journey of the Prophet Muhammad and his followers from Mecca to Medina in 622 CE. As miriam cooke argues, the Prophet's *hijra* is rhetorically invoked in literary travel tropes in part because "Islam's insistence on actual and symbolic travel allows for simultaneous self-positionings in the local and the global and then back to another local, in the present and the past and then back to a transformed present" (158). Waṭṭār inverts the sura, demonstrating Bū al-Arwāḥ's spiritual journey as one toward religious disillusionment rather than enlightenment.

Constantine, the urban backdrop of Bū al-Arwāḥ's *hijra*, provides the ideal setting for *Al-zilzāl*'s apocalyptic unfolding. Situated on an elevated plateau and framed by a deep ravine, Constantine is a city intersected by seven bridges—a revered number in both the Qur'an and Sufism. In the novel, the city is suspended between unfulfilled dreams of colonial grandeur and the harsh reality of postrevolutionary life, as the promise of modernity is replaced by the destruction of the very idea of a future: "This is what happens to every netherworld [*al-ʿawālim al-suflā*]. It deteriorates, crumbles, until nothing of it remains except its lowliness [*sufliyyatihā*]" (Waṭṭār, *The Earthquake* 109/112). Structured over seven chapters that are each named after one of Constantine's bridges, the novel's narrative progression mirrors the spatiality of the city. Relics of the colonial past, the architecturally impressive suspension bridges were constructed as part of the French geopolitical remapping of Algeria.[21] The bridges function as physical signposts along the way to Constantine's foretold demise. Beginning with Bāb al-Qanṭara, the reader then moves to Sīdī M'sid, Sīdī

Rashīd, Majāz al-Ghanam (Bridge at Flock Crossing), Jisr al-Maṣʿad (Elevator Bridge), Jisr al-Shayāṭīn (Demons' Bridge), and finally Jisr al-Huwāʾ (Bridge of the Abyss). The successive movement across these threshold bridges echoes the novel's eschatology, which ends with the psychotic breakdown of Shaykh Bū al-Arwāḥ and the city's (either imagined or actual) demise.

As Bū al-Arwāḥ traverses Constantine, he is disturbed by what he perceives as a perverted social/ist order that unites people of all classes, ethnicities, and genders. He reads this social upheaval as symptomatic of the departure of the French, who maintained order through a clearly demarcated social hierarchy. Bū al-Arwāḥ is also highly critical of socialist programs that allow for upward mobility: affordable medical care, social welfare, and even public education. With an almost ethnographic attention to phenotypes and dialects, he criticizes the hybridization of the city and interprets it as a sign of the coming apocalypse: "The faces are all distinct in Constantine. Facial features vary from one person to another, as do people's physiques. At the time of the occupation, features were more generic: Arab and European, but not now. Today, you can tell the difference between the Shawi Berber from ʿAin al-Baidaʾ or ʿAin M'Lila, from Batina, Khanshala or Shalghoum al-ʿId. . . . Their facial features, like their smells, blatantly proclaim their true identities in this city" (29/10–11, translation modified).[22] Bū al-Arwāḥ's sudden awareness of Constantine's diversity reveals a reality previously occluded by the racial dynamics of French imperialism; Algeria is not simply "Arab." His preoccupation with the ethnic diversity of the Imazighen demonstrates not only the heterogeneity of Algeria's indigenous populations but also their increased presence in urban spaces. While Bū al-Arwāḥ's surprise exposes his own perceptual blindness, it also reflects the evolving social and economic realities of postrevolutionary Algeria, which were fueled in large part by socialist policies that nationalized and centralized industrial development and agriculture.

As with Assia Djebar's *L'amour, la fantasia*, Waṭṭār's representation of Constantine's hybridized social makeup undermines nationalist discourses of Algerian cultural homogeneity. His satirical portrayal of Bū al-Arwāḥ's inability to reconcile himself with postrevolutionary Algerian socialism further calls attention to the complicity of the religious elite in conscripting a monolithic Algerian national identity. More crucially, *Al-zilzāl*'s use of eschatological symbolism allows Waṭṭār to critique these modes of thinking from within the very discourses themselves. Through the complex reworking of the Qur'an, Arabic, and lived Islam, Waṭṭār seems to be breaking away from atavistic understandings of religious consciousness and national identity in ways that complicate his remarks on Djaout's death.

Bū al-Arwāḥ even justifies Constantine as the epicenter of the earthquake of the apocalypse by invoking the country's repeated occupations:

> Maybe that's the city's history from its inception. It ended with the end of the Berbers and started with the beginning of the Romans. It continued beginning and ending between Berbers and Romans and other peoples until the Arabs came. The city resumed its history with them until the Turks arrived. It ended and began until the French came. And now it is ending and beginning all over again. The earthquake which is going to be the demise of this whore of a city has not come yet. When it does, it will do so with a vengeance against her dark and soiled past. (Waṭṭār, *The Earthquake* 81/75–76, translation modified)[23]

Algerian history is eschatologically represented as recursive colonial occupations repeated until the city's inevitable demise. Bū al-Arwāḥ further describes Constantine within the sexual economy of prostitution, claiming that the apocalypse will come in order to avenge its sordid colonial past. While Waṭṭār seems to be contesting a "pure" Algerian ethnic, linguistic, or religious genealogy, it is worth noting that he begins the historical narrative with the destruction of the Berbers. In light of Waṭṭār's Amazigh background and vocal support of Berberophone communities, as well as his choice to write in Arabic and study Islamic jurisprudence, no singular form of cultural self-identification seems privileged here. However, his animosity toward the French colonial legacy is sharply palpable in the novel's critical representation of Bū al-Arwāḥ's nostalgia for French rule and the bourgeois privilege it afforded his class.

Bū al-Arwāḥ is particularly disturbed by the Soviet influence on Algeria's postrevolutionary model of Arab nationalism. His fervent defense of Arabism and Islamism borrows from the reformist rhetoric of Shaykh Bin Bādīs, under whose tutelage his character studied. Like Bin Bādīs, Bū al-Arwāḥ proposes a conservative model of Islamic jurisprudence that relies upon the Qur'an, hadith, and practices of the first generation of Muslims known as *al-salaf al-ṣāliḥ*. However, whereas Bin Bādīs situated his reformist rhetoric in opposition to French colonialism, Bū al-Arwāḥ romanticizes French rule. He blames all of Algeria's challenges on the new socialist regime, which he argues has deviated from the proper Islamic path: "Religion is being loyal to our ancestors [*al-salaf*]. Any reckless innovation [*bidʿa*] is an aberration [*ḍalāl*]" (Waṭṭār, *The Earthquake* 31/12, translation modified).

Bū al-Arwāḥ distinguishes between the model of Algerian nationalism promoted by the Bin Bādīs school of reformers, and that of the postrevolutionary state. He even historically situates the reformist school as the "true" ethnically Arab people:

> Ibn Khaldūn will burn in hell for what he wrote, that it was the Arabs who brought the one, true, monotheistic religion, and that it is impossible that they symbolize the destruction of life. But the fact of the matter is that they not only destroyed life, they destroyed religion as well. The Arabs build with one hand and destroy with the other. . . . These are not Arabs, nor are they Berbers, nor Vandals, nor Tatars, Mongols, or Copts. They are either Russians whom God has sent to devastate our land, or they are people without roots, religion, or denomination. When we as Arabs, pure and free of mind, labored to defend Arabism and our religion, alongside Ben Bādīs and his companions and disciples, men of nobility and learning, we did so as builders and not destroyers. We spread the pure Arabic language, the language of the Holy Qur'an, and we opened people's hearts to the traditions of the Prophet Muhammad and the sacred customs of the *Salaf*. (Waṭṭār, *The Earthquake* 47/33–34, translation modified)[24]

Bū al-Arwāḥ's animosity toward Ibn Khaldūn (1332–1406) stems from his disagreement with the Tunisian polymath's universal glorification of Arabs. He believes that independent Algeria is governed and populated by an entirely different genus of Arab. His alignment of modern Algerians with Russians, or people without racial or religious affiliation, demonstrates his fear of Soviet-influenced Arab nationalism. More crucially, Bū al-Arwāḥ sees the socialist policies of the new regime as incompatible with the true principles of Arabism and Islamism espoused by Bin Bādīs and his followers: the promotion of the pure Arabic language (*lughat al-ḍād*), Qur'anic Arabic (*lughat al-qur'an al-karīm*), the practices of the Prophet Muhammad (hadith and *sunna*) and the conventions of *al-salaf al-ṣāliḥ*.

What is striking about Bū al-Arwāḥ's speech on the decline of Algerian civilization is the relative invisibility of French imperialism. He cites the major groups who had an occupying presence in the region—the Arabs, Berbers, Vandals, Tatars, Mongols, and Copts—with the exception of the French. This touches on a critical point in Bū al-Arwāḥ's revisionist history. Although Bin Bādīs's rhetoric was largely anticolonial in its condemnation of French decadence, the Algerian reformist movement of the 1930s also generated an elite class of religious figures who prospered under French rule. Bū al-Arwāḥ's family lineage is testimony to the various collusions that helped facilitate France's occupation of Algeria. From his great-grandfather through his father, his patrilineage is littered with figures who cooperated with the French in exchange for illustrious military honors and large quantities of land. This anticlerical critique of the ʿulamāʾ and religious elite is echoed across the works of Abdelwahab Meddeb, Assia Djebar, and Driss Chraïbi.

While Bū al-Arwāḥ's criticisms of Algerian socialism are largely inspired by his material self-interest, they also reveal the contradictory logic of the new state order. *Al-zilzāl* highlights the incongruity of postrevolutionary socialist rhetoric and reforms with the reality of the country's rampant capitalism. Bū al-Arwāḥ maps Qurʾanic apocalyptic rhetoric onto the growing overconsumption and waste that plague the city of Constantine: "Perhaps it's the incessant feeling of the earthquake that compels people to spend every bit of money that falls into their hands and to snap up every good that hits the market. They pillage away like criminals sentenced to die [*innahum yanhabūna laʿallahum, ka-l-maḥkūm ʿalayhim bi-l-iʿdām*]" (48/35, translation modified). Waṭṭār goes further, offsetting his character Bū al-Arwāḥ's critique by linking the country's capitalist consumption with the French economic investment in Algerian infrastructure under the occupation: "It is jam-packed with merchandise and loaded with millions of tons of goods, hundreds of thousands of gas bottles, millions and millions of tons of lead and cement, canals and pipes. . . . From this netherworld the water seeps out and escaping in its every drop is a particle of earth and a fragment of this wretched rock" (50–51/37, translation modified).[25] The materiality of this list highlights Algeria's geographic restructuring according to French colonial policies of expansion, settlement, and development. The apocalyptic city represents the corrupt legacy of a French colonial order romanticized by Bū al-Arwāḥ, while also serving as a literal receptacle for the destructive forces of global capitalism.

Aborted Pasts, Sterile Futures

Upon arriving in Constantine, Bū al-Arwāḥ attends a Friday prayer in which the sermon is on the Qurʾanic description of the earthquake of the end of times. The imam employs the image of destruction and upheaval to describe the moral and spiritual implications of the end of times: "Disorientation, terror, and the filling of the soul with darkness [*al-lawn al-dākin*]: this is how Almighty God has described the condition at the final hour, and the Almighty has chosen to use the earthquake to allegorically illustrate that final hour" (33/14–15, translation modified).[26] The imam invokes the Qur'an's metaphoric use of the earthquake to describe a spiritual and psychological experience. He even uses the literary term *isti'āra*, meaning to engage in metaphor or allegory, to demonstrate its figurative use in the sura. It is Bū al-Arwāḥ who interprets the passage literally and envisions an actual earthquake destroying Algeria. I read this divergence as a critique of literalist scriptural interpretations that fail to account for rhetorical language. The Qur'an's literariness thus signals that ways in which hermeneutical practices simultaneously serve an aesthetic and ethical function within Islam.

Even though Bū al-Arwāḥ interprets the earthquake physically, he himself experiences it psychically, spiritually, and ethically as a darkness invading his soul (*al-lawn al-dākin*). Bū al-Arwāḥ complains of a viscous liquid (*al-mādda al-sā'ila*) that spreads throughout his body: "The darkness was spreading in his heart. That viscous fluid was melting. It was getting hotter. He was growing weak in the knees. His neck was getting stiff and his head was pounding. He felt an enormous weight on his shoulders" (87/82–83, translation modified).[27] In these moments Bū al-Arwāḥ enters a trance-like state and is often driven to violent thoughts and acts. As with *Talismano*, *Al-zilzāl* uses the grotesque to reconfigure the world symbolically and materially, thereby inverting social and political hierarchies. While Bū al-Arwāḥ manipulates religious discourse to serve his own personal and financial interests, it is ultimately the Qur'anic sura that turns on him. The Day of Reckoning forces Bū al-Arwāḥ to confront his past and ultimately be defeated by his former indiscretions, both ethical and religious. As Debbie Cox astutely observes, "That this critique [of the religious elite] is expressed in Bu al-Arwah's Quranic language functions to subvert the link between Arabic and the religious elite since the Arabic of the Quran is mobilized by the text *against* Bu al-Arwah" ("The Novels" 103). While Bū al-Arwāḥ's literal interpretation of the sura speaks to his inability to ethically engage in hermeneutical acts, his internalization of the sermon nonetheless signals the importance of embodiment to Qur'an praxis.

Bū al-Arwāḥ's corporeality operates on multiple registers: first, it marks the novel's use of the grotesque as a narrative device for social and political critique. It also calls attention to the relationship between bodily comportment and ethics in Islam. Bū al-Arwāḥ's moral decrepitude manifests both inside and outside his body—swimming through his veins and his soul. Waṭṭār describes his rotund off-kilter physique with "his feet tripping over each other and his stomach and buttocks jiggling. His head lolled around, at times in half circles, and at other times in full circles. His arms dangled as the sweat rolled down his face. His anger was so fierce it made his muscles twitch in spasms" (Waṭṭār, *The Earthquake* 57). Bū al-Arwāḥ's vulgar corporeality is inseparable from his moral decay, a reality that painfully manifests in his violent relations with women.

Plagued with sterility, Bū al-Arwāḥ comes from a family of murderous men with an incestuous history of sexual violence against women. His first marriage is to a child-bride named ʿĀʾisha when she is nine and he fifteen. On their wedding night, they are unable to consummate the marriage until Bū al-Arwāḥ's father forces them to sleep together. The father later attempts to rape ʿĀʾisha and strangles her to death when she refuses him. The cycle of sexual violence continues with Bū al-Arwāḥ, who becomes sexually involved with his father's sixteen-year-old wife, Ḥanīfa, whom he eventually strangles to death. Bū al-Arwāḥ then kidnaps the wife and nine-year-old daughter of a sharecropper, both of whom he rapes and murders.

Waṭṭār's choice of the name ʿĀʾisha for Bū al-Arwāḥ's first wife, and the synchronicity of her age with that of the Prophet Muhammad's third wife, ʿĀʾisha bint Abī Bakr, at the time of their marriage, is crucial to understanding the broader implications of how gender is represented in the novel.[28] Often considered his most beloved wife, ʿĀʾisha stayed married to the Prophet until his death when she was eighteen years of age. She spent the last fifty years of her life as a powerful political, social, and religious figure in her community, as well as in early Islamic history.[29] One of the better-known *muḥaddithāt*, or female transmitters of hadith, ʿĀʾisha was also a trusted exegete of the Qurʾan: "ʿAisha, as Moḥamad's favorite wife, received the state's highest pension: acknowledged as having special knowledge of his ways, sayings and character, she was consulted on the Prophet's *sunnah*, or practice, and gave decisions on sacred law or custom" (L. Ahmed 689).[30] Upon the murder of the third Caliph ʿUthmān ibn ʿAffān, who was a notable supporter of a woman's right to practice her faith publicly, it was ʿĀʾisha who led an army into battle against ʿAlī ibn Abī Ṭālib to avenge his death (689–690).[31]

Referred to as Umm al-Muʾminīn (Mother of the Believers), ʿĀʾisha represents a coeval female Islamic intellectual tradition. I read *Al-zilzāl*'s reference to ʿĀʾisha as indicative of a parallel Islamic genealogy, one that actively includes women as political, social, and ethical agents—a genealogy under threat by Bū al-Arwāḥ and his ilk. The attempted rape and murder of ʿĀʾisha's character in the novel exposes the occlusion and silencing of this very history.[32] Moreover, Bū al-Arwāḥ's mirroring of the Prophet's life in taking a nine-year-old bride demonstrates the dangers of transposing cultural practices from seventh-century Arabia onto twentieth-century Algeria. *Al-zilzāl* therefore undermines not only literalist interpretations of the Qur'an but also early Islamic practices. This has broader implications for the manner in which Islam is recorded, transmitted, interpreted, and practiced. Through his satirization of Bū al-Arwāḥ, Waṭṭār yet again demonstrates the diverse hermeneutical possibilities within Islam. He also seems to be suggesting that Islam be contextualized and adaptive; or, to borrow the words of Leila Ahmed, that we question "whether the religion is to be allowed to remain permanently locked into replicating the outer forms of the specific society into which it was revealed, or whether the true pursuit and fulfillment of the Islamic message entails, on the contrary, the gradual abandonment of laws necessary in its first age" (677).

Unable to locate any suitable heirs who are not martyrs, government officials, or communists, Bū al-Arwāḥ abandons his mission. As he crosses his sixth bridge, Jisr al-Shayāṭīn (Demons' Bridge), he finds himself part of a carnivalesque procession of faceless people. Overpowered by the viscous fluid, he runs toward Jisr al-Huwā' (Bridge of the Abyss), where he sees scores of children whom he imagines to be the impossible progeny of his barren marriages. Bū al-Arwāḥ is forced to reconcile with the women of his past as they appear to him one by one and mock his sterility before he throws each of them into the ravine. It is then that the apocalypse begins: tanks explode, flesh sizzles, and the earth begins to buckle. Bū al-Arwāḥ's final appeal before he attempts to hurl himself off the bridge is to the daughter of 'Uqbah bin Nāfi' (622–83), an Arab general of the Umayyad dynasty who led the Islamic invasion of the Maghreb and eventually died in battle in Algeria. Bū al-Arwāḥ's appeal to her speaks to his attempt to trace a lineage, and notably a feminine one, with the original invaders responsible for Algeria's Arabization and Islamicization. He further reconciles with his own lack of progeny, for it is precisely before his attempted martyrdom that Bū al-Arwāḥ asks her to mourn for him in lieu of a daughter of his own: "You, daughter of 'Uqbah bin Nāfi' from Biskra, exchange trances with me, yours against mine. Cry for me before I jump off this bridge. Cry for all us Bū al-Arwāḥs" (Waṭṭār, *The Earthquake* 178/197, translation modified). The inclusion of a female Islamic lineage, embodied in the figures of 'Ā'isha bint Abī Bakr and the daughter of 'Uqbah bin Nāfi', realizes the novel's eschatological vision by generating a nonfilial Islamic history. In so doing, Waṭṭār also ruptures a genealogical model of Algerian national history—a point I revisit in my discussion of Djebar's *L'amour, la fantasia*.

At the Threshold of the Abyss

In mapping Qurʾanic eschatology onto postindependence Algeria, *Al-zilzāl* creates an eerily fragmented temporality of Algerian national history.[33] The apocalypse unfolds in its narrative recounting of the physical chaos of the city of Constantine, the moral corruption of its inhabitants, but most crucially, in Shaykh Bū al-Arwāḥ's own psyche. However, *Al-zilzāl* is unique in that it does more than simply demonstrate a site of postcolonial rupture through the fractured consciousness of its narrator. Rather, it transforms the traditional form of allegory, whereby the personal narrative serves to explicate a larger political and often national agenda. Waṭṭār presents the national narrative (the postcolonial destruction of Algeria) as symptomatic of the personal narrative (Shaykh Bū al-Arwāḥ's psychotic breakdown), while also demonstrating their mutual imbrication.[34] Furthermore, the constant shifts in language, time, speakers, and states of consciousness deliberately disrupt the novel's temporal and spatial continuity, linguistic purity, and subjective coherence. *Al-zilzāl* then restructures the very temporality of Algerian nationalist discourse—linguistic, literary, religious, and gendered—through Qurʾanic intertextuality and the novel's narrative manipulations of Islamic eschatology.

Waṭṭār mobilizes the Qurʾan formally and thematically in order to explore the complex cultural and political histories of Islamism and Arabism in Algeria. *Al-zilzāl* reveals the disjuncture between Arabism's appropriation by state ideologies and reformist schools of Islamic thought, alongside its ability to function as a rich medium of cultural expression and resistance. For, as James McDougall argues, "the significance of Arabism has largely lain precisely in its ability to evoke a 'dream' or promise; it has been double-edged, nourishing aspirations, providing a powerful idiom of self-expression and political action, as well as serving to frustrate aspirations, attempting to enclose its own promised possibilities in the limiting power of the national state" ("Dream of Exile, Promise of Home" 253). Like much of Waṭṭār's literary oeuvre, *Al-zilzāl* touches on the fundamentally radical potential of Arabic and Islamic discursive traditions, as well as the dangers of binding them within exclusionary state or religious politics.

Al-zilzāl engages with structures of discursive authority in relation to other hegemonic orders: colonial, national, religious, filial, and sexual. Resignifying Qurʾanic eschatology along spatial and temporal registers, the novel upends authorized national narratives formally and discursively. In so doing, Waṭṭār authors a very different kind of "postcolonial novel," one that challenges the liberatory and progressivist rhetoric of both nationalist and orientalist accounts of postcolonial subjectivity. Instead, he offers a complex meditation on Algerian national identity that simultaneously mobilizes and unsettles the discourses of Arabism and Islamism. *Al-zilzāl* uses the language of the Qurʾan to demonstrate, on the one hand, the dangers of self-interested or literalist interpretations of scripture. On the other, Waṭṭār's deft reworking of the Qurʾan turns it into a living literary repository that functions as both a narrative and thematic intertext. The novel's satirical representation of Shaykh ʿAbd al-Majīd Bū al-Arwāḥ's psychic, physical, and material self-destruction through a fundamental misreading of the Qurʾan exposes the ethics of reading. In addition to revealing the multiple registers upon which the Qurʾan operates—the mind, the body, and the soul—*Al-zilzāl* demonstrates its literary complexity by mirroring its rhetorical code-switching and polyphonic narrative structure.

Before turning to Assia Djebar's *L'amour, la fantasia*, I would like to revisit Waṭṭār's incendiary remarks on the death of his former friend Tahar Djaout in 1993. Echoing this book's broader critical intervention, this chapter reads *Al-zilzāl* against the grain of the author's own false binary of Arabic (national) and Francophone (non-national) literature. The Francophone novels in this study—*Talismano*, *L'amour, la fantasia*, and *Le passé simple*—trouble this dichotomy through their lexical, grammatical, and rhetorical accenting of French with Arabic, as well as in their intertextuality with the Qurʾan. *Al-zilzāl* challenges the imbrication of Arab ethnic identity and Islam exclusively in Arabic precisely through its narrative use of Qurʾanic eschatology. Assia Djebar's *L'amour, la fantasia* similarly interrogates questions of Algerian national identity by disrupting teleologically staged historical narratives. She does so, however, through a feminist intervention into Islamic textual and hermeneutical practices—precisely the occluded history and genealogy alluded to in my discussion of gender in *Al-zilzāl*.

CHAPTER 4

The Polyphonic Hermeneutics of Assia Djebar's *L'amour, la fantasia*

> At the time of the French Empire, North Africa—like the rest of Africa on behalf of colonial England, Portugal or Belgium—suffered for a century and a half the dispossession of its natural resources, the breakdown of its social foundations, and for Algeria, the exclusion within education of its two identitarian languages [*ses deux langues identitaires*]: age-old Berber and the Arabic language—with its poetic quality, which for me cannot be perceived outside the Qur'anic verses that I hold dear. . . . In this sense, the French monolingualism established in colonial Algeria managed to devalue our mother tongues, driving us even further in the quest for origins.
>
> Assia Djebar, "Discours de reception"

Assia Djebar's 2006 address to the Académie française upon her induction as one of the forty *immortels* represented in its illustrious ranks confronted the complexities of her status as a French, and not merely Francophone writer.[1] As the Académie's first writer from a former North African colony, Djebar's unprecedented election inscribed her institutionally within French linguistic, literary, and cultural patrimony. Her speech situates Algeria's violent colonial history within the broader politics of nineteenth-century European imperialism, while simultaneously marking the country's exceptional status as a 132-year settler colony. It is the question of language, in particular, that for Djebar distinguishes Algeria's colonial past from the shared social, economic, and political "dépossession" endured across the African continent. Her emphasis on the institutionalized linguistic erosion of national identity highlights the particularly insidious nature of French colonial policy in Algeria. For Djebar, both Berberophone languages and Arabic signal Algeria's "*langues identitaires*" and "*langues maternelles*." While she designates indigenous Berber as Algeria's foundational "*séculaire*" language, Arabic signifies the language of the Qur'an—poetic, yet haunted "by the religious shadow" ("Dialogue" n.p.). Despite her fraught relationship to French, it nonetheless serves as a literary site for Djebar's utopic imaginings: "French then is the place where I excavate my work, the space of my meditations or reverie, the target of my utopia" (*Le français donc est lieu de creusement de mon travail, espace de ma méditation ou de ma rêverie, cible de mon utopie*) ("Discours de reception" n.p.).

As her address continues, Djebar recounts an Algerian cultural history that looks beyond its Arab and Islamic roots to the literary greats of her "*terre ancestrale*" (ancestral land)—from Apuleius, to Tertullianus, and St. Augustine—who wrote "an elevated written literature in Latin" (*une littérature écrite de haute, de langue latine*) (ibid.).[2] Djebar's invocation of these figures, in part, "echoes French colonial and Berber cultural postulations of shared 'Latinity' between French and pre-Islamic Amazigh cultures" (Tageldin, "Which *Qalam* for Algeria?" 472).[3] These intellectuals, she notes, "are part of our heritage [*patrimoine*]. They should be taught in schools in the Maghreb" (Djebar, "Discours de reception" n.p.). By highlighting their absence from Algerian curricula, Djebar reveals the importance of pedagogy to questions of cultural patrimony and national identity. Moreover, her account of Ibn Baṭūṭa, Ibn Rūshd, and al-Ghazālī emphasizes the colonial context in which they used Arabic: "The Arabic language then was also a vehicle of scientific knowledge (medicine, astronomy, mathematics etc.). Thus, it is again, in the language of the Other (the Bedouins of Arabia Islamicized the Berbers to conquer Spain with them) that my African ancestors wrote and invented" (*La langue arabe était alors véhicule également du savoir scientifique [médecine, astronomie, mathématiques etc.] Ainsi, c'est de nouveau, dans la langue de l'Autre (les Bédouins d'Arabie islamisant les Berbères pour conquérir avec eux l'Espagne) que mes ancêtres africains vont écrire, inventer*) (ibid.). Djebar resignifies colonial rhetoric, in which French signals the civilizing language of secular forms of knowledge, by casting Arabic as the conveyor of scientific knowledge—bypassing Ibn Baṭūṭa, Ibn Rushd, and al-Ghazālī's contributions to Islamic philosophy. By tracing a notably African ethnocultural lineage, she further decenters Arabness and Islam as Algerian cultural signifiers.

As a Francophone writer of Amazigh descent, Assia Djebar (b. Fatma Zohra Imalayen, 1936–2015) shares an ambivalent relationship to both Arabic and French—which she first studied at a colonial school where her father was a teacher.[4] Similar to Abdelwahab Meddeb and Driss Chraïbi, her glowing reception by the French intellectual establishment underscores the ways in which she is circumscribed within and overdetermined by the politics of Francophonie. I pair my discussion of Assia Djebar's novel *L'amour, la fantasia*—which many believe secured her admission into the

Académie française—with al-Ṭāhir Waṭṭār's *Al-zilzāl*, because when read together they complicate and enrich one another in unexpected ways. If my reading of Waṭṭār's novel reframes his dismissal of Algerian Francophonie, my reading of Djebar's fiction unsettles her easy absorption into French cultural patrimony. This chapter argues that Djebar models a practice of ethical reading in her renarration of official histories and archives—colonial, national, and Islamic. Much of the scholarship on Djebar's literary and cinematic oeuvres relies upon secular feminist and postcolonial frameworks that rarely engage Arab/ic literary and critical traditions.[5] Rather than reading gender and language politics as tangential to Qurʾanic intertextuality, I emphasize how they inform and shape Djebar's narrative ethics—largely through the novel's insistence on orality and embodiment.

Djebar's celebrated career began with the publication of her first novel *La soif* (The thirst) in 1957, followed by three more novels over the coming decade. She then took a nearly ten-year publishing hiatus, during which she studied Arabic while teaching film, literature, and history at the University of Algiers, in addition to working on her first feature film.[6] Djebar described the time as "a period of profound self-questioning," adding that she was "overcome . . . by the need to communicate with peasants, with villagers from regions with different traditions, and also by the need to reconnect with my maternal tribe, twelve years after independence" (qtd. in Hillauer 303). Her acclaimed 1977 film *La nouba des femmes du Mont Chenoua* foregrounds the importance of indigenous women in rural Algeria to the country's anticolonial history. The film, like *L'amour, la fantasia*, chronicles Algerian national history through matrilineal genealogies passed down in dialectical Arabic and Berberophone languages. Modeled after musical suites, the film and novel bridge narrative genres by inflecting the visual with the oral, and the textual with the musical. In their emphasis on orality and embodiment, *La nouba des femmes du Mont Chenoua* and *L'amour, la fantasia* confront the ways in which colonial and national archives fail to account for women's experiences and contributions. The works challenge generic taxonomies, formal conventions, and historical teleologies with their polyphonic accounts from the forgotten margins of histories.[7]

Written between 1982 and 1984, *L'amour, la fantasia* (translated as *Fantasia, An Algerian Cavalcade*, 1985) is the first of an "Algerian Quartet" that also includes *Ombre sultane* (translated as *A Sister to Scheherazade*, 1987), *Vaste est la prison* (*So Vast the Prison*, 1995), and *Nulle part dans la maison de mon père* (No part in my father's house, 2008). Blending autobiography, memoir, historiography, and oral history, *L'amour, la fantasia* formally experiments with genres and modes of representation. The book is composed of three parts: "La prise de la ville ou L'amour s'écrit" (The capture of the city or love-letters), "Les cris de la fantasia" (The cries of the *fantasia*), and "Les voix ensevelies" (Voices from the past). The chapters alternate between colonial archival records and personal accounts that include Djebar's memoirs, reports and eyewitness accounts from the occupation of Algeria in the 1830s, in addition to oral histories from women involved in the war of independence (1954–1962).[8] Capitalizing on Djebar's training as a historian, *L'amour, la fantasia* is the product of years of research into the French colonial archives and the recording of women's oral histories.

Moving between narrative voices, political orientations, and historical contexts, the novel upends authoritative accounts of Algeria's violent colonial history. This narrative polyphony is further complicated by Djebar's extemporaneous historical speculation, marginalia, and annotations on the process of reading and interpreting these archives, as well as her metatextual commentary on the practice of writing in French. According to Djebar, the novel served a cathartic function in her reckoning with the legacy of French settler colonialism in Algeria: "In writing *L'amour, la fantasia,* I settled my accounts, once and for all, with the French language" (*En écrivant 'L'Amour, la fantasia,' j'ai définitivement réglé mes comptes avec la langue française*) (Zimra, "Disorienting the Subject" 151). Similar to *Al-zilzāl, L'amour, la fantasia* exposes how dominant accounts of Algerian national identity rely upon the institutional legitimization of religious, linguistic, and ethnic mythologies of origin. It stages revisionist genealogies that remythologize Algerian history through the occluded voices of women and indigenous populations. Blurring the line between the historical and the literary, the novel performs a polyphonic hermeneutics that I read in relation to Djebar's anticlericalism and views on *ijtihād*, or independent reasoning in Islam.

Engendering Genealogies

In dialogue with prominent Islamic exegetes, particularly the canonical Persian scholar al-Ṭabarī (838–923), Djebar's 1991 novel *Loin de Médine: Filles d'Ismaël* (*Far from Medina: The Daughters of Ishmael*) at once rewrites and reimagines the early history of Islam. Bridging genres, the polyphonic work explores the lives of various influential female figures during the time of the Prophet Muhammad. It critically examines how hadith is legitimized through *isnād*, the chains of transmission that verify the validity of hadith according to the consensus of religious scholars. As with *L'amour, la fantasia*, the novel brings to the fore previously occluded sources while also casting doubt on those most commonly accepted. Djebar invokes *ijtihād* in terms of her own right as a Muslim to critically engage with the Qurʾan and its surrounding scholarship, as well as by rewriting the canonical history of early Islam. Interrogating the political and theological role of women within Islamic thought, the novel's title invokes a generation of women that existed "outside, geographically or symbolically, a place of temporal power that irreversibly breaks away from its original light" (*en dehors, géographiquement ou symboliquement, d'un lieu de pouvoir temporel qui s'écarte irréversiblement de sa lumière originelle*) (Djebar, *Far from Medina* xv/7, translation modified). The holy city of Medina thus serves as a symbolic site of patriarchal power tied to official modes of historical and theological inscription.

In her foreword to *Loin de Médine*, Djebar writes: "I have given the title 'novel' to this collection of narratives, scenes, sometimes visions, which my reading of some historians of the first two or three centuries of Islam (Ibn Hisham, Ibn Saʿd, Tabari) has nourished in me" (*J 'ai appelé 'roman' cet ensemble de récits, de scènes, de visions parfois, qu'a nourri en moi la lecture de quelques historiens des deux ou trois premiers siècles de l'Islam* [*Ibn Hicham, Ibn Saad, Tabari*]) (xv/5, translation modified). She qualifies the generically ambiguous work as a "novel" while simultaneously describing it as a repository for stories and visions. These extradiscursive visions were "nourished" by the most renowned scholars of early Islamic history—recalling the conceptual imagery associated with *adab* as a practice that cultivates ethical forms of intellectual edification.

Djebar closes the foreword by referring to the work as "*ma volonté d'Ijtihad*," implying both a wish and an effort or willpower (8). A footnote defines the concept: "*Ijtihād:* intellectual effort in the search for truth—coming from *Jihād*, internal struggle recommended for all believers" (*Ijtihad: effort intellectuel pour la recherche de la verité—venant de djihad, lutte intérieure, recommandée à tout croyant*) (8n2).[9] By tracing the etymological relationship to jihad, Djebar highlights the intellectual, political, and ethical dimensions of how Islam is practiced on both an individual and communal level. Her invocation of *ijtihād* in the context of this novel, which blends fictional imaginings of early Islamic history with the reinterpretation of officially sanctioned sources, transposes the concept onto a distinctly literary space. It generates a radical narrative ethics that treats creative and imaginative practices ("*cet ensemble de récits, de scènes, de visions*") as foundational to the hermeneutic process. Doing so in French further disengages these practices from the (gendered and gendering) canon of Arabic exegetical scholarship. Across Djebar's literary and cinematic oeuvre, orality functions as a form of embodied literacy seminal to both Muslim spiritual praxis and early Islamic history—signaling a polyphonic hermeneutics that operates across not only languages but also different modes of reading.

Scholars have argued that Djebar's *ijtihād* in *Loin de Médine* deviates from standardized interpretations within classic Sunni thought, in which it was "a ratiocinative procedure whose aim was to establish consensus among scholars alone"; whereas "Djebar so closely ties the question of isnad to alternative lines of narrative development that her *ijtihad* falls beyond ratiocination" (Lang 8). Operating across theological as well as literary registers, the novel "construct[s] . . . a montage of substitute fictional episodes that various isnad generate" (ibid). Invoking "the way the *Hādith* proliferates different narrations around the same event," *Loin de Médine* recasts the apostolic tradition through its very literary narrativization—as with Maḥmūd al-Masʿadī's *Ḥadatha Abū Hurayra qāl* (N. Rahman 23). By approaching the Qur'an as a textual object and hadith as a narrative mode, Djebar stages a *literary* intervention into Qur'anic hermeneutics.

Shaden Tageldin argues that *L'amour, la fantasia* is similarly modeled after hadith, positing that the novel incorporates French colonial accounts in order to "forge a new chain of textual (and sexual?) transmission between (post)colonial Algerian women and French men and to substitute that chain for one rooted in the Arab-Islamic literary tradition" ("Which *Qalam* for Algeria?" 477). While the novel certainly decenters the male colonial gaze, its self-conscious manipulation of these historical accounts speaks to yet another critique: *L'amour, la fantasia* stages these genealogical graftings in order to expose the precarity of authorized structures of transmission. Its use of multiple narrative voices and sources, as well as its resignification of authoritative colonial and Qur'anic discourses, troubles the originary narratives underwriting these genealogies. Across *L'amour, la fantasia* and *Loin de Médine*, Djebar at once theorizes and performs a narrative ethics that challenges colonialist historiography and the codification of certain schools of clerical thought.

L'amour, la fantasia critiques hegemonic interpretations of the Qur'an that rely upon a literal model of Muslim piety as submission rather than critical reflection.[10] Donald Wehrs proposes that Djebar's radical iconoclasm emerges from a critique of militant Islam as "renewed paganism" or "apostasy masquerading as reform," suggesting a retroactive reading of

L'amour, la fantasia from the perspective of Algerian Islamist militancy of the 1990s (Wehrs 4–5).[11] Rather than framing Djebar as an iconoclast, I situate her intellectual project within a long-standing critical tradition of Islamic thought. Championing *ijtihād*, Djebar critiques passive approaches to Qur'anic exegesis, writing: "In the transmission of Islam, an acid erosion has been at work: Tradition would seem to decree that entry is by submission [*entrer par soumission*], not by love. Love, which the most simple of settings might inflame, appears dangerous" (Djebar, *Fantasia* 169/239, translation modified). According to Djebar, adherence to a philosophy of submission is culturally motivated by tradition rather than driven by Qur'anic doctrine. She describes this process as a gradual "erosion" that has transformed the original message of Islam—again problematizing transmission over individual interpretation. By contrast, she proposes an Islamic ethos founded upon love rather than submission. While Djebar does not explicitly engage with *taṣawwuf*, her invocation of love and *ijtihād* as intersecting ethical imperatives of Muslim piety echoes Sufi poetic discourse.

Djebar introduces pious love in the figure of the Prophet Muhammad's first wife, Khadīja, as well as through her own family's matrilineal oral histories. She recounts a story her aunt would tell her about the Prophet's profound doubt during his early revelations—the very account fictionalized in Driss Chraïbi's *L'Homme du Livre*. Her aunt would describe Khadīja sitting the Prophet on her lap and comforting him, adding that "the very first Muslim woman or man, perhaps even before the Prophet himself, may Allah preserve him! was a woman. A woman was historically the first to adhere to the Islamic faith, 'out of conjugal love' [*par amour conjugal*]" (172/243, translation modified). By retelling this story in *L'amour, la fantasia*, Djebar demonstrates the ways in which oral traditions, particularly between and about women, are central to Islam. Refocusing the account of prophetic revelation onto Khadīja, the story casts her as both essential to the history of early Islam and to the Prophet's formation as an ethical subject. Moreover, by humanizing the Prophet Muhammad's vulnerability and intimacy with his wife Khadīja, who comforts him both physically and spiritually, Djebar foregrounds the body. It is practicing Islam "*comme en amour*" (as in love) that provokes in Djebar "*un désir d'Islam*" (a desire for Islam) (ibid., translation modified). In this sense, *désir* and *amour*—also referenced in the novel's title—are at the heart of Djebar's narrative ethics.

While it is romantic love that ignites faith for the Prophet Muhammad and Khadīja, elsewhere in the novel it is filial love. Specifically, it is the story of Abraham and his son Ishmael's profound faith that first instills in

Djebar "*une sensibilité islamique*" (an Islamic sensibility) (170/241, translation modified).[12] The parable demonstrates, however, that even submission may emerge from love: "I was deeply moved also by the son's submission: his veneration, the delicacy with which he bore his sentence" (*L'émoi me saisissait aussi devant la soumission du fils; sa vénération, sa délicatesse dans le poids de la peine*) (171/242, translation modified). In addition to the Abrahamic parable moving Djebar on a spiritual level, it inspires *Loin de Médine*, whose subtitle is *filles d'Ismaël*. From the son of Abraham to the daughters of Ishmael, Djebar reroutes filial piety through a feminist genealogy.

Linguistic Empires

Not only is *L'amour, la fantasia* the site of Djebar's self-described reckoning with the French language, but it also reveals her ambivalent relationship to Arabic as the privileged vehicle of Algerian nationalist discourse. Exposing Algeria's fraught ethnolinguistic landscape, the novel addresses the hegemonic history of Arabization in Algeria during the Islamic occupation of the seventh century, as well as upon independence in 1962. It opens by paralleling Djebar's induction into French education with the occupation of Algiers in 1830. In a short section titled "Biffure" (Deletions), she reflects upon the resonances between Arabic and French as imperial languages:

> *The conquest of the Unconquerable . . . Faint images flake off from the rock of Time. The flickering flames of successive fires form letters of French words curiously elongated or expanded, against cave walls, tattooing vanished faces with a lurid mottling . . . The mirror-image of the foreign inscription is reflected in Arabic letters, writ from right to left in the mirror of suffering; then the letters fade into pictures of the prehistoric Hoggar . . . To read this writing, I must lean over backwards, plunge my face into the shadows, closely examine the vaulted roof of rock or chalk, lend an ear to rising immemorial whispers, blood-stained geology. What magma of sounds lies rotting there? What stench of putrefaction seeps out? I grope about, my sense of smell aroused, my ears alert in this rising tide of ancient pain. Alone, stripped bare, unveiled, I face these images of darkness . . . How are the sounds of the past to be met as they emerge from the well of bygone centuries?. . . What love must be sought, what future must be planned despite the call of the dead? And my body reverberates with sounds from the endless landslide of generations of my lineage.* (46, translation modified)[13]

Djebar subtly weaves together the invasion of Algeria by French forces in the 1830s with the Arab-Islamic occupation of the Maghreb in the seventh century. She begins with a notably gendered description of Algiers based on the adage "*la Ville Imprenable*" (the Impregnable City) in reference to the city's infamous fortifications. The image also resonates with the novel's frequent metaphorization of Algeria as a woman, and its colonial occupation as a violent sexual act.[14]

The passage viscerally describes the inscription of the French language on the topography of the country and the very flesh of its inhabitants. Its extravagance conceals its colonial past, as with the florid narratives by French officials, woven throughout the novel, that chronicle the violent invasion of Algiers. This history, embodied in the "*diaprures rougeoyantes*" of French letters, is reflected and refracted in the parallel "*miroir de la souffrance*" of the Arabic language. Djebar highlights the Ahaggar (referred to in the text as Hoggar): a highland region in the central Sahara of southern Algeria almost exclusively occupied by the Touareg.[15] She employs the metaphor of the palimpsest to describe the images of the prehistoric Ahaggar buried beneath "*lettres arabes.*" The section's title alludes to the deleted history of Algeria's indigenous pre-Islamic populations, to whom Djebar expresses an ancestral and ethnic affiliation, describing them as "*des génerations-aïeules.*" Bearing witness to their "*douleur ancienne,*" she exposes the cultural hegemony of the Arab-Islamic and French occupations, as well as their mutual privileging of writing over orality.

As with al-Ṭāhir Waṭṭār's *Al-zilzāl*, the tension surrounding Algeria's Arab occupation manifests in the figure of the fourteenth-century North African historiographer and philosopher Ibn Khaldūn. Djebar includes a quote from the polymath's autobiography *Al-taʿrīf* that describes his role in the forced integration of Algeria's indigenous tribes: "*I myself had to lead an expedition into the mountainous region of Béjaia, where the Berber tribes had been refusing to pay taxes for some years. . . . After I had penetrated into their country and overcome their resistance, I took hostages to ensure their obedience*" (47/71). Ibn Khaldūn brazenly recounts his conquest of Amazigh tribes in Béjaia using the sexualized language of penetration. Djebar returns to Ibn Khaldūn when she discusses the politics of Arabization in relation to both the Berberophone tribes and the author's choice to write his autobiography in Arabic. A contentious figure in many ways, Ibn Khaldūn was born in Tunisia to an upper-class Andalusian family. The autobiography traces his lineage to the Prophet Muhammad through an Arab tribe in Yemen, although biographers have speculated that this might simply be an attempt to affiliate with Arab rather than Amazigh origins.[16]

Djebar appears drawn to Ibn Khaldūn's ability to simultaneously inhabit historical, fictional, and autobiographical discourses—embodied in the homophonic quality of the French words *histoire* (story) and *Histoire* (the discipline of history). However, she takes issue with his adoption of the "colonial" language of Arabic:

> Processions of new invasions, new occupations. . . . Shortly after the fatal turn that bleeds the country white from the devastation of the Banu Hilal, Ibn Khaldun, as great a figure as Augustine, rounds off a life of adventure and meditation by composing his autobiography. He calls it *Ta'arif*, that is to say, "Identity." Like Augustine, it matters little to him, the innovative author of *The History of the Berbers*, that he writes in a language introduced to his homeland through bloodshed! A language imposed by rape as much as love. (216, translation modified)[17]

Critical of Ibn Khaldūn's use of Arabic for his autobiography, Djebar compares him to Augustine of Hippo, who was born in Roman Algeria and infamously converted to Christianity. This passage follows an account of the violent introduction of Arabic into the Maghreb through the tribes of the Banū Hilāl. Referenced across Ibn Khaldūn's work, the Banū Hilāl were sent to various Berberophone tribes of the Maghreb on behalf of the Fatimids to enforce Shiʿa Islam and Arabic during the eleventh century.

Djebar's description of Ibn Khaldūn's *L'histoire des Berbères* as "*novateur*," in part, relates to the selective cropping of his larger manuscript on universal history titled *Kitāb al-ʿibar wa-dīwān al-mubtada' wa-l-khabar fī ta'rīkh al-ʿArab wa-l-ʿajam wa-l-Barbar* (Book of lessons, record of beginnings, and events in the history of the Arabs, foreigners, and Berbers) from which it was derived. As Abdelmajid Hannoum argues, the French translation of *L'histoire des Berbères* by William de Slane was perhaps "the greatest textual event in the history of French Orientalism. . . . [It] formed the foundation of French historical knowledge of North Africa . . . [and] became central in French colonial historiography" (62). Djebar's contention with Ibn Khaldūn stems from his identitarian claims to Arabness embodied in the title of his autobiography, as well as his affiliation with Muslims of Arab descent. While Djebar's *L'amour, la fantasia* similarly blends history with autobiography and is itself composed in French, she openly grapples with these concerns across the novel's formal and diegetic registers.

In addition to challenging the devaluation of oral forms of literacy, Djebar corrects revisionist histories that credit Arabic as the Maghreb's first written language. Citing the pre-Islamic alphabets of the region's indigenous inhabitants, she notes: "It is a question of a 'return' to a written language. . . . Arabic culture rests on the teaching (and thus the writing read and recopied) of the Book; whereas in the Maghreb, there is one of the oldest written cultures, with the women as privileged holders of the writing, the alphabet Tamazigh of Touareg" (Djebar qtd. in N. Rahman 37).[18] For Djebar, Berberophone languages signify the Maghreb's indigenous culture prior to its Arabization and Islamicization. Not only is the Tamazigh alphabet of the Touareg the region's earliest written culture, but it is associated with a matrilineal line of descent. By contrast, Arabic for Djebar often signals patrilineal or patriarchal structures. Arab ethnic and linguistic identity is inextricably linked not only to Islam but to the Qurʾan as an authoritative text whose pedagogy relies upon rote recitation.

Despite her skepticism around traditional Qurʾanic pedagogy, Djebar still finds those of her generation preferable to their later incarnation:

> I understood later that in the village I had participated in the last of an age-old, popular style of instruction. In the city, thanks to the Nationalist movement of "Modernist Muslims," a new generation of Arab culture was being forged. Since then these *medresas* have sprung up everywhere. If I had attended one of them . . . I would have found it quite natural to swathe my head in a turban to hide my hair, to cover my arms and calves, in a word to move about out of doors like a Muslim nun! (182–83, translation modified)[19]

In contrast to the schools of Djebar's childhood, those that emerged during decolonization were infused with the fervent ideology of the nationalist movement. The "*musulmans modernistes*" refer to Algeria's Islamic reformers, such as Shaykh ʿAbd al-Ḥāmid Bin Bādīs, who appears in Waṭṭār's *Al-zilzāl*. These reformers were prominent in the reformation of the Algerian educational system leading up to and following independence. In addition to their schools promoting an Arab and Muslim Algerian national identity, they vehemently fought against populist religious practices that were seen as *bidʿa*—unorthodox or even heretical forms of innovation that upend theological or juridical norms. The distinction between Djebar's village education and the urban schools of the reformers signals the complex and diverse history of Islamic education in Algeria.

Djebar's criticism of the practices of "cloistering" and veiling across the book are reflected in the passage's use of the mixed religious imagery of "*enturbanner*" and "*nonne musulmane*."[20] Her extravagant use of veiling imagery, which appears more than forty times in *L'amour, la fantasia* alone, has contributed to Djebar's celebration by Western feminist scholarship, in which she serves the role of both the oppressed and liberated Muslim woman.[21] While veiling and cloistering clearly double as metaphors for the repeated elision of women from the master narratives of history (colonial, national, and Islamic), Djebar is also commenting on and exercising her critical right as a Muslim. She defines the harem as "the taboo, whether it be a place of habitation or a symbol" (*l'interdit, qu'il soit d'habitation ou de symbole*), rendering it as both a physical space and a site of social as well as psychological exclusion (128/183). Fusing decolonial historiography with *ijtihād*, the novel also mobilizes the symbolic language of criminalization to describe cloistering—fathers, husbands, and brothers become "*geôlier*[*s*]" (jailors) and women "*prisonnières*" (prisoners) or the walking dead: "*fantômes blancs, forms ensevelies à la vertical*" (white ghosts, figures buried upright) (3/11; 45/67; 115/164, translation modified). Elsewhere, cloistering stands in for the lack of figurative representation in Islam, in which preserving a woman's image is "a duty regarded as their most sacred inheritance" (*ce devoir comme le legs le plus sacré*) (125/180, translation modified).

Across *L'amour, la fantasia*, language is intimately tied to social and cultural hierarchies—from gender and sexuality to ethnolinguistic and religious identity. Djebar writes of the four languages available to Algerian women: "While the man still has the right to four legitimate wives, we have at our command four languages to express our desire, before panting: French for secret missives; Arabic for our sighs before a stifled God; Lybico-Berber which transports us to our oldest mother-idols. The fourth language, for all women, young or old, cloistered or half-emancipated, remains that of the body" (180, translation modified).[22] By equating the four wives permissible in Islam to the four languages "*pour exprimer notre désir*," Djebar resignifies polygamy from a feminist perspective; French functions as the language of subversion, while Arabic bears the suffocating burden of an Islamic legacy ("*nos soupirs vers Dieu étouffés*"). By contrast, Berber represents not only pre-Islamic culture but also a matrilineal world of "*idoles mères*." It is the body, however, that serves as the lingua franca for all women—a site that allows for a feminist ethics of embodiment that transcends the fraught politics of the Maghreb's linguistic hierarchies.

Djebar's personal educational history, which she addresses across the autobiographical sections of *L'amour, la fantasia*, sheds light on her fraught relationship to Arabic. As she was educated predominantly in French schools, her exposure to Arabic was limited to her time at a madrasa, where she studied the Qur'an and learned Arabic "only for the sacred words" (*seulement pour les paroles sacrées*) (181/256, translation modified). Djebar's estrangement from Arabic seems to derive in part from the diglossic division between classical and dialectical Arabic. While she overaestheticizes the Arabic of the Qur'an, which is "cloaked in innocence and whispering arabesques" (*en pelure d'innocence, en lacis murmurants*), Djebar describes oral Arabic as "my long-lost mother-tongue" (*ma langue mère disparue*) (181/256; 213/298). This distinction is further underscored by her association of written Arabic with the Qur'an, and a specific interpretation of scripture: "Under the weight of taboos that I bear like a heritage" (*Sous le poids des tabous que je porte en moi comme héritage*) (214/298, translation modified).

Djebar's relationship to French and her "*langue maternelle*" are mediated by the colonial context of her education. She describes her ambivalence toward the two languages through the motifs of music and warfare that run throughout the novel:

> After more than a century of French occupation—which ended not long ago in such butchery—a no-man's-land still exists between two people, two memories: the French language, all body and voice, has established a proud *presidio* within me, while the mother-tongue, all oral tradition, all rags and tatters, resists and attacks between two breathing spaces. In time to the rhythm of the *rebato*, I am alternatively the besieged foreigner and the native swaggering off to die, illusory turmoil between the spoken and written word. (215, translation modified)[23]

Djebar depicts the linguistic landscape of postindependence Algeria as "*un territoire de langue*" that divides both people and memories. Granting her "*corps et voix*," the French language facilitates both bodily and narrative expression for Djebar. It instills within her, however, an "*orgueilleux préside*"—a technical term used to describe military garrisons under colonial rule, particularly in the context of the Spanish empires in Mexico and Morocco. Her mother tongue on the other hand, is the dilapidated language of resistance, "*en hardes dépenaillées*," that unseats the hegemony of French. While Djebar situates herself in limbo between writing and orality, between "*l'assiégé étranger et l'autochtone partant à la mort par bravade*," her work ultimately reveals a reluctant affiliation with French as the privileged language of literary writing.

Reading, Writing, Revelation

Despite Djebar's troubled relationship to Qur'anic Arabic, she nonetheless returns to the text of the Qur'an in order to demonstrate the intrinsic importance of critical reading to Muslim subject formation. When questioned as to why her daughter is not veiled, Djebar's mother responds with the phrase, "*Elle lit*" (she reads). In her reflections on this telling remark, Djebar connects the physical liberties afforded her by a French education, to the commandment by Gabriel to the Prophet Muhammad to read. As in Abdelwahab Meddeb's *Talismano*, Djebar mobilizes the sura "Al-ʿalaq" ("The Germ-Cell" or "The Clot"), in which Gabriel commands the Prophet Muhammad *iqraʾ* (read/recite), in order to highlight the embodied ethics of reading within Islam. Marrying the acts of reading, recitation, and revelation, the sura bridges textual, corporeal, divine, and hermeneutical registers. Commenting on her mother's remark, Djebar writes: "'She reads,' that is to say in Arabic, 'she studies.' I think now that verb 'to read' was not just causally included in the Qurʾanic revelations made by the Angel Gabriel in the cave. . . . 'She reads' is tantamount to saying that writing to be read, including that of the unbelievers, is always a source of revelation: in my case, of the mobility of my body, and so, of my future freedom" (180, translation modified).[24] The scene inverts the gendering of the parable by substituting Djebar's mother for Gabriel, who passes the gifts of revelation and reading to the Prophet Muhammad. It further removes the commandment from its Islamic context, suggesting that non-theological writing, even among "*des mécréants*," is inherently revelatory. In this case, Djebar's French literacy grants her mobility, and by extension, freedom. Djebar appropriates one of Islam's foundational narratives in order to generate a feminist genealogy that does not rely upon Arabic as the official language of piety.

The sura "Al-ʿalaq" is also referenced when Djebar revisits the story of an unnamed victim of Algeria's nineteenth-century occupation. Earlier in the novel, she recounts the death of a young woman killed during the violent siege of Algiers. The account is based upon the diaries of Eugène Fromentin, the official painter of the conquest, who describes coming across the severed hand of a woman that had been amputated in order to take possession of her gold bracelets. Disturbed by the image, Fromentin is unable to paint the hand and instead documents the story in writing. Djebar ends *L'amour, la fantasia* by returning to this unsettling image: "I intervene to greet the painter who has accompanied me throughout my wanderings like a second father figure. Eugène Fromentin offers me an unexpected hand—the hand of an unknown woman he was never able to draw. . . . Later, I seize on this living hand, hand of mutilation and of memory and I attempt to bring it the *qalam*" (226).[25] Granting this anonymous woman both a narrative and a voice, Djebar's historical intervention is at once literary and ethical. It is simultaneously mediated through French colonial history—in the figure of Fromentin, whom she describes as "*en seconde silhouette paternelle*"—as well as the Qurʾan—in her reference to the *qalam*.

The gesture of offering this woman a *qalam* recalls the sura "Al-ʿalaq" ("The Germ-Cell" or "The Clot").[26] By returning to the first Qurʾanic sura revealed to the Prophet Muhammad—one based on the relationship between reading, writing, and revelation—Djebar actively positions both herself and the unnamed woman within a Qurʾanic genealogy. As with Gabriel and the Prophet, Djebar initiates this woman into the world of spiritual literacy while also enshrining her within the novel's pages. She inserts her "prosthetic hand that bespeaks colonial amputation and gendered violence" within both Algeria's colonial history and scripture (Tageldin, "Which *Qalam* for Algeria?" 480). Moreover, the use of the definite article "le" for *qalam* indicates that these are authoritative traditions. By proffering the severed hand an instrument that signals knowledge as the foundation of Muslim piety, Djebar intervenes into patriarchal historiographies—French colonial and Islamic.

The story of the Prophet Muhammad's miraculous introduction to literacy through the Qurʾanic revelations also appears in Djebar's account of her childhood experience at a madrasa. She describes the corporeality of the practice of rote recitation often employed at Qurʾanic schools:

> The act of cleaning the tablet seemed like ingesting a portion of the Qurʾanic text. The writing—itself a copy of writing which is considered immutable—could only continue to unfold before us if it relied, clause by clause, on this osmosis. . . . This language which I learn demands the correct posture for the body, on which the memory rests for its support. The childish hand, spurred on—as if training for some sport—by willpower worthy of an adult, begins to write. "Read!" The fingers laboring on the tablet send back the signs to the body, which is simultaneously reader and servant. (Djebar, *Fantasia* 184, translation modified)[27]

Referring to the erasure of the tablet as an act of ingestion—similar to the practice of physically ingesting ink from memorization tablets—highlights the physical nature of Qurʾanic methods of study in which the body functions as both "*lecteur et serviteur*." This embodied piety recalls the Prophet Muhammad's first revelation and the command to read/recite. Problematizing the Qurʾan's unilateral inscription on the Muslim subject's body, Djebar invocation of *ijtihād* is a reminder that the Qurʾan is not an "immutable" textual object.

L'amour, la fantasia troubles various religious, linguistic, and ethnic genealogies mobilized within Algerian nationalist discourses. In the process of deconstructing these narratives, however, it stages some unlikely affiliations: "Djebar constructs her narrative around a tacit affinity and an equally tacit antipathy: the affinity of French with Algeria's occluded languages and the antipathy of those Algerian tongues (always gendered female) to the force imagined responsible for their occlusion—literary Arabic, always aligned with 'official' Islam" (Tageldin, "Which *Qalam* for Algeria?" 476). While French serves as Djebar's language of literary expression, the specter of both Arabic and the Qur'an loom large in the novel. As both a narrative text and a spiritual guide for Muslims, the Qur'an functions as a critical intertext to her broader literary project. That said, my reading of *L'amour, la fantasia* attends to the complex ideological and ethnolinguistic entanglements underwriting Djebar's narrative ethics.

Scholars have noted how Djebar's prose, similar to that of Abdelwahab Meddeb and Driss Chraïbi, is heavily inflected by the Arabic language. Anne Donadey, for example, taxonomizes the different ways in which Djebar's fiction "deterritorializes the French language through the lexical and syntactic presence of Arabic" ("The Multilingual Strategies of Postcolonial Literature" 34). She cites translated or transliterated Arabic words and concepts, as well as the use of diegetic, metatextual, and metaphoric references to "*the epistemic violence of colonialism*" through the literary tension between Arabic and French (31). As I have argued across this chapter, there is far more at stake in *L'amour, la fantasia* than simply anticolonial critique—particularly when read in relation to Djebar's broader literary and cinematic oeuvre. The ornate stylization of her prose, coupled with her extravagant use of densely conceptual language, ironically recall Djebar's assessment of classical Arabic: "The lushness of this language seems to me almost suspiciously profuse, in short, a verbal consolation" (*La luxuriance de cette langue me paraît un foisonnement presque suspect, en somme une consolation verbale*) (Djebar, *Fantasia* 214/298, translation modified).

Not only does Djebar write multilingually, but *L'amour, la fantasia* enacts and invites reading practices that traverse languages (French, classical and dialectical Arabic, as well as Berberophone languages) and modes of literacy (written, oral, and embodied). Donadey, like many scholars of Maghrebi literature, argues that this functions to disrupt all potential readers: "Such sophisticated vocabulary serves both to enrich her works and to decenter all her readers, since none of them can sustain the illusion of having complete mastery over the texts. The complex syntax, the almost Proustian sentences with their many subordinate, coordinate, and juxtaposed clauses, also contribute to the difficulty in reading—and even more so in translating—Djebar" (Donadey, "The Multilingual Strategies of Postcolonial Literature" 34). Michael Allan, on the other hand, notes the multiple ways in which the novel "draws our attention to the poetics of reading, missed modes of address, and unintended reception. Reading is not solely a matter of literacy in one particular language or another, but implicated in an interaction between languages, overheard, and respoken" (Allan, "Scattered Letters" 3). In the context of this study, my pairing of *L'amour, la fantasia* with al-Ṭāhir Waṭṭār's *Al-zilzāl* asks how a multilingual or polyphonic mode of writing/reading translates into a hermeneutical practice. It considers the ethics of reading performed and fostered in Djebar's novel, in addition to its relationship to questions of embodiment and orality.

In advocating for *ijtihād* as a practice that is seminal to Muslim ethics, Djebar mobilizes the Qur'anic dialectic between *ẓāhir* (exoteric) and *bāṭin* (esoteric) meanings. As *Talismano* reminds us in the context of Ibn ʿArabī, to access the *bāṭin* meaning of a text entails precisely a process of unveiling known as *kashf*. In this vein, I read Djebar's (un)veiling imagery as participating in a hermeneutical practice of *ijtihād*. The recurring invocation of the sura "Al-ʿalaq" suggests that the invitation to read and write is one embedded within a Qur'anic narrative and ethical episteme. This is echoed in the correspondence between the text's palimpsestic narrative structure and Djebar's interrogation of the politics of transmission and interpretation in the Qur'an and hadith. Her textual and interpretive liberties reveal the multivocality of theological and literary discourses, as well as the ethical imperative underlying aesthetic choices across these traditions. Finally, Djebar's uncoupling of Muslim ethics from the Arabic language as the privileged site for Qur'anic discourse suggests a polyphonic modality of critical Muslim subjectivity also reflected in the novels of Abdelwahab Meddeb and Driss Chraïbi.

PART III

Genealogies of Transmission

CHAPTER 5

Tense Eruptions in Driss Chraïbi's *Le passé simple*

> Had there *only* been the Protectorate and colonialism, everything would have been simple. Indeed, my past, our past, would have been simple. No, Mr. Sartre, hell is not others. It is also within us.
>
> Driss Chraïbi, "Questionnaire"

In a decades-long controversy known as *l'affaire Chraïbi*, Driss Chraïbi's 1954 novel *Le passé simple* (*The Simple Past*) was the subject of a heated debate among Moroccan intellectuals, journalists, and politicians that resulted in a government ban until 1977.[1] The warm reception of the novel by French intellectuals on the right only fueled the political flames, reifying readings of *Le passé simple* as an orientalist portrayal of Moroccan culture and a heretical attack on Islam.[2] The above remarks were published in an interview with Chraïbi from a 1967 special issue of the Marxist-Leninist literary journal *Souffles* (Breaths) entitled "Driss Chraïbi et nous" (Driss Chraïbi and us). The special issue speaks to the continuing influence of the controversial novel on Moroccan intellectuals—particularly those on the Left.[3] Chraïbi's comments stress the ways in which *Le passé simple* attempts to rethink the colonial encounter outside of a binary of colonizer/colonized and oppressor/oppressed. His aside to "Monsieur Sartre" simultaneously invokes and satirizes the French literary canon, turning it into an indictment of both the self and the other. That he addresses Jean-Paul Sartre, a symbol of the French anticolonial Left and *littérature engagée* (engaged literature), further sheds light on the political complexities of Chraïbi's literary project.[4]

Published by the French press Denoël two years before Morocco's official independence from France, *Le passé simple* is often cited as the paradigmatic novel of the "1952 Generation" of Maghrebi writers.[5] It traces the rebellion of nineteen-year-old French-educated Driss Ferdi against his seemingly pious father, Haj Ferdi, a wealthy tea merchant, landowner, and claimed descendant of the Prophet Muhammad. The novel employs the grammatical tense of the *passé simple* as a metaphor for critiquing a teleological model of history. Defined as "the privileged tense of narrative, the only one capable of constructing a chronology of events," the *passé simple*, or preterit, is the literary tense par excellence and is rarely used in the first person or for direct speech.[6] Unlike the *passé composé*, or compound past—which is connected to the present temporally and spatially through its use of an auxiliary verb (either *avoir* or *être*)—the *passé simple* indicates an action, event, or situation that has a definitive beginning and end. The tense subsequently implies temporal detachment and distance from the present moment. As it is the preferred tense for historical writing, the *passé simple* also bears a certain discursive authority. By inscribing his novel within the preeminent tense of French literary and historical writing, Chraïbi at once demonstrates his mastery and subversion of the French language. As a metaphor, the tense contests the idea that history may be represented as a fixed chronology of events divorced from either the present or future.

This chapter argues that *Le passé simple*'s formal and diegetic disruption of historical temporality stages a double critique against colonial and nationalist teleologies—a tension that emerges most explicitly in its engagement with the Qur'an. I investigate the novel's critique of imbricated modes of genealogical historical inscription under Protectorate Morocco: French imperial discourses of civil society and the Moroccan monarchy's—and Hajj Ferdi's—filiation with the Prophet Muhammad. What many critics have reduced to "Muslim patriarchy," I instead read as a critique of the codification of institutional forms of hegemony through distinctly patriarchal structures. The novel demonstrates the ways in which a patriarchal model of genealogical authority is used to legitimize and sustain familial, socioeconomic, religious, and political expressions of power. I propose that Chraïbi offers an alternative mode of historical inscription in the recurring image of *la ligne mince*, or the thin line: a hallucinatory apparition that appears throughout the novel. Reading it in relation to both the Qur'an and Sufi philosophy, I argue that *la ligne mince* envisions history, identity, and language as epistemological sites of slippage and disruption.

L'affaire Chraïbi

Le passé simple is organized around five chapters, whose names follow the metaphor of alchemy. The first chapter, "Les éléments de base" (base elements), introduces the Ferdi family as they wait for Haj Ferdi's permission to break their fast during a Ramadan *ifṭār*. The theatrical opening sets the stage for the Ferdi family drama and Driss's rebellion against his father. Haj Ferdi, known as *Le Seigneur*, is a wealthy tea merchant and landowner who rules his family with fear. Driss's mother hides in the kitchen reciting her prayers to "saints of the Greeks and Russians," because, as she states: "I have invoked our saints but they have not heard my prayers. They are devoted to my lord and master [*mon seigneur et maître*]" (Chraïbi, *The Simple Past* 9/26–27). Driss fantasizes about patricide as his eldest brother, Camel, is out drinking, and his remaining five brothers sit obediently still. In chapter 2, "Période de transition" ("Transitional Period"), Driss escorts his mother to her native city of Fès during Laylat al-Qadr (The Night of Power), where he clashes with a sheikh named Si Kettani who leads a prominent Sufi order or *ṭarīqa*, and the chapter marks the beginning of Driss's spiritual rebellion.[7]

The third chapter, "Le réactif" ("The Reagent"), centers on Driss's discovery that his nine-year-old brother, Hamid, was murdered by his father after he was caught stealing money for their journey to Fès, which provokes Driss to rally his brothers in the attempted murder of their father. After his failed patricide, Driss is expelled from the Ferdi household and disowned by his father. In the fourth chapter, "Le catalyseur" ("The Catalyst"), he wanders the city of Casablanca seeking refuge with his *lycée* friends, in a church, and at school, only to discover that all doors are closed to him due to his father's expansive power. During his exile, Driss passes the exam for his baccalaureate by writing an essay entitled "La théocratie musulmane" (Muslim theocracy), instead of the assigned topic of "*liberté, egalité, fraternité*." He returns home only to learn that his mother has committed suicide. In the final chapter, "Les elements de synthèse" ("Elements of Synthesis"), Driss and his father settle accounts on the family farm. Haj Ferdi then takes him to receive benediction from the Sultan Muḥammad V, the future king of Morocco, before Driss leaves for France, determined to return and complete his revolt.

While French critics across the political spectrum hailed *Le passé simple*'s innovative literary style, reactions by French conservatives were notably pointed. Following the publication of the novel, for example, the right-wing French periodical *Bulletin de Paris* published a laudatory article that read: "From this novel . . . it seems that the real conflict is not between Morocco and France but between two different generations of Moroccans, or rather between a small minority who have been won over to Western civilization, and the bulk of the population (and their leaders) whose beliefs and traditions are still Islamic. . . . We can only hope that the French read the book . . . and understand the secret appeal that it makes" ("La Révolte," qtd. in N. Harrison 31).[8] Conflating colonialism with modernity, the article mobilizes *Le passé simple*'s supposed critique of Islam in order to validate the French *mission civilisatrice*. It interpellates the novel as a transgenerational tale of ideological incommensurability between Islam and Europe that serves as a "secret appeal" for Western civilization on behalf of Morocco's youth. Collapsing Morocco into the signifier "Islamic," the anonymous article opposes Western civilization and secular modernity to the Islamic "beliefs and traditions" responsible for Morocco's civilizational lag.

These kinds of readings incited claims by Arab critics that the book justified France's colonial presence during a crucial period in the country's battle for independence. *Démocratie*, the primary periodical of the Moroccan nationalist Parti Démocratique d'Indépendance (PDI), published an anonymous article denouncing the writer.[9] Titled "Driss Chraïbi, assassin de l'espérance" (Driss Chraïbi, assassin of hope), the piece claimed:

> Not content to have insulted his father and mother with the stroke of a pen, spit upon all national traditions, including the religion that he now claims to practice, Mr. Chraïbi is now addressing the Moroccan problem. In the name of an Islam he ridiculed, in the name of a sudden interest in a cause that had never been his. . . . This Judas of Moroccan thought never felt the need to talk about the values of his people. Passionate denigrator, he prefers to cling to the values of others, though they are not valid for us, insofar as we respect and love our own. (*Démocratie* January 14, 1957, qtd. in Dziri 13)[10]

The scathing article casts Chraïbi as a Judas-figure betraying the values of his family, nation, and religion. Focusing on Chraïbi's representation of Islam, it collapses the familial with the national, and the ethical with the political. The author suggests that Chraïbi's lack of participation in the nationalist fight for independence delegitimizes his ability to speak on behalf of his country.

Published three years after *Le passé simple*, the article reignited the controversy to such an extent that Chraïbi responded by publicly repudiating the novel in a letter to the editor (Chraïbi, "Je renie"). After the intervention of Abdellatif Laâbi, who edited the special issue of *Souffles*, Chraïbi eventually retracted the act. It was in fact Laâbi who offered one of the timeliest analyses of the novel:

> He did not carry out a sociological assessment of the colonial system, though he may have demonstrated the tangible causes that deepened and nourished colonization. In this sense, he is probably the only writer from the Maghreb who had the courage to expose an entire people's cowardice, reveal their stagnation and the origins of their hypocrisy, this self-colonization and oppression exerted over one another: the landowner over the agricultural laborer, the father over his children, the husband over his spouse-object, the lecherous master over his apprentice. (Laâbi, "Défense" 20)[11]

Laâbi makes two crucial points in response to the arguments lodged against Chraïbi: first, that one cannot reduce a literary work to an ethnographic or sociological project; and second, that the novel offers a personal portrait of the various factors that helped sustain French imperialism in Morocco. Laâbi's Marxist analysis highlights the dialectical feudal (landowner-laborer), familial (father-children), sexual (husband-wife), and economic (master-apprentice) forms of injustice addressed within *Le passé simple*.

Within contemporary scholarship on *Le passé simple* there remains a telling slippage between the individual and the national: "In making Chraïbi a spokesperson and his text an act of testimony, his critics appeared to oversimplify the relation between the literary and the political, confusing, or slipping between, radically different orders of representation" (N. Harrison 32).[12] Many critics have favored psychoanalytic readings that highlight the autobiographical overtones of the novel, which Ellen McLarney argues "has resulted in a near complete elision of [the novel's] . . . political implications" (McLarney 2).[13] She instead reads it as a political allegory, modeled after the French Revolution and the genre of family romance novels, that shows the various factions vying for power in the years leading up to independence: the Sultanate, Imazighen chieftains or Caïds, the Sufi *ṭarīqas*, as well as the emergent classes of merchants and French-educated intellectuals.[14] McLarney maintains that although the novel is a national allegory, it is one that critiques the social, political, and feudal structures out of which both the nation and the novel have emerged. While I agree that symptomatic readings often occlude pertinent political realities, the lens of national allegory can pose somewhat parallel challenges.

Rather than family dynamics merely standing in for national politics, *Le passé simple* demonstrates the ideological as well as structural complicity of private and public interests. It subverts discursive codes emerging from the various centers of power within pre-independence Morocco: the colonial administration, the Sultanate, the religious elite, Sufi orders, feudal systems, and the emergent class of capitalist merchants. Each of these orders is itself intimately bound within the text's representation of familial and national structures. Moreover, by situating this intervention in a Francophone novel that undermines the grammatical and literary dictates of French, Chraïbi also "implodes conventional and traditional markers of Euro-centric rational-critical and bourgeois discursive participation" (Graiouid 151). *Le passé simple* subsequently follows Abdelwahab Meddeb's *Talismano* and Assia Djebar's *L'amour, la fantasia* in its double critique of colonial and nationalist ideologies through Qur'anic intertextuality.

The troubled relationship between private and public spheres plays out most explicitly in the figure of Haj Ferdi, the most controversial yet least examined dimension of the novel.[15] The protagonist's father, Haj Ferdi, is an autocrat par excellence, whose "empire" traverses a number of social orders: he is the head of the Ferdi family, a feudal lord with extensive landholdings, a haj, the owner of a successful tea company that dominates the market, as well as a descendant of the Prophet Muhammad. Haj Ferdi's power over his family and community is legitimized and sustained by two critical factors: his collusion with the French Protectorate and the invocation of his Sherifian heritage.[16]

Genealogical descent from the Prophet Muhammad is a crucial component of Morocco's political and religious institutions of power, insofar as it is used to legitimize both the monarchy and heads of the Sufi *ṭarīqas*. In *Le passé simple*, however, it serves a subversive political function. Haj Ferdi descends from the Idrisī rather than the ʿAlawī line represented by the Sultan Muḥammad V (1909–1961). Muḥammad V took control of Morocco upon independence and had a rather contentious relationship with the Protectorate. At the time of the novel's publication, the sultan was in exile, and French authorities, as well as a number of Moroccan nationalist and religious groups, were questioning his claim to the throne—a history alluded to in the plot of the novel (267, 271). Chraïbi's subtle incorporation of this history highlights the complex relationship between the Moroccan monarchy and its self-legitimization through filial ties to the Prophet Muhammad. Paralleling Haj Ferdi's authority with that of the Moroccan monarchy, *Le passé simple* undermines their respective genealogical claims to power.

Genealogies of Patriarchy

Across his literary oeuvre, Driss Chraïbi unsettles authoritative narratives of Islamic history: from the revelations of the Prophet Muhammad in *L'Homme du Livre* (The Man of the Book, translated as *Muhammad*, 1994), to the Islamicization of the Maghreb. His trilogy—*Une enquête au pays* (*Flutes of Death*, 1981), *La mère du printemps (L'oum-er-bia)* (*Mother Spring*, 1982) and *Naissance à l'aube* (*Birth at Dawn*, 1986)—for example, investigates the complex history of the Arab-Islamic conquest of North Africa from the perspective of its indigenous Amazigh communities. As with Djebar's *L'amour, la fantasia*, the trilogy contests dominant accounts of Moroccan national identity: "By writing about the origins of Islam in the Maghreb, Chraïbi provides a genealogical perspective that restores the complexity of struggles and competing interests to the image of a reality from which oversimplified myths of origin spring" (Marx-Scouras 141).[17] His novels are attentive not only to the narrativization of mythologies—colonial, national, and religious—but to the very genealogical structures that legitimate them.

A key figure signaling this history in Islam is Abraham, and his parable serves as a crucial intertext in the works of both Djebar and Chraïbi. *Le passé simple* opens with an invocation of Abraham's youngest son, Ishmael: "At the hour when a descendant of Ishmael can no longer distinguish a black thread from a white one" (*A l'heure où un descendant d'Ishmaël ne pourra plus distinguer un fil noir d'un fil blanc*) (Chraïbi, *The Simple Past* 1/13). The line rewrites a Qur'anic passage on the guidelines of fasting during the month of Ramadan from the sura "Al-baqara" ("The Cow"):

وَابْتَغُواْ مَا كَتَبَ اللَّهُ لَكُمْ وَكُلُواْ وَاشْرَبُواْ حَتَّى يَتَبَيَّنَ لَكُمُ الْخَيْطُ الأَبْيَضُ مِنَ الْخَيْطِ الأَسْوَدِ مِنَ الْفَجْرِ
ثُمَّ أَتِمُّواْ الصِّيَامَ إِلَى اللَّيْلِ وَلاَ تُبَاشِرُوهُنَّ وَأَنتُمْ عَاكِفُونَ فِي الْمَسَاجِدِ تِلْكَ حُدُودُ اللَّهِ فَلاَ تَقْرَبُوهَا كَذَلِكَ
يُبَيِّنُ اللَّهُ آيَاتِهِ لِلنَّاسِ لَعَلَّهُمْ يَتَّقُونَ

> [A]nd avail yourselves of that which God has ordained for you, and eat and drink until you can discern the white streak of dawn against the blackness of night, and then resume fasting until nightfall. (Qur'an 2:187 trans. Asad)[18]

In this scene, Haj Ferdi has forbidden the family from breaking fast even though it is after sunset—a violation of even the most stringent interpretations of the Qur'an—which demonstrates Haj Ferdi's control across both familial and religious spheres of life. Inverting the Qur'anic image to designate a liminal ethical zone, Chraïbi mobilizes the sura to critique religious overreach.

The word *fil* in the passage harkens not only to the repeated image of *la ligne mince* but also to lines of descent in its resemblance to the word *fils*, or son. The passage invokes Driss's descent from his father, and by extension, the Prophet Muhammad. It also suggests the shared lineage of the Abrahamic faiths: Abraham's son Ishmael marking the lineage of Muhammad, and Isaac that of Jesus and Moses. Notably, Driss expresses a proclivity for the Christian and Jewish faiths throughout the novel. He seeks asylum in a Catholic church where he considers conversion, and repeatedly refers to his affinity with Moroccan Jews. The novel's opening subsequently stages many of the book's prominent motifs: the parable of Abraham, Manichean dualism in relation to both colonial policy and religious imagery, as well as the politics of Sherifian descendance in Morocco.

Described in the Qur'an as a paradigm of piety and selfless faith, Abraham was willing to sacrifice his first-born son Ishmael based upon on a dream that he interpreted as divine commandment.[19] Not only does Abraham signify absolute submission to God's will, even at the expense of his own progeny, but he represents patriarchal structures more broadly.[20] By framing Driss as the son unwilling to be sacrificed at God's altar, the parable of Abraham forms the thematic backdrop of *Le passé simple*, in addition to being integrated into the diegesis. The murder of his youngest brother, Hamid, at the hand of Haj Ferdi provides the catalyst for Driss's revolt and serves as a realization of the parable. He interprets Hamid's death, in lieu of his own, as a sacrifice to Haj Ferdi's theocracy. Driss even mockingly refers to himself as an Abrahamic figure enslaved by Islam: "There is of course the offering, a sort of holocaust, for I am a kind of Abraham, tattooed by Islam, or to translate: Orient, and oriental parable" (*Il y a certes l'offrande, une sorte d'holocauste, je suis une espèce d'Abraham, un tatoué de l'Islam, or traduisez: Orient, parabole orientale*) (Chraïbi, *The Simple Past* 156/270). Despite dismissing the story as a didactic "parabole orientale," Driss nonetheless identifies with the figure of Abraham through their shared inscription within patriarchal structures.

Driss similarly parodies the genealogical structure of hadith and his father's selective reliance upon the corpus: "'The son of Adam So-and-So tells us that one So-and-So had heard it said that one So-and-So heard someone tell So-and-So that he remembered that one So-and-So . . .' etc. . . . etc. . . . Here a dogma followed by its usage: not to comprehend, not to judge, to believe, that is all that is asked of you. Amen!" (*'Le fils d'Adam Untel raconte qu'Untel avait ouï dire qu'Untel entendit un jour qu'il se rappelait qu'Untel . . .' etc. . . . etc. . . . ici un dogme suivi du mode d'emploi: à ne pas comprendre, à ne pas juger, à croire, c'est tout ce qu'on vous demande. Amen!*) (27/58). While the validity of a specific hadith relies upon its ability to document and justify an uninterrupted chain of transmission, this passage satirizes the process as gossip. Moreover, since *isnād* requires a continuous chain, Driss is deliberately interrupting the process by trailing off with an incomplete account. The use of the name Adam, coupled with the absence of the Prophet Muhammad, suggests a reorientation of the chain of transmission from the Prophet Muhammad, as the prophetic progenitor of Islam, to Adam, as the origin of humankind. Critiquing hadith as the institutionalization of hearsay into "*dogme*," Driss challenges the opacity of a process that forgoes comprehension for belief.

Haj Ferdi embodies a patriarchal order mired within a network of French colonial, Moroccan nationalist, and Islamic rhetoric. His designation as *Le Seigneur* echoes the novel's constant blurring of the line between the sacred and the secular, the political and the personal, the private and the public. In the context of the *ancien régime*, which serves as one of the novel's main framing devices, the title refers to a noble or feudal lord (McLarney 12–14). It may also connote a master, divine being, or God. Critics have further suggested that it is a translation of the colloquial Moroccan title *m'sid*, meaning sir, or *sayyid*, that references a descendant of the Prophet Muhammad (Kadra-Hadjadji 48). *Le passé simple* employs the term to highlight the intersecting hegemonic forces within the Protectorate: the French administration, the religious elite, feudal lords, as well as the sultanate, while simultaneously exposing the structural similarities with the *ancien régime*. As Driss states: "The Lord awaits me. His law is indisputable . . . I become once more a simple pedestrian on the Straight Path, the path of the chosen of God over which those He has damned never shall pass . . . [The] Lord, the embodiment of Islam" (*Le Seigneur m'attend. Sa loi est indiscutable . . . je suis redevenu un simple piéton du Chemin Droit, chemin des élus de Dieu et par où ne passent jamais ceux qu'Il a maudits . . . (Le) Seigneur, cristallisation de l'Islam*) (Chraïbi, *The Simple Past* 1–2/14, translation modified). This passage illustrates the overlapping feudal, Islamic, and colonial significations of the term *Seigneur*. As McLarney observes, it also "puns on the notion of *droit de Seigneur*," a medieval concept that references the unspoken right of a feudal lord to bed his serfs' virgin daughters (McLarney 12). The title thus highlights the manner in which economic and social power also provide sexual and gendered privilege—a notable dimension of Haj Ferdi's authority to which I will return.

Chraïbi's attempt to parallel the history of France's *ancien régime* with Protectorate Morocco does more than simply shed light on the logic of French imperialism in North Africa. It also demonstrates the structural affinities of revolutionary France with the emerging social structures of the Protectorate that will come to shape local politics following independence in 1956. These similarities are most pronounced in the hierarchies embedded within feudal and religious orders. Driss's attempt to incite a populist *coup d'état* with his brothers, alongside his appeal to the revolutionary ideals of *liberté, egalité, fraternité,* further weaves these two histories together: "And if, at the same time, the Lord had said to me 'There is something in you that we do not understand and that frightens us, you are no longer a part of our world. Speak, explain your wishes. We grant you that.' I would reply: 'Liberty' and refuse it" (Chraïbi, *The Simple Past* 22/49, translation modified). By expressing a desire for "*liberté*" but also refusing it, Driss subverts *Le Seigneur*'s feudal order, as well as the French revolutionary ideals of *liberté, egalité, fraternité.*

Although *Le Seigneur*'s authority is spiritually sanctioned by his Sherifian lineage and title of haj, it is also economically enforced. This is demonstrated in his control over land, resources, and material goods within the context of both his family and the Protectorate. Haj Ferdi represents a new social class fostered by the centralized and capitalist state structures upon which the colonial order rests. For example, his thriving tea business in Casablanca manipulates import and export regulations determined by the Protectorate and the U.S. involvement in World War II. Moreover, Haj Ferdi's public gestures of piety are contradicted by his private indulgence in alcohol, drugs, and sex: "You perform your five prayers a day, and your prayer beads weigh a kilo. Everybody respects you. You have the beard of a patriarch. You are a man of God. . . . You are a saint. A direct descendant of the Prophet. . . . Well hidden inside that pious felt bag *there are a hundred grams of kif.* The spiritual and the temporal at the same time, isn't that right? That's life. Allah is great!" (90/165, translation modified).[21] Driss satirizes his father's *tartufferie*, aptly exposing the intermingling of "*Le spirituel et le temporel*" in his father's empire. He reveals the hypocritical manner in which Haj Ferdi's piety serves as a mask for his indulgences, even going so far as to reveal the fully stocked bar of premium French liqueurs and wines that hide behind his collection of rare religious manuscripts and scrolls. Ferdi's collusion with the French is figuratively and literally veiled by his ostentatious displays of religiosity.

Driss's critique of religious dogma extends to his time at a Qur'anic school before he enrolled at the elite Lycée Lyautey: "Over the course of four years, the Qur'anic schools taught me Law, dogma, the limits of dogma, and hadiths, with cudgel blows to the head and on the soles of my feet—administered with such mastery that, even until the Day of Judgment, I will never forget them" (*Les écoles coraniques m'ont enseigné la Loi, dogmes, limites des dogmes, hadiths. Pendant quatre ans. A coups de bâton sur mon crâne et sur la plante des pieds—si magistralement que, jusqu'au jour du Jugement dernier, je n'aurai garde de l'oublier*) (3/16, translation modified).[22] Chraïbi employs the same rhetoric of *loi, dogma, jugement,* to discuss the methods employed in Qur'anic school and the domestic rule of *Le Seigneur.*[23] This further highlights the significance of Driss's participation in a new symbolic order exemplified by the elite educational institutions of the French Protectorate. However, it is an entry sanctioned and even facilitated by *Le Seigneur.*

Haj Ferdi's decision to enroll Driss in a French school is motivated by his nationalistic desire to cultivate a new generation to lead Morocco after independence:

> Our role as father is the role of guide. Learn everything you can and as well as you can, so that all you have learned will serve you as a useful weapon, first of all for your examinations and secondly for the comprehension of the Occidental world. We are in need of young people capable of navigating between our oriental lethargy and the Occident's insomnia, and capable of assimilating today's science and of teaching it to our future generations. Don't ever let yourself be tempted by what you have learned, by these mirages that until now you had never heard of and which you seem content to treat as if they were dogma. Don't forget that all existing civilizations are based on postulates. (7, translation modified)[24]

Haj Ferdi's prophetic words explain not only his interest in Driss arming himself with scientific knowledge—part of the very weaponry of French imperialism—but also the fear that his son may become seduced by this world. His acknowledgment that all civilizations are founded upon postulates exposes the danger in transforming ideology into institutional dogma, and ironically echoes Driss's own critiques of his father's religious practice.

Haj Ferdi's authority reflects not only his self-interested appropriation of Qur'anic rhetoric but also the centralization of power that occurred under the French Protectorate. McLarney suggests that the father symbolizes the king, and his *grenier* (storeroom) denotes the Makhzen, or centralized infrastructure of the Moroccan government (McLarney 5).[25] If *Le passé simple* represents the different factions that constituted the Moroccan political scene, then the figure of Haj Ferdi represents the vast consolidation of power under the nationalist banners of Arabization and Islamicization that were facilitated by the centralization of the colonial administration. In Driss and his father, we witness two emerging forms of power cultivated by French imperialism. As the old guard, Ferdi signifies the feudal structures supported by the Protectorate but also the emergent class of merchants capitalizing on French economic policies and class divisions. Driss, on the other hand, is representative of the French-educated (and also France-bound) class of the intelligentsia fostered to harbor skepticism toward Islam. Invariably, these two generations violently clash in the novel, suggesting that they reflect the divide-and-conquer policies of the Protectorate.

Another complex figure in the novel signaling the imbrications of religion with political as well as socioeconomic power is Si Kettani. *Le passé simple* seems to be referencing a prominent historical figure in the years leading up to Moroccan independence. Si ʿAbd al-Ḥayy al-Kitānī was the president of the Federation of Religious Brotherhoods. Along with the Pasha of Marakesh, Thami El Glaoui, al-Kitānī formed the Movement for Opposition and Reform that attempted to usurp the throne of Sultan Muḥammad V, allegedly in collusion with the French.[26] Driss encounters the sheikh at his uncle's home in Fès during a trip with his mother to visit the shrine of her father. He is a saintly *marabout*, whom Driss describes as "a saint, number 2740 in the catalogue" in mockery of the prolific, almost bureaucratic, saint culture in Morocco (Chraïbi, *The Simple Past* 47).[27] In line with the novel's depiction of Haj Ferdi's hypocrisy and the "*pédérastie appliquée*" (applied pederasty) of the Qur'anic schools, Driss emphasizes Si Kettani's religious hypocrisy and exploitation of his authority (16/39). He also comments extensively on the sheikh's sexuality, particularly his well-known predilection for young boys.

The relationship between religion and sexuality is a recurring preoccupation in *Le passé simple*. After Driss is expelled by Haj Ferdi, he seeks a Catholic priest for confession and conversion, only to find himself envisioning the priest as a young, attractive woman. During this dreamlike sequence, the priest, signifying the interplay of colonialism and Christianity, is simultaneously eroticized and feminized. Driss's "rape" of this symbol of Christianity "destined uniquely for the satisfactions of the flesh," is an inversion of the missionizing role of Christianity in Protectorate Morocco (108). As Jarrod Hayes argues, sex in the novel is a signifier for power, whereby the outdated binary of "active" and "passive" demarcate positions of power and powerlessness respectively ("Rachid O" 507–8). This is evident in Driss's disdain for his mother, whom he sees as a "*Coffre à grossesses*" (a receptacle for pregnancies), and in his rejection of Si Kettani's sexual proposition on the grounds that it requires him to be sexually "passive" (Chraïbi, *The Simple Past* 71/133).[28]

Similarly, Driss's former French lover Roche, a reminder that the French ruling class "see Morocco as one vast Gomorrah," cuts off sexual relations when Driss wishes to switch to an "active" position (157). The relationship between social power, wealth, and sexual prowess—often coded in the text as aggression—is most apparent in the figure of Haj Ferdi. His authority, as both a father and a landowner, is imbricated within a distinctly libidinal economy. This is represented in his position as the Ferdi family patriarch, as well as in his sexual relationship with a young woman named Aisha, who resides on his estate and with whom he has fathered two children.[29]

In addition to outing Si Kettani for his sexual proclivities, Driss exposes the manipulations that facilitated the sheikh's professional and material success:

> One morning you wrapped yourself in an almost white sheet and went from door to door, from one street corner to another, from one mosque to another, shouting that you had seen the Prophet discuss the world situation with Franklin Delano Roosevelt in a dream. You were given a *zaouïa* where you suddenly retired and a substantial pension that you accepted with disdain for the vanities of this world. You subsequently had other dreams that were quickly blessed by specific donations, notably the office of jurisconsult and a Cadillac. The Resident named you counselor general of the *Makhzen* and everybody in Fez society wanted you as a guest. (45, translation modified)[30]

Driss itemizes the various material gifts and honors bestowed upon Si Kettani for his allegedly holy visions: imam of the Sherifian schools, head of a *zaouïa* (*zāwiya*), the office of jurisconsult, and counselor general of the Makhzen.[31] As with Haj Ferdi, Driss satirizes Si Kettani's feigned disdain for the material world despite his substantial wealth and privilege. Moreover, his vision of the Prophet Muhammad discussing world politics with President Roosevelt, and his newly acquired Cadillac, demonstrate the structural parallels of global capitalism and religious authority.[32]

While Driss problematizes Islam's institutional codification, particularly in Qurʾanic schools, he also shares an ambivalent relationship to French colonial education. French schooling offers an escape from the symbolic order of his father, while simultaneously cultivating in him a critical suspicion of Islam. As he declares to Si Kettani: "Let's say that a high school graduate . . . will have the same power and consideration as a *fqih*. . . . [T]he elite of the future will all be people with a baccalaureate. . . . Times have changed Monsieur" (42–43/82–83, translation modified). Addressing Si Kettani as Monsieur according to French rather than Moroccan or Muslim rules of etiquette, Driss suggests that the religious elite will soon be replaced by a French-educated generation. What he fails to acknowledge, of course, is that his very access to the privileged Lycée Lyautey was possible only because of his father's religious stature and vast wealth. This tension between the material and the spiritual is most clearly exhibited in the recurring image of *la ligne mince*.

Technologies of Inscription

An enigmatic motif throughout the novel, *la ligne mince* is a spectral vision that appears to Driss in two key scenes: following a failed revolt against his father and when he is at the mosque on Laylat al-Qadr (The Night of Power). While little critical attention has been given to the complex image of *la ligne mince*, except as "a symbol of the frontier between two worlds, like the line of demarcation between the Orient and the West" (*le symbole de la frontière entre deux mondes, comme la ligne de démarcation entre l'Orient et l'Occident*), it is essential to understanding the novel's intertextuality with Qur'anic cosmology (Kadra-Hadjadji 43). Anthropologist Stefania Pandolfo argues that *la ligne mince* builds upon the Islamic concept of the *barzakh* as a liminal space between spiritual worlds. She reads *la ligne mince* as

> a Quranic concept. It is the image of the *barzakh*—a partition, isthmus, limit, or barrier—which establishes a difference and which it is forbidden to pass (*Qur'an* 23:99–100). In its Sufi interpretation, and in the thought of Ibn ʿArabi in particular, the *barzakh* is a pivotal concept: a theory of the Intermediate World of absence-presence, region of the boundary and domain of the Imagination, in which contraries come together, bodies are spiritualized, and spirits become manifest in corporeal forms. Both a limit and an *entre-deux*, the entre-deux of the limit, the *barzakh* is a thin line. ("The Thin Line of Modernity" 121)

As a *barzakh*, the thin line functions as a liminal space (epistemological, ontological, and spiritual) with imaginative and ethical potential—similar to Maḥmūd al-Masʿadī's *Mawlid al-nisyān* and Abdelwahab Meddeb's *Talismano*.[33]

Expanding upon Pandolfo's analysis of *la ligne mince* as a site of rupture, the image also functions as an intervention into the French language and genealogical modes of historical inscription—at once colonial, nationalist, and religious. Driss initially experiences *la ligne mince* after an altercation with his father in the first chapter. After Haj Ferdi confronts Driss for his inability to commit patricide, Driss beckons for *la ligne mince*:

> *Thin Line*, *Thin Line*, I call out to you like a sleepless child would call out for a maternal lullaby. . . . And it is through the *Thin Line* that I escape. It descends on this room like a flash. Lord, look at your puppet. Behind my eyes so desperately closed in my tension to find sleep, it is first like the thread of a spider's web, a thread so thin, so impalpable that it is unreal. This thread is a letter, a number or a broken line. It does not move, but I see it growing, oh! so slowly, so softly, so imperceptibly at first. And as it becomes more precise, as it grows, letter, broken line or number are transformed into matter and move, pendulum-like, dancing faster and faster. The *Thin Line* becomes as thick as a finger, bigger than an arm, takes the form of a motor-valve, an airplane propeller, the trajectory of a rocket, becomes as enormous as a mountain, but keeping its form of number, letter or broken line. And as the speed and size of the *Line* attain paroxysm, its materiality becomes visible, palpable, acquiring a kind of sound, muffled at first, then growing clearer and clearer, then like the whistling of a bullet, as precise, as strong, as violent, as thundering as the sound of a car wheel on a tar road, on a paved highway, on a rocky road, to finally become the gigantic clamor of a moving train. And all of that is behind my eyes so desperately closed in my tension to go to sleep, inside my eyes injected with fear, in my brain completely deafened by this din, crushed by this weight, minced by this speed. Then the gamut of sound generates a tone, then another, then even another. The speed diminishes, the mountain becomes a block, the block a beam, letter or number, behind my eyes so desperately closed in my tension to find sleep, is nothing more than a *Thin Line* without sonority or movement, like the thread of a spider's web, a thread so thin, so impalpable that it is unreal. (Chraïbi, *Le passé simple* 30–31, translation modified)[34]

In this first encounter, Driss not only likens himself to a child, but he also summons the line "*comme une berceuse maternelle*." His invocation of *la ligne mince* as a maternal figure is contrasted with the shifting imagery of the passage. Its appearance is sudden and visceral, "*comme un flash*," but the line is also elusive, otherworldly, and "*irreal*." Initially, Driss describes it as "*une lettre, un chiffre ou une ligne brisée*." The discontinuity of the broken line reflects the Latin script, in contrast to Arabic script, where the letters are interlinked and more closely resemble a continuous line. Delicate and innocuous at first, *la ligne mince* metamorphoses as it gradually acquires size, speed, and sound.

A phantasmagoric vision, the line defies all rules of logic; it transforms from the delicacy of a spider web into the enormity of a mountain. It also vacillates between stasis and movement, the impalpable and the material, as well as silence and sound. However, it manages to maintain its form as a mode of textual inscription: "*toujours avec sa forme de chiffre, de lettre ou de ligne brisée.*" In addition to visually suggesting the French language, *la ligne mince* also stands in for French discourses of modernity. The French language represents the various technologies employed to disseminate colonial ideology; hence the analogies to cars, trains, planes, rockets, paved roads, and highways. Although he initially beckons the line to comfort him, it soon becomes overwhelming, and Driss is "*assourdi par ce tintamarre, écrasé par ce poids, haché par cette vitesse.*" Therefore, while *la ligne mince* is the very medium of Driss's escape ("*par quoi j'échappe*"), its violence also traps him "*comme un fil de toile d'araignée.*" Driss eventually recuperates this mode of inscription as an instrument of subversion.

In this passage, *la ligne mince* begins faintly and then grows in size, movement, and finally sound, only to shrink back to its original form. The line's shape-shifting nature gestures toward a rhizomatic model of subjectivity. Chraïbi does not seem to be privileging a romantic notion of hybrid identity, however, as the encounter with *la ligne mince* is clearly a painful one. It is in this state of being located between sleep and consciousness, reality and imagination, that Chraïbi situates a site of ethical agency. In this regard, *la ligne mince* represents the generative possibilities of the *barzakh* as a spiritual, epistemological, and ontological space. Throughout the novel, Driss's imagination functions as a means of both subversion and creation, as it does in *Mawlid al-nisyān* and *Talismano*. He tells his father "I escape you, through my imagination, which is vast, as you yourself have recognized" (*Je vous échappe. Par mon imagination. Elle est vaste, vous-même l'avez reconnu*) (23/50).

Driss next encounters *la ligne mince* at a mosque in Fès on Laylat al-Qadr; one of the most sacred days in Islam, it commemorates the descent of the Qur'an and entails a night of reflection and prayer. Possessed by *la ligne mince* on this holy night, Driss is able to confront "*mon état d'âme*" (the state of my soul), as he listens to Si Kettani's recitation of "Āyat al-kursī" (The verse of the throne) from the sura "Al-baqara" ("The Cow") (55/105). The sura reads:

اللَّهُ لاَ إِلَهَ إِلاَّ هُوَ الْحَيُّ الْقَيُّومُ لاَ تَأْخُذُهُ سِنَةٌ وَلاَ نَوْمٌ لَّهُ مَا فِي السَّمَاوَاتِ وَمَا فِي الأَرْضِ مَن ذَا الَّذِي
يَشْفَعُ عِنْدَهُ إِلاَّ بِإِذْنِهِ يَعْلَمُ مَا بَيْنَ أَيْدِيهِمْ وَمَا خَلْفَهُمْ وَلاَ يُحِيطُونَ بِشَيْءٍ مِّنْ عِلْمِهِ إِلاَّ بِمَا شَاء وَسِعَ
كُرْسِيُّهُ السَّمَاوَاتِ وَالأَرْضَ وَلاَ يَؤُودُهُ حِفْظُهُمَا وَهُوَ الْعَلِيُّ الْعَظِيمُ

> God—there is no deity save Him, the Ever-Living, the Self-Subsistent Fount of All Being.
>
> Neither slumber overtakes Him, nor sleep. He is all that is in the heavens and all that is on earth. Who is there that could intercede with Him, unless it be His leave?
> He knows all that lies open before men and all that is hidden from them, whereas they cannot attain to aught of His knowledge save that which He wills [them to attain].
>
> His eternal power overspreads the heavens and earth, and their upholding wearies Him not. And He alone is truly exalted, tremendous. (Qur'an 2:255 trans. Asad)

During his recitation of this celebrated passage on the omnipotence and omniscience of God, Si Kettani transforms before Driss's eyes: "He was no longer ugly, he was no longer bestial" (Chraïbi, *The Simple Past* 55). *La ligne mince* then takes hold of Driss, addressing him in accusation:

> It said to me: You are a black. You are a black from the generations that crossed with white. You are about to *cross over the line*, to lose your last drop of authentic black blood. Your facial angle opened up, and you are no longer woolly-haired or thick-lipped. You were issued from the Orient, and through your painful past, your imagination and your education, you are going to triumph over the Orient. You have never believed in Allah. You know how to dissect legends, you think in French, you are a reader of Voltaire and an admirer of Kant. Only the occidental world for which you are destined appears to you to be strewn with nonsense and ugliness, almost exactly the same ugliness and nonsense from which you are fleeing. Moreover, you feel that it is a hostile world, that it is not going to accept you right away, and . . . you have some setbacks. That is why I appear to you. Since the very first day I appeared to you, you have been nothing but an open wound. (56, translation modified)[35]

La ligne mince confronts Driss with the implications of his French acculturation and deracination. It casts his transformation as both visceral and intellectual—reflected in the shape of his face, the texture of his hair, and the size of his lips, as well as his thoughts, ideals, and beliefs. Employing decidedly racialized tropes of blackness, *la ligne mince* describes Driss's transformation as a literal whitewashing and cautions him that he is on the brink "*de perdre ta dernière goutte de sang authentiquement nègre.*" The use of charged racial phenotypes, such as "*crépu*" and "*lippu,*" emphasizes the power discrepancy between Driss and the line, further suggesting its relationship to the authority of the French language.

La ligne mince tells Driss that he will triumph over the Orient precisely through his French education, imagination, as well as his "*passé douloureux.*" Tellingly, the passage situates faith in the *passé compose*: "*tu n'as jamais cru en Allah,*" thereby relegating Islam to an inaccessible and distant past. His French acculturation, by contrast, is cast in the present tense: "*tu sais disséquer les legends, tu penses en français, tu es lecteur de Voltaire at admirateur de Kant.*" *La ligne mince* suggests that it is precisely because of rational Enlightenment thought, represented by the figures of Voltaire and Kant, that Driss is able to dissect the mythology of Islam. An influential intellectual figure of the French Revolution, Voltaire was a known advocate for social reform, and his satirical works took aim at religious institutions and dogma. Kant's philosophical writings were also critical of the hierarchical institutionalization of religious doctrine. In this regard, *la ligne mince* warns Driss that the world he aspires to join is riddled with "*les mêmes laideurs et les mêmes bêtises*" as the Orient. The text thus draws a connection between the anticlericalism of the Enlightenment and Driss's own ambivalent relationship to Islamic institutions and the religious elite.

Driss's encounter with *la ligne mince* signifies his cultural, linguistic, and ethical disorientation, transforming him into "*rien d'autre qu'une plaie.*" His rejection by the authorial voice of empire, however, inspires a spiritual transformation. While under the spell of *la ligne mince* on Laylat al-Qadr, Driss is mesmerized by Si Kettani's recitation of the Qur'an. He interrupts the sheikh so that he may continue the recitation, during which he begins to rewrite the Qur'an. Si Kettani is reciting "the overture to the Chapter Hard *H M*" (56/106, translation modified). Chraïbi's attempt to represent the Arabic letters of *Ḥa'* and *Mīm* as "*H dur M*" renders legible the incommensurability of certain modes of inscription but also a desire to mediate this gap. Each beginning with the incantation *Ḥā' Mīm* (H M), this series of seven suras from the late Meccan period includes "Ghāfir" (40: "Forgiving"); "Fuṣṣilat" (41: "Clearly Spelled Out"); "Ash-Shūrū" (42: "Consultation"); "Al-zukhruf" (43: "Gold"); "Al-dukhān" (44: "Smoke"); "Al-jāthiya" (45: "Kneeling Down"); and "Al-aḥqāf" (46: "The Sand-Dunes"). Speculation on the meaning of the Arabic letters *Ḥā' Mīm* that adorn this series of suras is rather divided in Qur'anic exegesis.[36] The commentator Yusuf Ali explains that "The general theme of the whole series is the relation of Faith to unfaith, Revelation to Rejection, Goodness to Falsehood" (1260). One interpretation suggests that the letter *Mīm* connotes the Day of Judgment, while the letter *Ḥā'* implies that "the Beginning is only for the End, the Present for the Future," emphasizing "the eschatological element in Faith" (ibid.). Driss's intervention into these eschatological suras, coupled with the novel's metaphor of the *passé simple*, ruptures a teleological model of historical time.

Driss interrupts Si Kettani's recitation of the sura and begins his own that is both a reading and a rewriting. The night of Laylat al-Qadr—signifying spiritual renewal, reflection, and rebirth—becomes a creative and subversive space for Driss. While possessed by *la ligne mince*, he is finally able to confront God:

> Yes, my God, you speak truth. You see I still accept you . . . and even when you thunder out your maledictions or detail for us the punishments of the Last Judgment, you explain yourself in incantatory rhythms. You see my God, Haj Ferdi Fahmi taught me to love you, in fear for the body and the desolation of the soul. He applied your law, to a woman whom he has tortured, tortured so thoroughly, severe, punctual, worthy, that, without this torture, she would collapse into dust. To sons that he tied up and bound, cut up, and crushed, duty and honor he says . . . I still love you. And so, although from you to me, from you who determine for me what is determined, a prayer would be useless, grant that I may love you for a long time still. These verses I chant in your house and in the ears of your faithful, I say them... because you ought to be something other than the Allah of *m'sids* and shackles. I repeat to you that I am shackled. (Chraïbi, *The Simple Past* 56, translation modified)[37]

Driss's recitation demonstrates an intimate knowledge of the Qur'an, as well as this particular series of suras. Chraïbi thus works from within Qur'anic discourse itself in order to undermine its appropriation and misuse by the religious elite.

Driss critiques the fear-based religious doctrine enforced by figures such as Haj Ferdi and Si Kettani. He suggests that it is his father's selective interpretation of the Qur'an that has transformed him into an abusive husband and father. Notably, while each of the suras in the series addresses questions of disbelief, sin, punishment, and the Day of Judgment, they are also about God's benevolence ("Ghāfir"), knowledge ("Fuṣṣilat"), guidance ("Ash-Shūrū"), truth ("Al-zukhruf"), humility ("Al-dukhān"), justice ("Al-jāthiya"), and patience ("Al-aḥqāf"). If the first passage on *la ligne mince* depicts the authoritative voice of French as a mode of inscription used to codify colonial modernity, then the second demonstrates its relationship to hegemonic Islamic institutions. Through *la ligne mince* as a liminal *barzakh* space, however, Driss intervenes into the discursive authority of French imperialism, as well as the patriarchal order of his father. He attempts to generate a new genealogy between himself and God—a god he cannot entirely believe in, but one he loves all the same.

The Alchemy of Change

The tension between faith and Enlightenment discourses of modernity is perhaps most visible in the formal construction of *Le passé simple* as a novel. Structured around the theme of alchemy, each of the novel's five chapters traces the gradual transformation of base metals into gold: "Les éléments de base," "Périod de transition," "Le réactif," "Le catalyseur," and "Les éléments de synthèse." They further echoe the novel's paroxysmal structure, as Driss attempts to reconcile his French education with his Moroccan Muslim upbringing, only to realize in the end that "I have lived my life like an alchemist. No doubt I have a few years ahead of me, twenty or sixty, that I will lead like a chemist" (157/273, translation modified). Through this dichotomy between chemistry, as a traditionally "rational" science, and alchemy, as a reputedly "mystical" science, Chraïbi seems to suggest that rather than attempting to transform base elements, the emerging intelligentsia must create anew—as the concept of *ibdʿa* proposes.

In the prologue to his novel *L'âne*, published in France in 1956, Chraïbi revisits some of the criticisms of *Le passé simple* around the question of Islam. He also addresses the autobiographical readings that dominate critical reception of the novel:

> The hero of *Le passé simple* is named Driss Ferdi. Perhaps it is me. In any event, his despair is mine; despair in faith. This Islam in which he believed—that speaks of the equality of rule, of God's part in every individual creation, of tolerance, of liberty, and of love—he saw it [as] a fiery teenager trained in French schools, reduced to a pharisaism, a

> social system armed with propaganda. All things considered, he embarked for France: he needed to believe, to love, to respect someone or something. . . . Choose? I have already chosen, but I genuinely wish to no longer have to do so. For if I chose to live in France—and perhaps to die there, though that is not up to me—I continue to participate in this world of my childhood, as well as in this Islam that I believe in more and more. (Chraïbi, *L'âne* 13–14)[38]

Chraïbi responds to accusations lodged against him that *Le passé simple* reflects the views of a native informant against Islam. He frames his literary intervention into Moroccan social and ethical issues as both personal and political. Chraïbi critiques the self-righteous institutionalization of Islam as a propaganda-laden "*système social.*" He acknowledges, however, that this awareness emerged in part from his French education. One could even note a structural parallelism between the Muslim values he lists and the tripartite motto of the French Revolution: *tolérance/egalité*, *liberté/liberté*, and *l'amour/fraternité*. While Chraïbi's tone evokes a sense of resignation, the novel seems to suggest other avenues of ethical engagement.

Le passé simple's double critique of colonial and nationalist genealogies of power culminates in Driss's baccalaureate essay on the subject of *liberté, egalité, fraternité*. The essay very consciously performs the troubled "symbiosis of my rejection of the Orient and of the skepticism that the Occident generated in me" (*symbiose de mon rejet de l'Orient et du scepticisme que fait naître en moi l'Occident*) (Chraïbi, *The Simple Past* 115/205, translation modified). In it, Driss describes himself as an "*Arabe habillé en Français*" (Arab dressed as a Frenchman) crafting an orientalist "good novel of the old-school genre: Morocco, land of the future, of sun, couscous . . . the slums, pashas, factories, dates, mueddins, mint tea, fantasies" (116–17/206–8, translation modified). Driss further reveals the tools of his performance, telling the French examiners that he will write about the topic "as an Arab. Without a plan, without technique, gauche, belabored" (117). More revealing than Driss's orientalist performance, however, is the manner in which he exposes the similarities of these two narrative worlds: "The subject is 'Liberty, Equality, Fraternity.' I am not fully qualified to speak on the subject. On the other hand, I can easily substitute another subject to replace it, one with which I am familiar: 'Muslim Theocracy.' Using such a theorem of similar triangles, I presume that the result will be the same, or at least very similar" (ibid.).[39] Chraïbi parallels the French revolutionary ideals of *liberté, egalité, fraternité* with "*la théocratie musulmane*," claiming that one could easily be substituted with the other. According to Driss, the two are linked by their mutual reliance on foundational myths of origin. The motto represents a progressivist model of modernity used to legitimize the *mission civilisatrice* in the Maghreb. Similarly, Haj Ferdi's "Muslim theocracy" relies on his religious and material authority, both of which are legitimized through his Sherifian lineage.

Chraïbi's use of the *passé simple* as a metaphor challenges the authority of French literary and historical discourse. Similar to Meddeb's *Talismano*, Waṭṭār's *Al-zilzāl*, and Djebar's *L'amour, la fantasia*, the novel's engagement with a variety of discursive traditions simultanesosuly exposes and upends social hierarchies. *Le passé simple* critiques the institutionalization of Islam by undermining the use of patrilineage to legitimize familial, socioeconomic, religious, or political authority. This is performed in the text's satirization of the collusion between the religious elite and the French Protectorate, claims to Sherifian descent, the corpus of hadith as a chain of transmission, and the parable of Abraham. Similarly, the novel disrupts French discourses of modernity by resignifying the revolutionary rhetoric of *liberté, egalité, fraternité* and the technologies of the *mission civilisatrice*. Chraïbi offers an alternative, however, in the recurring image of *la ligne mince*. In its invocation of the *barzakh*, the spectral image represents a space of temporal and epistemological rupture that also functions as a site of ethical formation.

This chapter has argued that *Le passé simple*'s complex representation of Islam is enriched by attending to its critical engagement with the Qur'an as a literary intertext. The novel's reception by French critics on the right as a disavowal of Islam and appeal to Western secularism has informed its literary celebration as the paradigmatic modernist Francophone Maghrebi novel. As with my discussion of both *Talismano* and *L'amour, la fantasia*, my analysis of *Le passé simple* has sought to attenuate the ease with which Qur'anic intertextuality is whitewashed when novels are interpellated as championing secularism. All three novels engage critically with Islam as a national signifier associated with Arabization, particularly in light of their representation of the collusion of Islamic institutions with colonial administrations. Rather than reading this as inimical to Islam, I argue that it is instead part of the critical exercise of Muslim ethics. In the process, I also seek to disentangle secularizing reading practices from the taxonomy of modern narrative forms—a point to which I now turn in my discussion of Muḥammad Barrāda's *Luʿbat al-nisyān* (*The Game of Forgetting*) as the exemplar postmodern Arabic novel.

CHAPTER 6

Threads of Transmission in Muḥammad Barrāda's *Luʿbat al-nisyān*

> Each generation has its truth . . . a *Zeitgeist* that tempts the artist above anyone else. . . . There is no single voice that represents an entire generation; rather, there is a diversity of voices. Their melodies distinguish themselves to the extent of conflicting and clashing with one another. . . . The value of a generation is determined by its ability to understand and express its individual "truth" or historical trajectory as well as its ability to mobilize social powers. . . . Insofar as literature is a form of expression that transcends collective and individual realities, it must act to eliminate, through its own means and norms, signs of underdevelopment and stagnation. . . . The goal is not innovation for the sake of newness, or to reach an avant-garde aesthetics by the easiest means (such as adapting foreign and Western artistic forms). The problem at hand is to see literature, and the arts in general, become one of the tools that will form the society that we aspire to become. Societal innovation is fundamentally a response to biological, psychological, and human needs. The dream of creation is behind every leap forward and innovation.
>
> MUḤAMMAD BARRĀDA, "GENERATION DRIVE"

In this 1968 contribution to the Marxist-Leninist journal *Souffles-Anfas* (Breaths), writer and theorist Muḥammad Barrāda (b. 1938) appealed to Morocco's literary avant-garde.[1] He argued that this new generation of writers were in a uniquely challenging yet generative moment within the cultural history of the Maghreb. Barrāda describes an epochal "truth" that binds each generation together, such as the project of cultural decolonization that marked his own. Employing the Marxist discourse of base, superstructure, and historical dialecticism, he theorizes the cultural avant-garde in terms at once ideological, ethical, and intellectual. Barrāda, who translated Bakhtin's theory of heteroglossia/heterology in "Discourse in the Novel," advocates for a dialogic approach to historical formations and their attendant cultural products, in which conflicting perspectives generate artistic innovation and creativity. This polyphony is not only explicitly argued in his theoretical works but also performed in his fiction, particularly his first novel, *Luʿbat al-nisyān* (*The Game of Forgetting*, 1987).

Unlike most of the writers in this study, Muḥammad Barrāda had a predominantly Arabophone education in Moroccan nationalist schools under the French Protectorate before studying Arabic literature at the University of Cairo and Muḥammad V University in Rabat.[2] He headed the Arabic program of the National Broadcasting Services before joining the Faculty of Arts of Human Sciences at Muḥammad V University as a professor of Arabic literature and criticism. While many Maghrebi intellectuals turned to Europe, Barrāda turned to the Mashriq, even writing his doctoral dissertation on contemporary Egyptian critic Muḥammad Mandur and the "theorization of Arabic literary criticism" (Boullata, introduction 2).[3] One of the founders of the Moroccan Writers' Union, Barrāda was its president from 1973 to 1983, in addition to editing its literary journal *Āfāq* (Horizons). His role as a cultural critic, however, extends beyond the union and its in-house publication. In addition to his theoretical monographs—*Al-riwāya al-ʿarabiyya wa-rihān al-tajdīd* (The Arabic novel and the wager of renewal), *Al-riwāya dhākira maftūḥa* (The novel: An open memory), *Faḍāʾāt riwāʾiyya* (Novelistic spaces), and *Asʾilat al-riwāya, asʾilat al-naqd* (Questions of the novel, questions of [literary] criticism)—Barrāda served on the Advisory Board of the literary magazine *Prologue* and was a regular contributor of essays, op-eds, and short stories to a number of regional periodicals.

While Barrāda published in Arabic, his views of Francophonie were more forgiving than those of al-Ṭāhir Waṭṭār. Like Maḥmūd al-Masʿadī, he actively draws upon both Arabophone and Francophone philosophy and literary criticism. Moreover, Barrāda translated a number of theoretical works from French to Arabic, including Abdelkébir Khatibi's *Le roman Maghrébin* (*Al-riwāya al-maghribiyya*, 1971), Roland Barthes's *Le degré zéro de l'écriture* (*Al-daraja al-ṣifr li-l-kitāba*, 1981), and Mikhail Bakhtin's "Discourse in the Novel" (*Al-khiṭāb al-riwāʾī*, 1987). His career-long theorization of the Arabic novel is part of a larger critical interest in semiotics, narratology, and genre studies.

The limited body of Anglophone scholarship on Barrāda's experimental novel *Luʿbat al-nisyān* emphasize its postmodernist aesthetics (Boullata, Phillips, and Younssi), linguistic code-switching (Sellman), and political commitment (Al-Nowaihi). This chapter examines the novel in dialogue with narrative techniques central to the Qurʾan and hadith, as well as the vast body of Islamic hermeneutical and embodied practices. By framing Qurʾanic intertextuality as commensurable with literary postmodernity, it challenges the ways in which the periodization of literary genres is often enmeshed within secular epistemes. The very formal qualities that make *Luʿbat al-nisyān* legible as a postmodern novel, I propose, can be read within this study's model of Qurʾanic narratology. In what follows, I explore how Barrāda's theorization of the novel in his critical writings works dialogically with the narrative practices of his fiction. Specifically, I examine how *Luʿbat al-nisyān* interrogates the generative possibilities of polyphonic modes of cultural, political, or religious discourse. The novel's unique narrative stylization enacts an ethics of writing, reading, and transmission that I read alongside its diegetic engagement with embodied and textual forms of Islamic praxis.

Polyphony and the Novelistic Text

Written in 1987, *Luʿbat al-nisyān* narrates a multigenerational story that spans the 1930s through 1980s. Resisting the temporal linearity of a pre- to postcolonial trajectory, the experimental text moves disorientingly between and through these periods. While the book was published as a novel, Barrāda introduces it with the title *naṣṣ riwāʾī*, or "novelistic text." The use of the adjectival form novelistic (*riwāʾī*), rather than the noun for novel (*riwāya*) casts the work as a text with novelistic qualities rather than as a novel as such. Both *Luʿbat al-nisyān* and Barrāda's broader critical oeuvre theorize the novel as a discursive mode rather than a fixed genre. Novelistic discourse, according to the critic-writer, often coexists with other narrative or rhetorical modes, such as Islamic textual traditions. In this regard, Barrāda's approach to the novel as a genre is deeply resonant with the work of Bakhtin, particularly his seminal 1935 essay "Discourse in the Novel." Translated as "Al-khiṭāb al-riwāʾī" (Novelistic discourse), the essay was published in Cairo by *Dār al-Fikr* in 1987—the same year as *Luʿbat al-nisyān*.

Bakhtin's theorization of the novel relies upon the critical concepts of *heteroglossia* and *heterology* introduced in the essay. Heteroglossia (*raznoiazychie*) references the multiplicity of national languages within a particular culture; meanwhile, the neologism heterology (*razorechie*) addresses the "coexistence within one natural language ('national' in Bakhtin's terminology) of 'socio-ideological languages' . . . the internal heterogeneity of one single natural language" (Zbinden 69).[4] The heterological dimensions of discourse account for the extralinguistic conditions—theological, sociocultural, political, and psychological—that bring together "a multiplicity of social voices and a wide variety of their links and interrelationships" into a singular utterance (Bakhtin, "Discourse in the Novel" 263). As Bakhtin elaborates, the novelistic genre provides the optimal platform for heterologic discourse, particularly in its reliance on multiple voices, as well as oral and written modes of address (Bakhtin, *Speech Genres* 60). Moreover, because of the frequent use of reported speech and dialogue within most novels, both of which are heavily present in *Luʿbat al-nisyān*, the genre works reciprocally with living forms of language that operate outside of the world of the text.[5] Bakhtin's understanding of the internal, external, and relational dimensions of language within novelistic discourse reiterate his reading of "literature as a *public* site through which *social* meaning is generated" (H. El Shakry, "Heteroglossia and the Poetics of the *Roman Maghrébin*" 9).

Barrāda's translation of "Discourse in the Novel" relied upon the French edition translated by Daria Olivier in 1978: *Esthétique et théorie du roman*, alongside Tzvetan Todorov's analysis in *Le principe dialogique*. Olivier's French edition collapses heteroglossia and heterology into the term *plurilinguisme*, in a translational oversight that has carried over into the almost exclusive use of "heteroglossia" in subsequent English editions. For polylingualism, Barrāda employs the two terms *al-taʿaddud al-lughawī* and *al-taʿaddud al-lisānī*. Appearing side by side in the critical index that accompanies his translation, the use of *lughawī* (related to language) alongside *lisānī* (etymologically from *lisān*, or tongue, and therefore related to speech) bespeaks a subtle understanding of the two concepts in Bakhtin's work.[6] In addition to a French-Arabic critical index of terms, Barrāda's translation includes a lengthy introduction, in which he writes of the importance of Bakhtinian semiotics to Maghrebi literature and criticism (Bakhtin, *Al-khiṭāb*, trans. Barrāda 20–23).[7]

Barrāda's theorization of novelistic discourse and *tajrīb*, or literary experimentation, will help contextualize this chapter's discussion of *Luʿbat al-nisyān* as well as this book's critical intervention into the periodization of literary genres.[8] While Barrāda predominantly focuses on the Arabic novel, his understanding of novelistic discourse relies upon a broader vision of the genre's synchronic and diachronic evolution. In reference to the history of the "world novel," Barrāda writes that the genre cannot be locked within a single national or linguistic tradition: "The novel is a form of human(ist) expression that has existed since ancient times, [and] that was enriched with numerous additions by creative artists belonging to different cultures and civilizations. . . . It is an open form, accommodating various additions, with narrative and aesthetic components that transcend any ethnic or cultural 'origin.' It is an assemblage that employs narrative, imagination, plot, polylingualism, and polyphony—all of which are components of this constantly evolving human(ist) novelistic heritage" (Barrāda, *Al-riwāya al-ʿarabiyya wa rihān al-tajdīd* 49).[9] Denouncing the Eurocentric and orientalist rhetoric that treats the Arabic novel as a mere adaptation or acculturation of an imported genre, Barrāda adds that the development and transformation of literary forms is an inherently nonlinear and asynchronous process: "We have transcended the debate over the importation of form. Translation has contributed to the diversification of global forms and criticism, in addition to crystallizing an awareness that all cultures have contributed to the crystallization and enrichment of the forms of expression" (Barrāda, *Faḍāʾāt riwāʾiyya* 70).[10]

As with those of Maḥmūd al-Masʿadī, Barrāda's critical writings emphasize the importance of literary creativity, or *ibdāʿ*. For both writers, literary innovation does not imply an aesthetic rejection of literary heritage or *turāth*. Rather, as Barrāda writes of the concept of *tajrīb*, it often entails "the revival of elements from the narrative tradition and the synthesis of the language of the classical historians and the lexicon of the Sufis, as well as the blending of literary genres in the expanse of novelistic texts" (Barrāda, *Al-riwāya al-ʿarabiyya wa-rihān al-tajdīd* 37).[11] Barrāda distinguishes between *tajrīb* (experimentation), *taqlīd* (imitation), and *tajdīd* (renewal)—which more closely resonates with the reformist and revivalist rhetoric associated with the *nahḍa* (14, 20, 48–49). He theorizes *tajdīd* as a self-conscious narrative strategy that requires theoretical awareness (*waʿy naẓarī*) (49). In this sense, one cannot extricate Barrāda's critical and fictional writings, insofar as his very understanding of literary experimentation is *as a theoretical practice*.

Barrāda takes issue with the privileging of novelty in the concept of *al-riwāya al-jadīda* (the new novel), which peaked in literary circles of the late twentieth-century. He argues that the binary between old and new suggests that newness is chronologically determined rather than an experience generated through a reader's engagement with the text at a particular moment in time:[12]

> The source of the problem lies in defining the meaning of "novelty" and "the new," as this word and its derivatives usually contain a positive connotation vis-à-vis what is old. However, in the area of literary and artistic creation [*ibdāʿ*], it is difficult to associate the new, automatically, with excellence and superiority over what is "old," i.e., what preceded

> it chronologically. Literary and artistic works have a long lifespan, and those bearing the age of centuries and decades maintain their "newness" by jolting the feelings and ideas of recipients living in a new and current time. (46)[13]

Arguing for a transtemporal view of literary modernity, Barrāda proposes that *tajrīb* disrupts the reader's very experience of time through the manipulation of narrative continuity. Experimental novelistic discourse, he writes, upsets classical narrative forms that "relied upon linear narrative and a commitment to a single perspective" (*al-muʿtamid ʿalā sard khaṭṭī, wa-iltizām manẓūr uḥādī*) (51).[14] This book's theorization of the Qur'an emphasizes precisely its multivocal and nonlinear narrative structure. Following Barrāda's asynchronous approach to literary modernity, the Qur'an—as a narrative (inter)text—aligns with his understanding of experimental novelistic form.

Returning to my discussion of *adab* in the Introduction, Barrāda attends not only to the literary experience but also to the praxis of writing. His model of *tajrīb* emphasizes writing as a process that captures the dialectic between the self and social at the level of form: "In our view, writing is the site where the writer's consciousness is expressed through different literary genres and through the function of language and form, which shifts and changes aesthetic standards. It represents the interaction of the writer's consciousness with his historical conditions" (32).[15] It is around the question of language—and specifically heteroglossia and heterology, or the heterogeneity both between and within languages—that Barrāda situates his theory of *tajrīb* in the context of novelistic discourse:

> When I think about the essential qualities of Arab literary creativity [*ibdāʿ*], my theory in this instance draws, above all else, on the phenomenon of polylingualism [*al-taʿaddud al-lughawī*] as a manifestation of the changing creativity of the concept of literature and its ideological weight, as well as of the method of its reading. It has become commonplace to argue that a literary text's achievement takes place in and through language. What I will try to present here, however, is an examination of the relationship of the literary product to language—especially in the novel—from the perspective of the inevitability of polylingualism [*al-taʿaddud al-lughawī*] within each narrative text, and to consider pluralism [*al-taʿaddudiyya*] as an internal component connected to a text's genesis and its formal, rhetorical [or discursive, *khiṭābī*], and ideological realization. (Barrāda, *As'ilat al-riwāya, as'ilat al-naqd* 30)[16]

Barrāda's theory of novelistic innovation centers on the narrative multiplicity of a text, which he argues occurs across the registers of form, discourse, and ideology. Polylingualism (*al-taʿaddud al-lughawī*) speaks to the ways in which literary creativity or *ibdāʿ* ultimately entails a reimagination of "the concept of literature" itself—as this study is attempting to do with a model of Qurʾanic narratology.

Qurʾanic Postmodernism

Reading *Luʿbat al-nisyān*'s narrative stylization in relation to the novel's formal and thematic engagement with Islam expands how we understand literary (post)modernity. Returning to my discussion of genre in the Introduction, conventional accounts of the modernist and postmodern novel have championed their antitheological orientation. According to this formulation, self-conscious experimentations with form—such as authorial decentering; the demystification of ideological, social, or political discourses and institutions; the deconstruction of the narrative, semiotic, or psychic construction of the self; and finally, the use of metanarrative techniques to call attention to the limitations of language and literary forms to represent phenomenological or metaphysical human experiences—signal a disavowal of theological logocentrism. This conflates religious doctrine with hermeneutical codification and belies an understanding of religious praxis as fundamentally incompatible with modes of critique associated with modern subject-formation.

As with all the novels discussed in this book, *Luʿbat al-nisyān* renders legible the imbrication of the Qurʾan's ethical, aesthetic, and narrative dimensions. The Qurʾan and tradition of hadith offer an alternative conceptual framework for reading the work's multivocality, nonlinearity, and architectonics as a "novelistic text." Similarly, the novel allows us to see the dialogism and polyphony inherent to Qurʾanic narrative practices. Frequently moving between diegetic and metanarrative accounts, the work is composed of multiple narrative voices. It alternates between the first, second, and third person, as well as singular and plural—a narrative device that I read in relation to Qurʾanic code-switching. Despite being very form-driven, the novel nonetheless experiments with some of the aesthetic practices more broadly associated with *al-wāqiʿiyya al-ishtirākiyya* (social[ist] realism)—a genre that had particular political and cultural cachet among the Arab Left in the mid-twentieth century. Spanning the 1930s through 1980s, the plot is grounded in the historical moments it covers, even as it flits between them asynchronously. It achieves this, in part, by balancing narrative multiplicity with distinctly individualized voices and perspectives.

Luʿbat al-nisyān is composed of seven sections, each of which is divided into subsections recounted by different narrators.[17] The narrators are largely members of the nuclear and extended family around whom the plot centers, in addition to their friends. Some of the narrators are individuals, while others are collective, such as the chorus of women living in family homes in Fès and Casablanca. Barrāda explicitly names some of the narrators, others can be inferred, while others still are anonymous—as in the case of an unnamed guest at a family member's wedding. The central figure and primary narrator within the text is al-Hādī, a leftist journalist and intellectual consumed with recalling and recounting his childhood.

At the metanarrative level, the text presents an omniscient narrative figure titled rāwī al-ruwwā, or the "Narrators' Narrator," to whom we are introduced in the second chapter.[18] These subsections begin with "*yaqūl rāwī al-ruwwā:*" (The Narrators' Narrator says:), invoking the narrative style of hadith. We are expressly told that the Narrators' Narrator is not the author (*al-muʾallif*) of the text. However, he directs and influences the narrative at various moments, all the while divulging his critical interventions to the reader. There is also a figure whom Issa Boullata refers to as the "implied author," who engages in creative debates and arguments with the Narrators' Narrator but never directly addresses the reader.

Most sections end with a series of subsections titled "iḍāʾatan" (illumination, lighting, enlightenment), followed by another titled "taʿtīm" (obscuration, darkening). These sections mirror the Qurʾanic, and particularly Sufi, dialectic of the *ẓāhir* (exoteric) and *bāṭin* (esoteric) that I discussed in relation to Maḥmūd al-Masʿadī, Abdelwahab Meddeb, and Assia Djebar. The *ẓāhir* and *bāṭin* frequently refer to registers of clarity and opacity in the Qurʾan as a divine object of revelation; they can also reference hermeneutical strategies; finally, in Sufism they distinguish the material world inhabited by the body from the realm of the soul and inner spiritual knowledge. Barrāda's mobilization of the *ẓāhir* and *bāṭin* as narrative techniques signals a model of literary innovation that echoes Qurʾanic discursive and interpretive practices.

While the narrators of the "Illumination" subsections vary, as does the register of Arabic employed, the "Obscuration" subsections are all narrated by al-Hādī in Modern Standard Arabic (MSA). Reported speech and dialogue are delivered in either the Fèsian or Rabatian dialect of Moroccan vernacular, further calling attention to the novel's polyphony. The first two "Illumination" subsections are narrated by a chorus of women living in the family home in Fès. These women are part of the extended family community, but not blood relatives. The subsequent "Illumination" subsection is narrated by the collective women of al-Hādī's next home in Casablanca; and the fourth and final, by an unnamed attendee of the wedding of ʿAzīz, al-Hādī's nephew.[19] The novel's disjointed movement between narrators, narrative perspectives, and addressees invokes the principle of *iltifāt*, or the frequent rhetorical and grammatical shifts that occur across the Qurʾan. These can include changes in the addressee or subject, gender, case marker, personal pronouns and/or their gendering, or verb tense. If, as many scholars argue, Qurʾanic code-switching serves to disrupt the potential anthropomorphization of God, in a literary context it can similarly be read as an attempt to destabilize the centrality of the author or narrator.

Luʿbat al-nisyān's sections are titled and thematically organized along a circular narrative arc that traces the death of al-Hādī's mother. They highlight his difficulty coping with the loss of the family matriarch, and on a more abstract level, his existential origin story. The sections are "In the Beginning Was the Mother"; "Si Tayyib"; "Our Prehistory"; "The World Grew in Our Eyes"; "I Said: How Many Lovers Are Infatuated with You?"; "Another Time"; and "Who of You Remembers My Mother"? The first section, "In the Beginning Was the Mother" (*Fī al-bidʾ kānat al-ʾumm*), opens with three attempts at a beginning: *mashrūʿ bidāya awwal* (First project of beginning); *mashrūʿ bidāya thānin* (Second project of beginning); and *thumma sārat "al-bidāya" hākadhā* (Then the "Beginning" became thus).

The use of the term *mashrūʿ* sets the tone for the experimental structure of the novelistic text as a decentralized and collective undertaking composed of a series of narrative acts and actors. While the first and second openings are presented as false starts, the title of the third shifts grammatically and conceptually. First, it qualifies and problematizes the very idea of a "beginning" with the use of quotation marks. It also employs the passive voice to describe the evolution of the "beginning," which is presented as *having become* rather than in a state of becoming or being. This subtle semantic shift carries authorial and revelatory undertones; it calls the readers' attention to the various figures directing the narrative process, in addition to flagging narration as a constructed process. This foregrounds the chasm between phenomenological experience and narrative modes of representation—a central preoccupation of Sufi poetics, which rely upon opacity and symbolization.[20]

Narratives of Transmission

Referencing the words (*ḥadīth*) and deeds of the Prophet Muhammad, the corpus of hadith and body of scholarship that surround it are referred to as *ʿulūm al-ḥadīth* (hadith sciences). As written documentation was fairly limited around the death of the Prophet, the process of verifying and collecting hadith relied upon a strict and rigorous system of authentication. Each hadith needed to be genealogically traced directly to the Prophet Muhammad, generally through one of his companions or wives. An uninterrupted chain (*silsila*) of transmission subsequently determined the authenticity and strength of a hadith within a delineated ranking system. In addition to its polyphonic narrative structure, *Luʿbat al-nisyān* gestures at concepts central to hadith studies, namely transmission, veracity, and narration.

The novel invokes hadith in both its formal architecture and diegetic narrative, where it is woven into the quotidian lives of the characters. At one point in the text, for example, al-Hādī recounts the period of his political formation, when nationalist party meetings and lectures were supplemented by studying key literary figures of the *nahḍa* (Muṣṭafā Luṭfī al-Manfalūṭī, Jurjī Zaydān, Ṭāhā Ḥusayn) alongside hadith. Barrāda describes al-Hādī's great respect for the hadith scholar Madani Bel-Housni, with whom he studied:

> He admired the scholar's method of interpreting hadith. . . . He narrated a particular hadith by first starting with its endless chain of transmission, interrupting himself to explain the genealogy of each Companion or Follower of the Prophet in the chain, and to authenticate the persons, the ideas, and sources. Then he began to explain the hadith, moving from considerations of history, geography, the Prophet's biography, to anecdotes and jokes . . . with Si al-Madani Bel-Housni, speech and pronunciation regained all their power, and the form of narration all its authority. . . . For he spoke naturally and without affectation or abstruseness, as though he was in a private session with a group of friends. (Barrāda, *Game of Forgetting* 49, translation modified)[21]

By placing the study of hadith alongside both a formal education in *adab* and anticolonial political mobilization, Barrāda highlights its importance within the Moroccan cultural as well as nationalist consciousness. He even refers to it as "reading and ijtihād," signaling the ethical dimensions of reading as a critical practice (ibid., translation modified).

Al-Hādī thoughtfully recounts al-Madani Bel-Housni's interdisciplinary approach to teaching and interpreting hadith (*tafsīr*). His methodology highlights the complex textual, historical, and hermeneutical practices comprising hadith studies. As with *adab*, teaching hadith marries intellectual and ethical, as well as a personal and social practices. Al-Hādī describes the animating power of the scholar's narration, parsing out its unique combination of scholastic theology (*al-kalām*), elocution (*al-lafẓ*), scholarly rigor, and even humor. These intersecting qualities of person, process, and pedagogy are also central to *adab*. Al-Hādī goes on to explain his physical imitation of the scholar's habits, which further emphasizes the mimetic qualities entailed in the study of the Qur'an and hadith (ibid.). These "Corporeal knowledge practices" refer back to the ways in which the Prophet Muhammad is venerated as an ethical exemplar who bridges embodied and textual forms of spiritual praxis (Ware 57).

Given the vast number of narrators dictating the diegetic narrative, hadith also functions as a metaphor for *Luʿbat al-nisyān*'s polyphonic structure. In this regard, the Narrators' Narrator operates as a kind of *muḥaddith*, or transmitter of hadith. He comments on and criticizes the veracity and genealogy of various accounts, as with the *isnād* that verifies hadith. Throughout the text, he calls attention to lacunae within various narrators' accounts, offers supplementary or background information, and compares contradictory accounts. He also reminds the reader repeatedly of his unique vantage point, seemingly unbiased perspective, and privileged narrative powers. The Narrators' Narrator further confesses his ethical responsibility to the reader, particularly when recounting his conflicts with the author over the relationship between narrative continuity and truthfulness.

Contemplating his metanarrative function, the Narrators' Narrator writes that he is "holding the threads of narration [*khuyūṭ al-sard*], and transmitting them [*al-nāqil lahā*] from one to another" (56/53). He then questions whether narrative continuity is possible within the polyphonic structure of the novel. He divulges to the reader: "I ask myself whether I am not a kind of censorship which the writer practices through what I say. I am supposed to know more than all the other narrators do, and my words are supposed to have greater importance than theirs, because I have knowledge of the backgrounds and of some of the details that the writer has confided to me, knowledge which I can use to undermine what the others have narrated" (56/53, translation modified).[22] As the use of the word *raqāba* (censorship) suggests, the Narrators' Narrator easily slips from facilitating the narrative's veracity and flow into controlling its content. He adds that he may displace (*uzaḥziḥu*) the narratives of others based on proprietary information.

The politics of narration are highlighted by the repeated use of terms derived from the root *w-z-n*—meaning to weigh, measure, or balance. The Narrators' Narrator refers to himself as *ʿunṣur tawāzun*, or an element of balance upon which the author can rely for the narrative's cohesion. He then describes his narrative power as having greater weight (*waznan*) than the other narrators, characters, and even the author himself. Words derived from *w-z-n* appear throughout the Qurʾan, where they reference: the scales of justice on the Day of Judgment (23:102; 18:105), holistic balance in the universe of creation (55:7); equitability in transactions with others (6:152; 7:85; 11:84; 83:3); as well as the ethical import of weighing right and wrong that the Qurʾan asks of believers (26:182; 42:17; 55:8–9; 57:25). The use of *w-z-n* within this passage, and more broadly across *Luʿbat al-nisyān*, reiterates the novel's use of the Qurʾan and hadith to reflect upon the ethics of narration.

As with Driss Chraïbi's *Le passé simple*, genealogical motifs move between *Luʿbat al-nisyān*'s religious, political, and familial registers. Its characters struggle to reconcile the realities of postindependence Morocco with the nationalist rhetoric leading up to decolonization. During the wedding of al-Hādī's nephew ʿAzīz, these tensions surface in an intergenerational debate on the relationship between religion, culture, politics, and state repression. One unnamed character, for example, positions both colonialism and capitalism in opposition to Muslim ethics:

> Conditions have devolved into such a state because we neglected our spiritual fundamentals and sacred teachings, so that we no longer knew whether we lived in an Islamic society or in one of the Metropole's annexes. . . . Those who still held to the true teachings and to Muhammadan *sunna* found themselves strangers in the midst of those who thought only of profit and adultery, and did not refrain from deceit, lying, and usury. . . . [I]s this the correct path? Do you find in your daily life any traces of justice, modesty, solidarity, tolerance, and all the other virtues which Muhammad ibn ʿAbd-Allah embodied and advised believers to adhere to? (121–22, translation modified)[23]

This social critique emphasizes the erosion of Muslim values in the face of colonialism and capitalism. Pitting greed and deceit against the virtues of justice and tolerance, the appeal frames postindependence solidarity within a distinctly Muslim model of ethics. It does so by turning to the Prophet

Muhammad as the spiritual (*sunna*) and literal embodiment (*jasadhā*) of Islamic virtue.

Fattāḥ, the son of al-Hādī's brother al-Ṭāyi', offers a very different social diagnosis based on a Marxist reading of "the logic of history" (*manṭiq al-tārikh*) that resonates with some of the rhetoric of the Islamic reformist movement.[24] Addressing both the disgruntled leftism of his uncle and the religious resignation of his formerly militant father, he argues:

> We cannot defend ourselves against transformations, which are the essence of life, by returning to a societal model realized in our Golden Age. . . . I believe that the logical thing is to put our civilizational, cultural, and religious heritages in a dialogic and interactive relationship with the questions of the present and with the dilemmas created by those transformations and their contradictions. We cannot begin by just denying the life we live today and by hypothetically adopting former solutions based on the conditions of a previous era that had its own specificities and historical determinants. (122, translation modified)[25]

Fattāḥ is clearly taking aim at religious movements calling for a return to the ways of the Prophet Muhammad and his followers. He instead proposes placing Islamic scripture within the historical context of seventh-century Arabia, in order to distill the foundational principles of Islam in dialogue with the realities of historical and cultural evolution. A similar point is articulated by Fattāḥ's father al-Ṭāyi' when he quotes "a well-known saying of Imam 'Ali urging fathers to coach their sons in behavior that suited their times" (114). This quote redirects filial obligations to suggest that one's spiritual and parental duty should be oriented toward the present or future rather than the past.

In a section narrated by al-Hādī's brother-in-law Si Ibrahim, he recounts a story about 'Ali ibn Abi Talib—the cousin and son-in-law of the Prophet Muhammad presumed by Shi'a Muslims to be the rightful successor to the caliphate (64–65). After an apocalyptic dream in which the natural order of the world becomes off-kilter, 'Ali approaches the Prophet, who interprets his dream as a foreshadowing of the decadence to befall the fourteenth century AH (1883–1980 CE). The Prophet's description resonates with the Qur'anic account of the Day of Judgment—particularly in its reference to greed, moral corruption, and self-interest.[26] As in al-Ṭāhir Waṭṭār's *Al-zilzāl*, Qur'anic eschatology is mobilized for social and political critique; here, imperialism and capitalism are symptomatic of the erosion of "Muhammadan ethics" (63).

Embodiment, Ritual, Praxis

Luʿbat al-Nisyān's intertextuality with the Qurʾan and hadith serves a formal, diegetic, and discursive function. As much of the novel consists of dialogue and reported speech, many passages blend dialectical and regional Arabic with Modern Standard Arabic (MSA). Into these, Barrāda seamlessly integrates Qurʾanic references and even suras, similar to Waṭṭār's *Al-zilzāl*.[27] This marks the ways in which the Qurʾan can serve as both a model of polyphonic narration, and an intertext that can be organically woven into different discursive and linguistic registers. Beyond the influence of the Qurʾan and hadith on its narrative and rhetorical stylization, *Luʿbat al-nisyān* is deeply embedded within the quotidian practice of Islam. This is largely framed through motifs of birth, marriage, death, and the afterlife. As with Chraïbi's *Le passé simple*, this genealogical framework resonates with the novel's broader problematization of the Moroccan monarchy's Sherifian lineage.

The novel's opening section, "First Project of Beginning," introduces a citation from the sura "Al-mulk" ("Sovereignty"):

تَبَارَكَ الَّذِي بِيَدِهِ الْمُلْكُ وَهُوَ عَلَى كُلِّ شَيْءٍ قَدِيرٌ

> Hallowed be He in whose hand all dominion rests, since He has the power to will anything. (Qurʾan 67:1 trans. Asad)

The sura appears in the context of al-Hādī's mother's funeral, as it is said to protect the recently deceased from the trials of death, based upon various hadith traced back to the Prophet Muhammad. This opening draws the reader into textual rituals that surround understandings of the afterlife, while also subtly invoking the unique relationship between Islamic and state sovereignty in the Moroccan context.[28] The metaphysical overtones of the talismanic sura incanted by the Qurʾanic reciters at the funeral contrast with al-Hādī's blunted affect in the opening lines to the novel: "'From now on, I shall see her no more,' I said to myself" (Barrāda, *Game of Forgetting* 16, translation modified). This is echoed in his brother-in-law's words of consolation that she has left behind *dār al-bāṭil* (the world/dwelling of falsity) for *dār al-ḥaqq* (the world/dwelling of truth—also one of God's ninety-nine names).

The proceeding ayas of the sura "Al-mulk" are read by Qurʾanic reciters in the subsequent family death, that of al-Hādī's uncle Si Tayyib:

الَّذِي خَلَقَ الْمَوْتَ وَالْحَيَاةَ لِيَبْلُوَكُمْ أَيُّكُمْ أَحْسَنُ عَمَلا وَهُوَ الْعَزِيزُ الْغَفُورُ {٢} الَّذِي خَلَقَ سَبْعَ
سَمَاوَاتٍ طِبَاقًا مَّا تَرَى فِي خَلْقِ الرَّحْمنِ مِن تَفَاوُتٍ فَارْجِعِ الْبَصَرَ هَلْ تَرَى مِن فُطُورٍ {٣} ثُمَّ
ارْجِعِ الْبَصَرَ كَرَّتَيْنِ يَنقَلِبْ إِلَيْكَ الْبَصَرُ خَاسِئاً وَهُوَ حَسِيرٌ {٤}

> He who has created death as well as life, so that He might put you to a test [and thus show] which of you is best in conduct, and [make you realize that] He alone is almighty, truly forgiving. [Hallowed be] He who has created seven heavens in full harmony with one another: no fault wilt thou see in the creation of the Most Gracious. And turn thy vision [upon it] once more: canst thou see any flaw? Yea, turn thy vision [upon it] again and yet again: [and every time] thy vision will fall back upon thee, dazzled and truly defeated. (Qur'an 67:2–4 trans. Asad)

Lu'bat al-nisyān traces the recitation across these two pivotal deaths that bookend al-Hādī's family history, while also structurally and thematically framing the novel. By continuing the sura *in medias res* where the last recitation ended, Barrāda uses to the language of the Qur'an to generate a narrative and conceptual thread that runs throughout the work. The recitation at Si Tayyib's funeral is followed by sung eulogies of praise (*al-amdāḥ*). These offer al-Hādī more consolation than the Qur'anic verse traditionally recited at funerals, in which death is framed as a trial. Al-Hādī compares his uncle's shrouded body to being surrounded by a sublime world of words (*wa-mā tansajihu min 'awālim 'ulwiyya*). The metaphysical, spiritual, and libidinal euphoria (*al-nashwa*) elicited from these eulogies tempers the absurdity (*al-'abath*) that al-Hādī experiences when confronted with the bodily finality of death (Barrāda, *Game of Forgetting* 33/27).

In his commentary on the sura, Qur'anic translator Muhammad Asad writes that it captures "man's inability to ever encompass the mysteries of the universe with his earthbound knowledge, and, hence, his utter dependence on guidance through divine revelation" (Qur'an, trans. Asad 1002). The sura opens with an invocation of God's immense power and omniscience. Referencing God and his singularity, the root *m-l-k* is etymologically related to dominion, sovereignty, and ownership/possession. Its connection to both a sovereign ruler and their monarchy, suggests another connotative layer to the Qur'anic citation—namely, the Moroccan monarchy's Sherifian lineage that traces the ruling family to the Prophet Muhammad.

Ruling the country since the seventeenth century, the Moroccan royal family are part of the Alouite dynasty, which traces its lineage to the Prophet through his daughter Fāṭimah and son-in-law 'Alī Ibn Abī Ṭālib.

The intersection between religious authority and centralized state power is a common motif within Arabophone and Francophone Maghrebi literature of the mid-twentieth century, as we saw in Driss Chraïbi's *Le passé simple* and Abdelwahab Meddeb's *Talismano*. Within this corpus, genealogical and filial themes are commonly mobilized to critique structures and agents of state authority. In *Lu'bat al-nisyān*, this opening passage employs the sanctioned Qur'anic rhetoric of divine power and omniscience, in order to call attention to the intersection of state and religious forms of power. Moreover, it foregrounds the novel's preoccupation with family structures and relations as a double for the political disillusionment of postindependence Morocco.

In addition to referencing the structural intimacy between state politics and religion through filial metaphors, related to either al-Hādī's family or the Moroccan monarchy, *Lu'bat al-nisyān* invokes quotidian forms of Islamic ritual. These include mentions of patron saints, shrines, incantations, supplications, recitations, chants, and rituals of remembrance (*dhikr*). It also emerges in the modeling of Muslim ethics after the life of the Prophet Muhmmad, and allusions to his son-in-law ʿAlī ibn Abī Ṭālib (Barrāda, *Game of Forgetting* 63, 122). Mentions of local patron saints are one means through which the novel simultaneously traverses Morocco's spiritual and political topography. The person and shrine of Moulay Idrīs, the patron Saint of Fès, are a focal point for sections of the novel that reference al-Hādī's early childhood. The great-great-great grandson of the Prophet Muhammad, Idrīs I (Idrīs ibn ʿAbd Allāh) founded the Idrīsid dynasty and was responsible for the Islamicization of the Maghreb in the eighth century. His son, Idrīs II, made Fès the capital of the dynasty and is buried in the Moulay Idrīs shrine, which is considered one of the holiest pilgrimage sites in Morocco.

The broader references to shrines in *Lu'bat al-nisyān* signal their function as physical and spiritual spaces for disempowered members of Moroccan society. They are spiritual havens for older women who often congregate around or tend to the shrines (17, 71), a refuge for political asylum seekers (59), a shelter for the distressed (102), and a sanctioned space for spiritual ascetics (111). Shrines are also sites for meditation, prayer, offerings, remembrances, and blessings, that surround pivotal events within the diegetic narrative—generally related to death, birth, or marriage. Al-Hādī's mother is even referred to as a saint because of her silent self-sacrifice for the welfare of her family and community (135). Similarly, eulogists, Qur'anic reciters, and mystics are frequently referenced in the novel as a source of spiritual communion and support (31, 63), providers of solace in the face of death (33), and prophetic seers (61). Demonstrating the diverse ways in which Islam is embodied and practiced, *Luʿbat al-nisyān*'s incorporation of the textual authority of the Qurʾan and hadith with the everyday practices of Moroccan Muslims mirrors the novel's blending of Qurʾanic and literary Arabic with the lived language of dialect.

Loose Threads

In the final section recounted by the Narrators' Narrator, he explains the deterioration of his relationship with the author over irreconcilable creative differences. The Narrators' Narrator recounts his insistence to the author that they share with readers the nature of their disagreement, which largely concerns the relationship between time, existence, and narration. Whereas the author believes each subjective (and therefore narrative) experience of time has its own ontology, the Narrators' Narrator argues that it is individual consciousness that molds to the continuous passing of time, which exists independent of phenomenological experience. The conflict not only reflects Barrāda's critical interest in narrative theory, but it speaks to an ethical investment in polyphony as central to his theory of literary experimentation, or *tajrīb*.

Barrāda's theorization of literary experimentation emphasizes the dynamic relationship between a text, author, and reader. In this vein, he echoes Maḥmūd al-Masʿadī's Sufi-inflected reading of literary creation as an ethical project that expands the imaginative horizons of the writer and reader alike. Barrāda situates this dialectical relationship not within the text as a closed hermeneutical circuit but rather in "a relationship of interpretation, vision, and recreation" (Barrāda, *Al-riwāya al-ʿarabiyya* 68, qtd. in El Younssi 11). As a narrative mode, *tajrīb* is premised on the dialectic between creation and recreation, moving us beyond the rehashed debates within Arabic literary criticism surrounding *turāth* (heritage), *aṣāla* (authenticity), and *taqlīd* (imitation). Returning to Barrāda's transtemporal reading of literary innovation, *tajrīb* challenges periodizations of literary modernity and genre.

Conventionally, postmodern literature is framed as antithetical to theological discourse. Religion, it is argued, relies upon singular, genealogical, or centralized discourses that codify exegetical and spiritual praxis. In exploring Barrāda's engagement with Islam's narrative, ethical, and embodied dimensions, this chapter offers an alternative approach to reading the relationship between literary modernity and religion. *Luʿbat al-nisyān*'s novelistic fragmentation is staged in conjunction with a narrative style suggestive of both the Qurʾan and hadith. It calls attention to the fact that chains of transmission cannot ever be unequivocally validated, no matter how rigorous the system of verification. This stems in large part from the phenomenological and revisionist nature of human consciousness referenced in the titular metaphor of forgetfulness as a game, and enacted through the novel's multiple unreliable narrators. The work mobilizes narrative techniques central to Qurʾanic discourse, as it simultaneously problematizes scripture as a closed hermeneutical circuit. *Luʿbat al-nisyān*'s literary stylization—which might otherwise be subsumed under a postmodern analysis that emphasizes the discursive decentering of theological discourses—epitomizes this book's reading of Qurʾanic narratology as a mode of narrative ethics.

Epilogue
Politics, Poetics, Piety

> Man must live up to the trust that God has placed in him;
> he must try, through his faith in God, to be an image of
> Him by creating and inventing whatever ideas he can.
> Isn't literature a type of philosophy that stems from an intellectual
> analysis of the problem of existence and that contributes to
> conscientious reflection on these subjects? That is to say,
> man undertakes literature out of his own inner tragedy and
> contemplation—not through logic and philosophical analysis,
> but rather through emotion and poetic expression. In this
> regard, literature can be called "conscientious philosophy."
>
> (Maḥmūd al-Masʿadī, *Collected Works* 3:344; 367).

When asked to elaborate on his creative process in an interview for *Al-aqlām* magazine, Tunisian novelist and critic Maḥmūd al-Masʿadī responded that he was driven "by the strength of faith" (*bi-quwwat al-īmān*) (al-Masʿadī, *Collected Works* 3:303).[1] Man's greatest "honor" (*sharaf*), he added, is that he is "the conscience of conscious existence" (*ḍamīr al-kawn al-wāʿī*) (ibid.). For al-Masʿadī, humanity reaches spiritual fulfillment in the ethical pursuit of creative endeavors. To attain "his highest status, the spiritual plane" (*ilā manzilatihi al-ʿulyā, al-manzila al-rūḥiyya*), man must "lift himself, with his words, his actions, his thoughts, his conscience" (*idhā rafaʿa nafsahu, bi-qawlihi wa-fiʿlihi wa-fikrihi wa-wijdānihi*) (ibid.).

In the spring of 1957, al-Masʿadī's esoteric views on the relationship between literature and Islam were at the center of a very public exchange with the "dean of Arabic literature," Ṭāhā Ḥusayn. The figurehead par excellence of the *nahḍa* and Arab modernist movement, Ḥusayn transposed al-Masʿadī's fiction into the politically charged debates on literary commitment and existentialism that preoccupied intellectuals across the decolonizing world. Reading this episode through the lens of competing frames of analysis, I argue, exposes a critical myopia around ethical approaches to literature. The exchange between al-Mas'adī and Ḥusayn sheds light on the ways in which the elision of cultural production from the Maghreb in critical literature on the *nahḍa* works in concert with the framing of Arab modernity as a secular project. Maghrebi intellectuals such as Maḥmūd al-Mas'adī, Abdelwahab Meddeb, al-Ṭāhir Waṭṭār, Assia Djebar, Driss Chraïbi, and Muḥammad Barrāda do more than simply trouble the narrative of cultural decline (*inḥiṭāt*) and flourishing (*nahḍa*) that places Cairo, Damascus, and Beirut at the center of Arab intellectual thought.[2] Their literary and critical works invite us to reimagine the very assumptions around culture, politics, and ethics upon which canonical accounts of the *nahḍa* rest.

Throughout the mid-twentieth century, there emerged a range of aesthetic and literary philosophies theorizing the relationship between art and politics that were inflected by the resurgence of Pan-Arabism,[3] as well as the political ideologies of communism, socialism, and Marxism-Leninism.[4] Across the political spectrum, however, the question of material, ideological, and cultural decolonization was often at the forefront. Attacking the elitism of literature of the "Ivory Tower" (*al-burj al-'ājī*), the dominant aesthetic philosophies were socialist realism (*al-wāqi'īya al-īshtirākīyya*) and dialectical materialism.[5] Moving away from what were deemed self-indulgent theories of art for art's sake, these theorists argued that literature is beholden to existing economic and political conditions—particularly the struggle against capitalist imperialism.

In the midst of these intellectual currents, there emerged a wave of existentialist writings that reimagined the social and political function of cultural production along more philosophical lines of inquiry. While existentialism in North Africa and the Middle East was certainly in dialogue with European philosophical thought, it was a distinct movement with uniquely local iterations across the region. To quote historian Yoav Di-Capua:

> Arab intellectuals did in fact devise a local existentialist tradition that transcended the narrow purview of anti-colonial nationalism, with its focus on physical liberation from foreign rule and a general sense of collectivity. . . . Arab existentialism functioned as a potent tool for social, political, and cultural self-criticism and was an important element in forging extra-regional alliances with the global front against imperialism. . . . Arab existentialism emerged not as a unified and accumulative phenomenon but as a multifocal intellectual system. Thus, interestingly, the fragmented nature of existentialism was not the result of a weak "borrowing" or "adaptation," but rather a multilayered

> cross-cultural process in which European existentialism lost its original meaning at the very same moment in which it was fused with local Arab thought and created anew. (Di-Capua 1064)

Di-Capua addresses a major lacuna within Arab intellectual history by capturing the dominant ideological poles between which existentialist philosophies were developing: internationalist anticolonialism and nationalism. The exchange between Maḥmūd al-Masʿadī and Ṭāhā Ḥusayn demonstrates how the Maghreb is at once germane to this narrative of "Arab existentialism," while also complicating its geopolitical trajectory of West to (Arab) East.

Existentialist philosophies both reflected and consolidated many of the tensions around the political work of literature with which Arab intellectuals had been grappling. Two key figures signaling this history are the prominent Egyptian philosopher ʿAbd al-Raḥmān Badawī (1917–2002) and the Lebanese intellectual Suhayl Idrīs (1925–2008), who fashioned existentialist philosophies infused with Sufism and Marxism respectively. The renowned Lebanese novelist, short-story writer, translator, journalist, and founder of the literary journal *Al-ādāb* Suhayl Idrīs argued for the necessity of a politically engaged model of existentialism in the context of Arab decolonization: "As for me, I did not understand existentialism as a philosophy but as a social and political doctrine which puts the values of liberty and responsibility, so urgently needed in the Arab world, into the centre of ethical behavior" (Idrīs qtd. in Klemm 55).

Idrīs was not alone in wanting to disengage existentialism from continental philosophy; the Syrian Marxist thinker Shahāda Khūrī similarly critiqued Sartre, Schopenhauer, and Kafka for their dependence on the theoretical scaffolding of philosophy, psychology, and theology (Klemm 53).[6] Idrīs's journal *Al-ādāb* even entered into a highly publicized debate with its competitor *Shiʿr* (Poetry) over the question of *adab al-iltizām* or *al-adab al-multazim* (committed literature). *Al-ādāb* aligned itself with a reworked Sartrean model of *engagement* that toned down the philosophy's existentialist origins while emphasizing art as a political weapon; meanwhile, *Shiʿr* privileged poetic and aesthetic autonomy.[7]

Somewhat on the other end of the philosophical spectrum, ʿAbd al-Raḥmān Badawī theorized the humanist relationship between existentialism and Sufism in his 1947 treatise *Al-insāniyya wa-l-wujūdiyya fī al-fikr al-ʿarabī* (Humanism and existentialism in Arab thought).[8] On his philosophical fusion, he explained that "between these two tendencies—existentialism and Sufism (mysticism)—there exist, in principal, deep affinities of method and ultimate goals. Sufism is based on a doctrine of subjectivity: by that we mean that it recognizes no true existence other than that of the individual" (al-Badawī qtd. in Mikhail 81). The writings of Badawī, whom Ṭāhā Ḥusayn claimed inaugurated "the birth of modern Arab philosophy," engaged with a diverse range of existentialist thought—from Alexandre Koyré, Martin Heidegger, Søren Kierkegaard, and Jean-Paul Sartre, to Ibn Rushd and al-Ghazālī (1061). For example, he examined the Sufi concepts of *al-insān al-kāmil* (the perfect human) and *qalaq* (anxiety) in dialogue with Kierkegaard and Heidegger (Somekh 55; Mikhail 81–94).

Historically, *al-insān al-kāmil* has referred to the Prophet Muhammed as the paradigmatic realization of humanity's divine attributes. Sufi writings, such as Ibn ʿArabī's *Fuṣūṣ al-ḥikam* (*The Bezels of Wisdom*), expanded the concept to encompass ascetics and mystics who have successfully mastered the various stages of *taṣawwuf* in their oneness of being (*waḥdat al-wujūd*) and ultimate fulfillment of divine destiny (Shaikh 71–75). The Sufi dialectic between the human and divine features extensively in Maḥmūd al-Masʿadī's *Mawlid al-nisyān* and Abdelwahab Meddeb's *Talismano*. It is also at the heart of the debate between al-Masʿadī and Ṭāhā Ḥusayn, who first introduced Sartrean *engagement* to an Arab reading public.

In his literary journal *Al-kātib al-miṣrī* (The Egyptian writer), Ḥusayn commented and elaborated on Sartre's series of essays published in *Les temps modernes* (Modern times), that were later anthologized as *Qu'est-ce que la littérature?* (What is literature?). Ḥusayn interpreted *engagement* as an ethical obligation to socially responsible writing but contested its applicability to Arab decolonization (Klemm 51–53; Di-Capua 1070–71).[9] Ironically, his critique gave the movement legs and a critical lexicon, as he was the first to bring the terms *iltizām* (commitment) and *multazim* (committed) into circulation within Arabic cultural criticism (ibid).

Nearly ten years after Ṭāhā Ḥusayn introduced *iltizām*, Maḥmūd al-Masʿadī was pulled into the debates on Arab existentialism following the publication of his play *Al-sudd* (*The Dam*).[10] In an open letter published in *Al-jumhūriyya* (The republic) in 1957, Ḥusayn crowned al-Masʿadī the founder of "Muslim existentialism" (*al-wujūdiyya al-muslima*). He wrote that unlike its secular French counterpart, Muslim existentialism acknowledges the limits of the individual in the face of the divine. Warning the author of the philosophy's atheistic proclivities, Ḥusayn compared al-Masʿadī's ethos to the Christian existentialism of the French philosopher Gabriel Honoré Marcel (1889–1973):[11]

> This [French] existentialism is founded upon the individual's unlimited faith in himself, which makes that person turn to himself as the measure of good and evil. It is the individual alone who bears the consequences of his actions. Those actions are questioned exclusively within himself; only after this are society and its laws taken into consideration. . . . The Existentialism that was . . . Islamicized in Tunisia at the hands of Professor al-Masʿadī, however, sets limits to man's faith in himself, the most important, strongest, and greatest of which is the limit of religion. . . . It is the power of Allah that keeps watch over a person's conscience, deceptive perception, and what is hidden in their hearts. (Ḥusayn, "al-Adab bayna al-Ittiṣāl wa-l-Infiṣāl," qtd. in *Al-sudd* 243–44)[12]

While Ḥusayn's reading acknowledges the spiritual undercurrent of al-Masʿadī's work, it minimizes the author's investment in the phenomenological nature of human experience as both an artistic and ethical project. He frames existentialism as a secular European philosophy that privileges the individual over divine authority. Ḥusayn's ontological distinction between the human and divine devalues the ability of art to surpass the earthly limitations of its creation. More troubling still, he treats existentialism as a static philosophical tradition imported from Europe. The very idea of an *Islamicized* existentialism assumes that there are no natural affinities between inquiries into the nature of existence, and Islam's various philosophical traditions—Sufi or otherwise.

In a response published in the Tunisian philosophical magazine *Al-fikr* (Thought) in May 1957, al-Masʿadī takes issue with Ḥusayn's framing of both his play and broader aesthetic philosophy. He writes that existentialism and commitment are concepts as old as literature and philosophy themselves but that they are frequently misunderstood in world literature debates (al-Masʿadī, *Collected Works* 3:55–56).[13] Al-Masʿadī defines literary commitment as an inherently existentialist practice, in which the individual is committed to a transcendental purpose:

> The proper meaning of literary commitment, in my estimation, is nothing other than the writer being committed to intrinsic matters, irrespective of the [false] ornament of elocution and [literary] craftsmanship. Commitment is for literature to be the aggregation of man's story and the quintessence of what he knows in his deepest depths and innermost heart. It is for literature to be a message from man to man, a message inspired by the divine aspect of his thought and soul. This sentiment or divine intuition—which encompasses thought and that which is beyond thought, reason and that which is beyond reason; it is

> imagination with science, knowledge with freedom and existence—is experienced completely and fully. (3:58)[14]

Al-Masʿadī defines artistic commitment as a state of being rather than an ideological stance. By investigating one's existential condition through the faculties of thought, spirit, knowledge, and imagination, one speaks to the broader concerns of humanity. In so doing, the committed intellectual engages in ethical labor *on behalf of* the divine.

Al-Masʿadī defines commitment as an ongoing "activity" (*nashāt*)—as necessary to conscious living as breathing or eating—to which the individual dedicates themself and their intellectual as well as spiritual energies (3:58). This life force needs to be consciously cultivated on the basis of manifest knowledge (*al-maʿrifa al-bayyina*) about oneself and the universe in relation to existence (*kiyān*) and Being (*al-kawn*) (3:58). Existentialist thinking, then, is a phenomenological activity in dialectical relationship with the committed writing that it engenders. He concludes: "If existentialist philosophical thought elucidates the concept, and committed literature expresses the approach and the position, then they both fall within the scope of the problem of existence, man's destiny and his position within the universe, his conduct in this life, and his fate after this life" (3:60).[15] By elevating artistic production to spiritual labor done in dialogue with the divine facets of humanity, al-Masʿadī posits a model of Muslim ethics in which the pursuit of knowledge is inseparable from the spiritual cultivation of the self.

Al-Masʿadī subsequently debunks the dichotomization of art of the "Ivory Tower" and politically engaged art that dominated debates on the role of the public intellectual in the context of decolonization. Following his epistolary debate with Ṭāhā Ḥusayn, he addressed the third Arab Writers' Conference in Cairo in December 1957 on "Protecting the Littérateur and Arab Nationalism" (*ḥimāyat al-adīb wa-l-qawmiyya al-ʿarabiyya*):

> Indeed, man is an individual being. It is what he must be and the secret to his sublime nobility in the world. As the manifest truth [of God], when man strengthens his individual essence it strengthens his humanity and accordingly, he fulfills his role in the universe. A writer may find that the consummation of his humanity lies in devoting himself to delving into the self and wandering through its dimensions. This makes him appear to be devoted to "art for art's sake" or "living in the Ivory Tower," as they say, and yet, through his art and his life, he attracts us to his consummate humanity, elevating us as individuals and as nations to the heights of the noble and sublime. (*Collected Works* 2:79–80)[16]

It is the artist's ethical devotion to self-exploration that for al-Masʿadī generates artistic production with social, political, and existential valences. While al-Masʿadī supported Tunisian self-determination, he was suspicious of the ideological machinery of Pan-Arabism, Pan-Islamism, and communism, which he believed subsumed autonomous artistic creativity under potentially oppressive political dogmatism.[17] I read al-Masʿadī's philosophical ethos as demarcating a turn away from the politicized aesthetics and didacticism of *al-wāqiʿiyya al-ishtirākiyya* (socialist realism) or *iltizām* (commitment). His existentialist theory of art is also an aesthetic theory of existence that casts the "completion" of one's humanity within creative acts and works.

Maḥmūd al-Masʿadī's nuanced framing of artistic creation—and notably, the readers' engagement with it—as an ethical practice underwrites my analysis not only of his novella *Mawlid al-nisyān* but also of Abdelwahab Meddeb's *Talismano*, al-Ṭāhir Waṭṭār's *Al-zilzāl*, Assia Djebar's *L'amour, la fantasia*, Driss Chraïbi's *Le passé simple*, and Muḥammad Barrāda's *Luʿbat al-nisyān*. Reading their novels through Qur'anic narratology and intertextuality unseats the dominant critical paradigms of anticolonial nationalism and literary commitment through which this body of literature is often mediated. Moreover, the concepts of *adab*, *ijtihād*, and *ibdāʿ* that run throughout this study introduce a new conceptual vocabulary for thinking through the relationship between narrative ethics and politics.

Ṭāhā Ḥusayn's misreading of al-Masʿadī's literary project renders legible the critical biases that codify false binaries of the secular/sacred, public/private, political/personal, and social/individual. Their competing frames of analysis speak to highly divergent understandings of the role of the public intellectual, especially in the context of decolonization. Ḥusayn's comments echo much of the rhetoric associated with the *nahḍa* movement, in his assumption that ethics operates outside of the realm of social or political agency. Meanwhile, al-Masʿadī's coconstitutional reading of literary commitment and existentialism reflects a philosophical ethos in which artistic creation is intimately bound to ethical Muslim subject formation. In the context of this study, the episode exposes the ways in which twentieth-century Maghrebi literature and criticism can enrich cultural histories of the Middle East and North Africa.

The Literary Qur'an: Narrative Ethics in the Maghreb has sought to challenge the polar tendencies to symptomatically read Maghrebi literature as either autobiographical or anticolonial. Francophone Maghrebi literature is always already tethered to a postcolonial studies framework by virtue of it being a disciplinary appendage to French (read: metropole) literature.

On the other hand, it is precisely the proliferation of Francophone literature that casts doubt on the "authenticity" of Maghrebi literature within Arabic literary studies. Maḥmūd al-Masʿadī, Abdelwahab Meddeb, al-Ṭāhir Waṭṭār, Assia Djebar, Driss Chraïbi, and Muḥammad Barrāda resist being exclusively conscripted within the critical paradigm of postcolonial resistance literature. They offer more complex visions of the public intellectual as an ethical subject engaged in narrative acts of creation—here read through the lens of Qur'anic narratology and intertextuality. Upending literary taxonomies and periodizations that privilege secularizing reading practices and modes of political intervention, their novels introduce critical modes of Muslim subjectivity at once aesthetic and ethical.

Glossary

adab—Belles lettres; cultural refinement; social comportement; etiquette; hospitality

adīb—(pl. *udabāʾ*) practitioner of *adab*

al-bayān—Eloquence

al-khiṭāb al-riwāʾī—Novelistic discourse

al-riwāya al-jadīda—The new novel; modern(ist) novel

al-taʿaddud al-lisānī—Polylinguistic (etymologically from *lisān*, or tongue)

al-taʿaddud al-lughawī—Polylinguistic (etymologically from *lugha*, or language)

al-wāqiʿiyya al-ishtirākiyya—Social(ist) realism

"Al-ʿalaq"—Qurʾanic sura 96: "The Germ-Cell" or "The Clot"; first sura revealed to the Prophet Muhammad

Amazigh—(pl. Imazighen) Indigenous populations of Maghreb; also referred to as Berbers

aṣāla—Authenticity

ʿaṣr al-inḥiṭāṭ—The age of decline/decadence

āya—Verse within a sura

ʿaẓīm—Magnificent; one of god's ninety-nine names in Islam

barzakh—Intermediate state separating two entities; isthmus

bāṭin—Esoteric; interior; hidden; spiritual; cf. *ẓāhir*

Berber—Indigenous populations of Maghreb; also referred to as Amazigh (pl. Imazighen)

bidʿa—(Heretical) innovation

duwār—Sufi state of vertigo

fanāʾ—Sufi state of annihilation or dissolution of the self

fiqh—Islamic jurisprudence

fqih—An expert in Islamic law, especially in North Africa

hadith—Sayings and practices ascribed to the Prophet Muhammad

ḥaqq—Truth; one of god's ninety-nine names in Islam

ḥayra—Sufi state of wonderment or bewilderment

hijra—Physical and spiritual journey of the Prophet Muhammad and his followers from Mecca to Medina in the seventh century
ibdāʿ—Creation; innovation; creativity
iʿjāz al-Qurʾān—Inimitability of the Qurʾan as a uniquely divine act of aesthetic expression
ijtihād—Individual reasoning independent of historical precedent
ʿilm—Science; knowledge; learning; information; cognition
ʿilm al-ʿarūḍ—Prosody
ʿilm al-balāgha—Rhetoric
ʿilm al-falsafa—Philosophy
ʿilm al-kalām—Scholastic theology
ʿilm al-lugha—Lexicography; linguistics; philology
ʿilm al-manṭiq—Logic
ʿilm al-tārīkh—History
iltifāt—Frequent rhetorical or grammatical shifts in the Qurʾan
īmān—Faith
iqraʾ—Read; recite; command to the Prophet Muhammad during first Qurʾanic revelation
ʿishq—Sufi state of love or desire
islām—Submission
isnād—Supporting scholarship verifying the veracity and rank of a given hadith
isrāʾ and *miʿrāj*—Prophet Muhammad's two-part evening journey from Mecca to Jerusalem and then to heaven
istighnāʾ—Sufi state of detachment
istiʿāra—To engage in metaphor or allegory
ittiḥād—Sufi spiritual union
kāna—To be
kashf—Unveiling; uncovering
kawn—Universe; world
khiṭāb—Discourse
maʿrifa—Knowledge or gnosis
medina—City; in the Maghreb, usually references precolonial city centers (*medina qadima* or "old city")
muḥaddith/a—Transmitter of hadith
mujtahid—Practitioner of *ijtihād*
nafs—Soul; self
nahḍa—Arab "awakening" or "renaissance" of late nineteenth to early twentieth-century
naqd—Critique; criticism

naṣṣ riwāʾī—Novelistic text
qalam—Writing implement; quill; reed; pen
qissa falsafiyya—Philosophical story
rasm—Consonantal skeleton of the Qurʾan absent of voweling
riḍāʾ—Sufi state of contentment
riḥla—Voyage; journey; literary genre of travel writing
riwāya—Novel
al-salaf al-ṣāliḥ—First three generations of Muslims
shawq—Sufi state of yearning
shāʿiriyya/ shiʿiriyya—Poiesis
Sherifian—Descendants of the Prophet Muhammad
Shiʿa—one of the two main branches of Islam; contrasts with Sunni Islam in its belief that ʿAli ibn Abi Talib (Muhammad's son-in-law) and the imams are the Prophet's rightful successors; cf. *Sunni*
silsila—Chain of transmission in the verification of hadith
ṭarīqa—Sufi school or order
sukūn—Sufi state of stillness
sunna—Practices and teachings of the Prophet Muhammad; Islamic law
Sunni—One of the two main branches of Islam; contrasts with Shiʿa Islam in its understanding of the sunna and acceptance of the first three caliphs as the Prophet Muhammad's rightful successors; cf. *Shiʿa*
sura—Chapter in the Qurʾan
tafātuḥ—Spiritual opening in Sufism
tafsīr—Qurʾanic exegesis; hermeneutics
ṭahāra—Sufi state of purity
tajdīd—Renewal
tajrīb—Experimentation
tajwīd—Qurʾanic elocution
ṭalab—Sufi state of searching
taqiyya—Rhetorical device of concealment common in the Qurʾan
taqlīd—Imitation
tartīl—Qurʾanic hymnody
taṣawwuf—Sufi path toward divine communion or unification
taṭawwur—Development; evolution
tawḥīd—Oneness of God; affirms that God alone is one (*wāḥid*) and unique (*awḥad*)
taʾwīl—Esoteric hermeneutics; allegorical or symbolic interpretive approach
taʿrīb—Arabization

muqaṭṭaʿāt—Shortened or abbreviated letters opening twenty-eight suras
turāth—Arab-Islamic cultural or literary heritage
umma—Community of Muslims
ʿurūba—Arabism
ẓāhir—Exoteric; manifest; literal; external; cf. *bāṭin*
zāwiya/s—Muslim temples that function as pilgrimage sites and shrines devoted to venerated patron saints or leaders of Sufi orders

Notes

PREFACE

1. The plural for hadith in Arabic is *aḥādīth*, whereas in English it can be rendered as "hadith" or "hadiths." This study will use the term "hadith" to reference the broader body of hadith literature.

2. Hadith literature is also critical to the establishment of sharīʿa, or Islamic law, and *fiqh*—Islamic jurisprudence that builds upon sharīʿa.

3. Quarante ans plus tard, un homme dans une grotte mourait à lui-même. Derrière lui se refermait le vantail du passé, tel un livre familier dont on eût tourné l'ultime feuillet et qu'on ne relirait plus jamais. Quelque part, entre reflet et ombre de la réalité, s'ouvrit un autre Livre. Les plumes étaient levées, l'encre était sèche depuis les temps sidéraux. Et on eût dit que le dernier mot de ce Livre avait été écrit avant que le premier ne fût formulé en quelque langue que ce soit. Quelqu'un en tourna les pages, depuis la fin jusqu'au début, du "il" au "je", calligraphia le premier mot:

—"*LIS*".

A peine formé, ce terme acquit la parole. Il dit—il dit d'une voix si paisible qu'elle en était effrayante:

—*LIS!*

La Révélation était là, surgie de la roche, simple, très simple, à emporter l'écoute et la raison. Et, parce qu'elle était là, Mohammed ramassa instantanément tous ses doutes anciens et futurs, toutes ses incrédulités, comme autant de pierres, les assembla en une muraille d'inertie entre le terrien qu'il était depuis sa naissance et "l'homme du Livre" qu'on lui demandait d'être (Driss Chraïbi, *L'Homme du Livre* [Casablanca: Balland-Eddif, 1995], 100–101).

INTRODUCTION

1. See Ziad Elmarsafy, *The Enlightenment Qur'an: The Politics of Translation and the Construction of Islam* (Oxford: Oneworld, 2009), 158.

2. See Rüdiger Safranski, *Goethe: Life as a Work of Art*, trans. David Dollenmayer (New York: Liveright, 2017), 118–20, 376–80.

3. On the relationship between Goethe's *Weltliteratur* and Islam, see Ayman El-Desouky, "Between Hermeneutic Provenance and Textuality: The Qur'an and the Question of Method in Approaches to World Literature," *Journal of Qur'anic Studies* 16, no. 3 (2014): 24–27.

4. David Damrosch edited a 2014 special issue of the *Journal of Qur'anic Studies* entitled "The Qur'an in Modern World Literature." On the impact of the Qur'an on current debates within world literature, see El-Desouky, "Beyond Spatiality: Theorising the Local and Untranslatability as Comparative Critical Method," in *Approaches to World Literature*, vol. 1, ed. Joachim Küpper, 59–84 (Berlin: Walter de Gruyter, 2013).

5. By contrast, literary critics frequently engage with the Bible as literary urtext (Northrop Frye), the philosophy of religion and political theology (Paul de Man, Paul Ricoeur, Emmanuel Levinas, Hannah Arendt), and Judaic messianism (Jacques Derrida, Walter Benjamin, Theodor Adorno, Max Horkheimer)—particularly in the aftermath of World War II. Even Donald Wehrs's study *Islam, Ethics, Revolt: Politics and Piety in Francophone West African and Maghreb Narrative* mobilizes French Jewish philosopher Emmanuel Levinas's ethical ontology to theorize Islamic ethics.

6. Parsing the distinction between *literary approaches* to the Qur'an and approaching the Qur'an *as literature*, Ayman El-Desouky notes the ways in which the Qur'an compels literary scholars to carve out "a conceptual language that is able to cross the borders of discourses of knowledge production, local and localised provenance of voice, and differing histories of reception and literary practice" ("Between Hermeneutic Provenance and Textuality" 15).

7. See Talal Asad, Wendy Brown, Judith Butler, and Saba Mahmood, *Is Critique Secular? Blasphemy, Injury, and Free Speech* (Berkeley, Calif.: Townsend Center for the Humanities, 2009).

8. See Jonathan Roberge, "What Is Critical Hermeneutics?," *Thesis Eleven* 106, no. 1 (2011): 5–22.

9. An earlier version of the essay "Pensée-autre" was published under the title "Le Maghreb comme horizon de pensée." For a discussion of this metaphor in Abdelkébir Khatibi's work, see Olivia Harrison, "Cross-Colonial Poetics: *Souffles-Anfas* and the Figure of Palestine," *PMLA* 128, no. 2 (March 2013): 365–66.

10. On how this instability can contribute critically and pedagogically to the fields of Arab/ic and comparative literature, see Hoda El Shakry, "Lessons from the Maghreb," in *Arabic Literature in the Classroom: Teaching Methods, Theories, Themes, and Texts*, ed. Muhsin J. al-Musawi, 109–29 (London: Routledge, 2017).

11. In "Heteroglossia and the Poetics of the *Roman Maghrébin*" (*Contemporary French and Francophone Studies: Sites* 20, no. 2 [2016]: 8–17), I theorize Maghrebi literature through the Bakhtinian concepts of heteroglossia and het-

erology. As I discuss in Chapter 6, Bakhtin's seminal essay "Discourse in the Novel" was translated into Arabic by Moroccan novelist and literary theorist Muḥammad Barrāda in 1987.

12. On the history of medieval North Africa—known as Ifrīqiyā—see Ramzi Rouighi, *The Making of a Mediterranean Emirate: Ifrīqiyā and Its Andalusis, 1200–1400* (Philadelphia: University of Pennsylvania Press, 2011).

13. Pan-Arabism is a political ideology, popularized in the late nineteenth and early twentieth centuries, that is based on the shared cultural, linguistic, and social affinity of Arabic-speaking peoples and nations. Although it evolved into various configurations over the latter half of the twentieth century, it most commonly entailed intergovernmental military, political, economic, and cultural alliances between sovereign Arab nations. Applications of the ideology included the formation of various Arab unions, such as Nasser's United Arab Republic in 1958, which joined Syria and Egypt; the Federation of Arab Republics, joining Jordan and Iraq in 1958; and the Federation of Arab Republics by Muʿammar al-Qadhdhāfī in 1972 that joined Libya, Egypt, and Syria. The League of Arab States was formed in 1945 with Egypt, Transjordan, Lebanon, Saudi Arabia, Syria, and Yemen; it now includes twenty-two member states.

14. It is estimated that Morocco's Berberophone community comprises approximately 40 percent of the population, with Algeria at about 25 percent (Chaker). In 2001, one study claimed that there were 20 million Tamazight speakers throughout Morocco and Algeria alone (El Aissati). On the complex history and forced assimilation of Algeria's indigenous populations, as well as the fraught politics of the signifiers "Berber" and "Amazigh" (plural: Imazighen), see James McDougall, "Myth and Counter-Myth: 'The Berber' as National Signifier in Algerian Historiographies," *Radical History Review*, no. 86 (Spring 2003): 66–88.

15. See Mohand Tilmatine, "French and Spanish Colonial Policy in North Africa: Revisiting the Kabyle and Berber Myth," *International Journal of the Sociology of Language*, no. 239 (May 2016): 95–119.

16. On the history and etymology of North African "Berbers," see Ramzi Rouighi, "The Andalusi Origins of the Berbers?," *Journal of Medieval Iberian Studies* 2, no. 1 (2010): 93–108; and Rouighi, "The Berbers and the Arabs," *Studia Islamica*, nouvelle edition/n.s., 1 (2011): 67–101. On the competing narrative mythologies mobilized by both European and indigenous writers in the Maghreb and broader Mediterranean, see Mohamed-Salah Omri, "History, Literature, and Settler Colonialism in North Africa," *Modern Language Quarterly* 66, no. 3 (September 2015): 273–98.

17. See Adam Guerin, "Racial Myth, Colonial Reform, and the Invention of Customary Law in Morocco, 1912–1930," *Journal of North African Studies* 16, no. 3 (2011): 361–80.

18. *Laïcité* was codified in France with the passing of the 1905 law separating the (Catholic) church from the state. David Fieni's "Decadent Orientalisms: Configuring the Decay of Colonial Modernity in French and Arabic" (Ph.D. diss., University of California, Los Angeles, 2006) contextualizes "contemporary French debates surrounding immigration, secularism, and the role of mass media" within "the discursive structures of Orientalism and decadence" (xii).

19. On the disciplinary politics of Maghrebi studies in the US academy, see H. El Shakry, "Lessons from the Maghreb."

20. Over the last decade, scholars such as Muhsin al-Musawi, Tarek El-Ariss, Elizabeth Holt, Boutheina Khaldi, Samah Selim, Shaden Tageldin, Jeffrey Sacks, and Stephen Sheehi have problematized the orientalist underpinnings of *nahḍa* narratives. Jens Hanssen and Max Weiss's recent edited volume *Arabic Thought in the Liberal Age: Towards a Critical History of the Nahda* (Cambridge: Cambridge University Press, 2016) is also an important intervention in the field.

21. See Wendy Brown's introduction to the volume *Is Critique Secular? Blasphemy, Injury, and Free Speech*, which offers a helpful overview of these different genealogies (7–19).

22. A number of critics have noted the fraught relationship that Arabic literature scholars share with Said's intellectual legacy in comparative literature and postcolonial studies. Hosam Aboul-Ela points out the challenge of reconciling Said's "career-long focus on the culture of the West and its Orientalizing gaze toward the Arabs . . . with the paucity of material focusing in direct and complicated ways on Arabic literature and ideas," adding that this dynamic "parallels an older and more conceptual tension between colonial discourse analysis as a pure critique of the West's gaze, and the need for a critical approach to the arts and ideas of the region that makes substantial statements about Arab actors" (Aboul-Ela, "Is There an Arab (Yet) in This Field? Postcolonialism, Comparative Literature, and the Middle Eastern Horizon of Said's Discourse Analysis," *MFS: Modern Fiction Studies* 56, no. 4 (Winter 2010): 733–34). See also Aboul-Ela, "Our Theory Split," Roundtable: Theory and Arabic Literature in the United States, *International Journal of Middle East Studies* 43, no. 4 (2011): 725–27; and Mohamed-Salah Omri, "Notes on the Traffic between Theory and Arabic Literature," ibid., 731–33.

23. Edward Said writes that secular criticism "trouble[s] the quasi-religious authority of being comfortably at home among one's people, supported by known powers and acceptable values, protected against the outside world" (Said, *The World, the Text, and the Critic* [Cambridge: Harvard University Press, 1983], 16).

24. Similarly, Said remarks that literary criticism that engages religious discourse is divorced from "the human and the circumstantial," reflecting "an

ultimate preference for the secure protection of systems of belief (however peculiar those may be) and not for critical activity or consciousness" (ibid., 291–92).

25. Beyond the authors discussed here, see Mathieu E. Courville, *Edward Said's Rhetoric of the Secular* (London: Continuum, 2009); William D. Hart, *Edward Said and the Religious Effects of Culture* (Cambridge: Cambridge University Press, 2000); and Tobias Döring and Mark Stein, eds., *Edward Said's Translocations: Essays in Secular Criticism* (New York: Routledge, 2012).

26. See Talal Asad, *Formations of the Secular: Christianity, Islam, Modernity* (Stanford: Stanford University Press, 2003).

27. Arjun Appadurai mobilizes the term to address the "politics of global cultural flow" in what he dubs the *global cultural economy* (Appadurai, "Disjuncture and Difference in the Global Cultural Economy," *Public Culture* 2, no. 2 [Spring 1990]: 3). Subsequent literary scholars—from Christopher Prendergast to Emily Apter—have expanded the concept to address the historiographic biases of literary criticism under the rubric of the "Eurochronology Problem" (see Prendergast, *Debating World Literature* [London: Verso, 2004]; and Apter, "Literary World-Systems," in *Teaching World Literature*, ed. David Damrosch, 44–60 [New York: Modern Language Association, 2009]).

28. Mikhail Bakhtin defines chronotopes as structuring principles for narrative time that demonstrate "the intrinsic connectedness of temporal and spatial relationships that are artistically expressed in literature" (Bakhtin, "Forms of Time and Chronotope in the Novel," in *The Dialogic Imagination*, ed. Michael Holquist; trans. Caryl Emerson and Holquist [Austin: University of Texas Press, 1981], 84).

29. Mohammad Salama notes that *tajdīd*, meaning both "renewal" and "renovation," is the founding principle of the *mujaddidūn* (renovators) school of rationalist exegesis; whereas according to more conservative schools of exegesis, "*ibdāʿ/ bidʿa* (invention, or the creation of something new, ex nihilo)... [can be] perceived as an act of transgression, namely, a blasphemous attempt to destabilize theological norms by adding to, altering, or criticizing the course of divinity which is already perceived to be complete in itself" (*The Qur'an and Modern Arabic Literary Criticism: From Ṭahā to Naṣr* [London: Bloomsbury Academic, 2018], 5).

30. Many of these fields were codified and documented by the fourteenth-century Iranian theologian, professor, and encyclopedist ʿAlī ibn Muḥammad al-Jurjānī in his famous lexicon *Kitāb al-Taʿrīfāt* [The book of definitions] (see Sarah bin Tyeer, *The Qur'an and the Aesthetics of Premodern Arabic Prose* [London: Palgrave Macmillan, 2016], 27–28).

31. Ira M. Lapidus reads *adab* in relation to *ʿilm* (knowledge/science), *taṣdīq* (knowing/belief), *islām* (submission), and *īmān* (faith) (Lapidus, "Knowledge,

Virtue, and Action: The Classical Muslim Conception of *Adab*, and the Nature of Religious Fulfillment in Islam," in *Moral Conduct and Authority: The Place of* Adab *in South Asian Islam*, ed. Barbara Daly Metcalf [Berkeley: University of California Press, 1984], 40).

32. Specifically, Allan situates *adab*'s codification as literature within "the rise of literary study as a modern discipline" through the Caireen Dār al-ʿUlūm (Michael Allan, *In the Shadow of World Literature: Sites of Reading in Colonial Egypt* [Princeton, N.J.: Princeton University Press, 2016], 15).

33. On the Qur'an and poetry, see Angelika Neuwirth, *Scripture, Poetry, and the Making of a Community: Reading the Qur'an as a Literary Text* (New York: Oxford University Press, 2014).

34. It is worth noting that Ṭahā Ḥusayn's *Fi al-shīʿr al-jāhilī* [On *jāhilī* poetry] controversially proposed that pre-Islamic poetry was fabricated after the Qurʾanic revelations (Cairo: Dār al-muʿārif, 1981). As Mohammad Salama argues, this undertheorized work challenges many of the assumptions and debates surrounding the relationship between pre-Islamic poetry and the Qurʾan's inimitability (2; 17–36).

35. See Adonis's chapter "Poetics and the Influence of the Qurʾān," in *An Introduction to Arab Poetics*, trans. Catherine Cobham (London: Saqi, 1990), 35–54; as well as his study *Al-naṣṣ al-qurʾānī wa āfāq al-kitāba* [Qurʾanic text and the horizons of writing] (Beirut: Dār al-ādāb, 1993).

36. There has been significant debate among Islamic scholars and historians as to the veracity of these accounts. For a popular overview of these debates, particularly as they were reinvigorated upon the discovery of early Qurʾanic manuscripts in Yemen in 1972 in which there were minor textual and verse order variations, see Toby Lester, "What Is the Koran?," *Atlantic*, January 1999, https://www.theatlantic.com/magazine/archive/1999/01/what-is-the-koran/304024/.

37. Qurʾanic studies remains a notoriously divisive field in which questions of historiography, ideology, politics, and even personal faith frequently blend with methodological concerns and practices. This is complicated by the largely orientalist origins of the field in the Euro-American context.

38. While this approach is most notable within Euro-American scholarship, it actually has roots in early Qurʾanic exegesis (Farid Esack, *The Qurʾan: A User's Guide* [Oxford: Oneworld, 2005], 64–66). Following the death of the Prophet Muhammad (ca. 632), the Qurʾanic revelations were historicized in relation to the Prophet's life. This occurred alongside the documentation and verification of hadith, as well as the literary-theological tradition of *sīra* biographies on the life of the Prophet.

39. References to and instructions in Qurʾanic recitation appear in (7:204), (17:45), (17:106), (73:4), (87:6). The Qurʾan is also referred to as truth (69:51);

divine proof (7:203); a reminder/*dhikr* (3:58), (15:9), (20:99), (25:29), (43:5), (43:44), (69:48), (81:27), (87:9); the exposition of everything (16:89); perfect wisdom (54:5); an instrument of knowledge (12:2), (15:1), (27:1), (29:49), (36:2), (41:3), (43:2), (43:3), (44:2); or a source of guidance through signs/*āyas* (29:49), (45:11).

40. In order to contextualize the controversy over the incendiary Danish cartoons about the Prophet Muhammad, Saba Mahmood explains how he represents a model of embodied ethics: "Those who profess love for the Prophet do not simply follow his advice and admonitions to the *umma* (that exist in the form of the *hadith*), but also try to emulate how he dressed; what he ate; how he spoke to his friends and adversaries; how he slept, walked, and so on. These mimetic ways of realizing the Prophet's behavior are lived not as commandments but as virtues where one wants to ingest, as it were, the Prophet's persona into oneself. It needs to be acknowledged of course that insomuch as Muhammad is a human figure in Islamic doctrine who does not share in divine essence, he is more an object of veneration than of worship" (Asad, Brown, Butler, and Mahmood, *Is Critique Secular?* 75–76).

41. Ware's ethnographic fieldwork on the epistemology of Islamic schooling in Senegal theorizes Qur'anic education as an *ethical* obligation at the level of both the community and the individual. This harkens to my earlier discussion of *adab* as an ethical pedagogical practice.

42. Yusuf Ali's translation reads: "Nay, here are Signs self-evident in the hearts of those endowed with knowledge: and none but the unjust reject Our Signs" (Qur'an 29:49 trans. Ali).

43. On narrative in relation to the Qur'an and *adab*, see bin Tyeer, *The Qur'an and the Aesthetics of Premodern Arabic Prose*, 11–12. On the Qur'anic distinction between "*qaṣaṣ* ('story' or 'narrative') and *usṭūra* ('myth' or 'legend')," see El-Desouky, "Between Hermeneutic Provenance and Textuality," 21; and El-Desouky, "Beyond Spatiality," 81.

44. El-Desouky historicizes these trends within the "classical literary approaches in the third/ninth and fourth/tenth centuries, from al-Naẓẓām (d. 232/846) through to al-Jurjānī (d. 470/1078)" ("Between Hermeneutic Provenance and Textuality," 30). On the question of Qur'anic (un)translatability in relation to world literature criticism, see El-Desouky, "Beyond Spatiality"; and Ziad Elmarsafy, *The Enlightenment Qur'an*.

45. For examples of *iltifāt* in the Qur'an, see Mahinnaz Mirdehghan, Keivan Zahedi, and Fatemeh Nasiri, "Iltifat, Grammatical Person Shift and Cohesion in the Holy Quran," *Global Journal of Human Social Science Research* 12, no. 2 (2012): 45–50; and M. A. S. Abdel Haleem, "Grammatical Shift for Rhetorical Purposes: *Iltifāt* and Related Features in the Qur'ān," *Bulletin of the School of Oriental and African Studies* 55, pt. 3 (1992): 407–32.

46. See Hussein Abdul-Raof, *Schools of Qur'anic Exegesis: Genesis and Development* (London: Routledge, 2010); Walid A. Saleh, *The Formation of the Classical Tafsīr Tradition: The Qur'ān Commentary of Al-Tha'labī* (d. 427/1035) (Leiden: Brill, 2004); Angelika Neuwirth and Michael A. Sells, eds., *Qur'ān Studies Today* (London: Routledge, 2016); Selwa M. S. El-Awa, *Textual Relations in the Qur'ān: Relevance, Coherence and Structure* (New York: Routledge, 2006); Bruce Fudge, *Qur'ānic Hermeneutics: Al-Ṭabrisī and the Craft of Commentary* (London: Routledge, 2011); and Angelika Neuwirth, Nicolai Sinai, and Michael Marx, eds., *The Qur'ān in Context: Historical and Literary Investigations into the Qur'ānic Milieu* (Leiden: Brill, 2010).

47. On the various disciplines in dialogue with Qur'anic exegesis, see Abdul-Raof, *Schools of Qur'anic Exegesis*, 13; on the different "genres" of exegesis, see 28–30 and 92–102. For a prototypical linguistic analysis of the Qur'an, see Abdul-Raof, "The Linguistic Architecture of the Qur'an," *Journal of Qur'anic Studies* 2, no. 2 (2010): 37–51. For approaches to the Qur'an inflected by literary studies, see Stefan Wild, ed., *The Qur'an as Text* (Leiden: Brill, 1996); and Travis Zadeh, "Quranic Studies and the Literary Turn" *Journal of the American Oriental Society* 135, no. 2 (April-June 2015): 329–42.

48. Amina Wadud's groundbreaking *Qur'an and Woman: Rereading the Sacred Text from a Woman's Perspective* (Oxford: Oxford University Press, 1999) is part of a growing movement of self-identified progressive and feminist Qur'anic exegetes.

49. For a morphological and semantic account of *ta'wīl*, see Abdul-Raof, *Schools of Qur'anic Exegesis*, 102. On the distinction between Qur'anic *ta'wīl*, *tafsīr*, and *tarjama* (translation), see El-Desouky, "Beyond Spatiality," 80–81.

50. For an explication of the sura, see Qur'an trans. Asad 80; for a broader discussion of symbolism and allegory in the Qur'an, see 1129–32.

51. Asad adds that "only a small segment of reality is open to man's perception and imagination" and that there is "a realm which is beyond the reach of human perception (*al-ghayb*)" (1129).

52. This is not to say that self-identified Sufi orders and leaders have not shared a complex relationship with the state and state-sanctioned religious institutions, particularly in the last decade, when Sufism is increasingly promoted by state organs across the Maghreb as an antidote to religious extremism. It is important, however, to distinguish these forces from readings of Sufism as intrinsically distinct from Islam "proper."

53. On *taṣawwuf* as a path, see Sa'diyya Shaikh, *Sufi Narratives of Intimacy: Ibn 'Arabi, Gender, and Sexuality* (Chapel Hill: University of North Carolina Press, 2012); Annemarie Schimmel, *Mystical Dimensions of Islam* (Chapel Hill: University of North Carolina Press, 1975); Carl Ernst, *Sufism: An Introduction*

to the Mystical Tradition of Islam (1997; Boston: Shambhala, 2011); and Michael Sells, *Early Islamic Mysticism: Sufi, Qur'an, Mi'raj, Poetic and Theological Writings* (New York: Paulist Press, 1996).

54. The terms *bāṭin* and *ẓāhir* also appear in the sura "Luqmān," in reference to *ni'amahu* (the outward/inward blessings) that God bestows upon his believers (31:20). In the suras "Al-An'ām" ["The Cattle"] (6:120) and "Al-A'rāf" ["The Heights" or "The Faculty of Discernment") (7:33), they reference sins that are either visible or hidden.

55. On the scholarly inclination toward Morocco over Algeria and Tunisia—particularly in relation to the archives of decolonization—see Hoda El Shakry, "Printed Matter(s): Critical Histories and Perspectives on Tunisian Cultural Journals," *ALIF: A Journal of Comparative Poetics* 37 (2017): 143–44.

56. The select students admitted into the al-Ṣādiqiyya educational pipeline were often expected to serve as colonial intermediaries—quite literally cultural and linguistic translators—or low-level clerks for the colonial regime.

57. The Arabic text reads:

ذلك عهد تأثرت فيه بأنغام القرآن وموسيقى القرآن. كنت أردّد وأقرأ ما تعلّمت منه على نحو من الترتيل. حفظت القرآن موقّعا في أذني حسب إيقاعات هي إيقاعات القرآن فعرفت أنه ليس كلاما فقط بل هو إيحاء. فيما بعد بدأت أتأثر بالقرآن فكريّا، ولكني أدركت أنه ليس فيه ما يدعو إلى عمليات عقلية منطقية. ففيه تخليص قارئ القرآن إن تساءل عن معناه من حدود المنطق إلى آفاق التصوّر الحرّ الذي يسمّى الخيال والذي هو عندي كلّ ما ينشاء داخل الضمير ممّا يحوي به من تقوى. وذلك العالم الحرّ الذي يجد الإنسان في نطاقه أو في مجال الله.

58. For an analysis of Meddeb's complex and often contradictory writings on Islam across his literary and critical oeuvre, see Hoda El Shakry "Abdelwahab Meddeb and the Po/Ethics of Sufism," *Expressions maghrébines* 16, no 2 (Winter 2017): 95–115.

59. These sentiments can also be found in his later poetic reflections on Sufism (*Tombeau d'Ibn Arabi*, 1995; *Portrait du poète en soufi*, 2014; *Instants soufis*, 2015).

60. The impulse to read Maghrebi fiction as simultaneously autobiographical and anticolonial reflects the orientalist assumption that (post)colonial intellectuals cannot not conceive of literature beyond their experience as subjects of empire.

CHAPTER 1

1. Unless otherwise indicated, all translations from Arabic and French are my own.

2. The Arabic text reads:

مشكلة الموت والحياة، أو مأساة الإنسان وهو يواجه حتمية الموت [. . .] أو هو، بعبارة أخرى، يعاني هذه الناحية من مأساته الوجودية التي جعلته لا يرضى بأن يكون فانيا زائلا، وجعلته يحاول بما لم تأت به الطبيعة أن يحصل على الخلود.

3. Al-Maʿarrī was a notoriously eccentric and controversial figure. The blind philosopher and poet lived an ascetic life of abstinence and veganism. His pessimistic heterodoxy took aim not only at Islam but also at Judaism, Christianity, and Zoroastrianism. Al-Maʿarrī's works, particularly his renowned *Risālat al-ghufrān* [Epistles of forgiveness], frequently parodied the Qur'an.

4. Al-Masʿadī wrote critical essays analyzing the works of al-ʿAtāhiya, al-Maʿarrī and al-Ghazālī early in his career: "Abū al-ʿAtāhiya kamā yarāhu Ṣāḥib al-aghānī" [Abu al-ʿAtāhiya through the eyes of the author of the Book of Songs (*Kitāb al-aghānī*)], *al-Mabāḥith*, no. 12 (March 1945); "Abū al-ʿAlā' fīmā baynaka wa bayna nafsika" [Abū al-ʿAlā' between you and yourself], *al-Mabāḥith*, no. 21 (December 1945); "Mushkilat al-maʿrifa ʿind al-Ghazālī" [The problem of knowledge in al-Ghazālī], *al-Mabāḥith*, no. 3 (February 10, 1940). On the individual influences of Abū al-ʿAtāhiya, al-Maʿarrī, al-Ghazālī, Abū Nuwās, and al-Tawḥīdī, see Maḥmūd al-Masʿadī, *Collected Works*, vols. 1–4, ed. Maḥmūd Ṭarshūna (Tunis: Dār al-Janūb li-l-Nashr, 2003), 3:346–47.

5. On how he was influenced by Baudelaire, Racine, Corneille, Greek philosophy, and Shakespeare, see al-Masʿadī, *Collected Works*, 3:344–45.

6. The notable exception is Mohamad-Salah Omri, who conducted a series of interviews with al-Masʿadī and whose articles and monograph on the author are an invaluable resource in Anglophone scholarship.

7. Al-Masʿadī wrote and spoke extensively on the *nahḍa*; see his 1975 interview with the Algerian newspaper *Al-aṣāla* [Authenticity] (*Collected Works*, 3:185–92).

8. While the density and difficulty of al-Masʿadī's prose certainly makes translations challenging, one can speculate that publication by a French press might have yielded greater circulation.

9. The Arabic text reads:

فالأدب هو الذي به يحقّق الإنسان درجة ما من الكمال، به يحقّق إنسانيته وكماله لأنه يقوم كلّه على التساؤل عن معنى الوجود وعن القيم التي بها يستطيع الإنسان أن يرتفع من درجة الحيوانية إلى درجة الألوهية.

10. Al-Ḥizb al-Ḥurr al-Dustūrī al-Jadīd (the New Constitutional Liberal Party) was formed under the French Protectorate in 1934 following the split of al-Ḥizb al-Ḥurr al-Dustūrī (the Free Constitutional Party). Instrumental in Tunisia's battle for independence, this nationalist party was largely populist and socialist in orientation. Despite undergoing a series of name changes—including al-Ḥizb al-Ishtirākī al-Dustūrī (the Socialist Constitutional Party) or the Parti socialiste destourien, and eventually al-Tajammu' al-Dustūrī al-Dīmuqrāṭī (the Democratic Constitutional Assembly) or the Rassemblement Constitutionnel Démocratique—the party remained in power until the toppling of President Zayn al-ʿĀbidīn bin ʿAlī in 2011.

11. On the significance of cultural journals to Maghrebi, and particularly Tunisian, decolonization, see Hoda El Shakry, "Printed Matter(s): Critical Histories and Perspectives on Tunisian Cultural Journals," *ALIF: A Journal of Comparative Poetics* 37 (2017): 140–68.

12. While al-Masʿadī penned the majority of his fiction between 1938 and 1941, most of his works were not published independent of literary journals until the 1970s.

13. The group's name references the café where its members congregated. For al-Masʿadī's reflections on the influential group, see *Collected Works*, 3:234–35.

14. See William Granara, "Ali al-Duʿaji (1909–1949)," in *Essays in Arabic Literary Biography: 1850–1950*, ed. Roger Allen (Wiesbaden: Harrassowitz Verlag, 2010); and Douja Mamelouk, "Ali al-Duʿaji and *al-ʿalam al-adabi* [The literary world]: A Voice of the Tunisian Avant-Garde under Colonial Rule (1930–1936)," *Journal of North African Studies* 21, no. 5 (2016): 794–809.

15. See the introduction to al-Gharībī's *Jadaliyyat al-aṣāla wa-l-muʿāṣira fī adab al-Masʿadī* (Tunis: Ṣāmid, 1994). The Epilogue expands upon the controversy with Ṭāhā Ḥusayn.

16. See H. El Shakry, "Printed Matter(s)," 153–54.

17. *Isnād* references the chain of transmission that is employed to verify the authenticity of a given hadith.

18. Irene Siegel expands upon this argument in her dissertation chapter on *Ḥadatha Abū Hurayra qāl* ("Authorizing Narrative: Negotiations of Belonging in North African Literature" [Ph.D. diss., University of California, Berkeley, 2009], 123–83).

19. The *conte philosophique* is a hybrid genre that employs fiction to explore philosophical and ethical questions. Such works often rely heavily on dialogue and questioning—as in the case of Voltaire's *Candide* or Plato's Socratic dialogues—in order to examine existence, the purpose of human endeavor, God, and/or the role of reason.

20. For a discussion of the etymology of *Salhawā*, see Mohamed-Salah Omri, *Nationalism, Islam and World Literature:* Sites of Confluence in the Writings of Mahmūd al-Masʿadī (London: Routledge, 2006), 7.

21. Variations of the word *hudā* appear more than seventy times in the Qurʾan with more than ten references in the sura "Al-baqara" ["The Cow"].

22. The number of stages in Sufism generally ranges between five and ten. The number seven is invoked by various Sufi orders, likely because of its significance in the Qurʾan. In addition to there being seven verses in the first sura of the Qurʾan, the number seven, and multiples thereof, appear across the text. There are also said to be seven levels of heaven in Islam through which

the Prophet Muhammad ascended on his night journey of the *miʿrāj*. Finally, the Kaʿba is circled seven times during the Hajj pilgrimage.

23. On the question of Ghazālī in relation to Aristotle's poetics, see Ebrahim Moosa, *Ghazālī and the Poetics of the Imagination* (Chapel Hill: University of North Carolina Press, 2005), 38–40, 78–80.

24. See al-Masʿadī, *Taʾṣilan li-kiyān* [Authenticating being] in *Collected Works*, 2:7–247.

25. See the sura "Al-anʿām" ["The Cattle"], 6:111–121. References to Satan's whisperings include "Al-ʾaʿrāf" ["The Faculty of Discernment" or "The Heights"], 7:20; "Al-anfāl" ["The Spoils of War"], 8:11; "Ṭā Ḥā" ["Ṭā Ḥā"], 20:120; and "Al-nās" ["Mankind"], 114:4.

26. See the sura "Al-baqara" ["The Cow"], 2:163.

27. See the sura "Al-dhāriyāt" ["The Winds That Scatter"], 51:41–46.

28. Portions of this passage are cited in Omri, *Nationalism, Islam, and World Literature*, 130–31; I have modified his translation. The Arabic text reads:

إني الان الحقُّ في حقّها . . . انظروا. فهذا قلبي سكت، وقد غلب السكونُ الزمان. انا لا أمُرُّ ولا أحُول. انا الوجود، انا الخلود، لم استَحِلْ منذ القدم . . . لكن من انا؟ أُولَدُ كلَّ ساعةٍ خَلْقاً جديدًا. انظروا آفاقي تَنَاءَى، فما أوسعَ أبْعَادي! ها سكن عني الحسُّ وآن الحُلُول. وعظمْتُ وشربْتُ السماءَ وحلَّتْ فيَّ الاكوانُ جميعا.

29. Qurʾanic commentator Yusuf Ali translates the sura as, "But will abide (for ever) the Face of thy Lord,—full of Majesty, Bounty and Honour," noting: "The most significant works of man—such as they are—are but fleeting. Ships, Empires, the Wonders of Science and Art, the splendours of human glory or intellect, will all pass away. The most magnificent objects in outer Nature . . . will also pass away in their appointed time. But the only One that will endure for ever is the 'Face' of God. 'Face' expresses Personality, Glory, and Majesty, inner being, essence, self, all the noble qualities which we associate with the Beautiful Names of God" (Qurʾan trans. Ali 1475n5189).

30. The Arabic text reads:

ما يحدث بين الأثر الأدبي وبين قارئه من تفاعل ومن تأثير وتأثّر على المستوى الوجداني والمستوى الفكري أو الخيالي أو الفلسفي، سرٌّ لا يعلمه إلا القارئ وحدَه لأنه لا يخضع إلى قاعدة كقواعد الكيمياء، لذلك نتحدث عن * ما وراء الكيمياء ولا نتحدّث عن الكيمياء، سرّ لا يَخضع إلى القواعد الطبيعية بل هو أمر غريب يتولّد عنه كل أثر أدبيّ.

* alchimie

31. [S]i l'Islam, non certes en tant que religion ou credo, mais en tant que mode d'interrogation et de réflexion de l'homme sur soi, ne devait plus susciter les efforts de création intellectuelle et spirituelle en Orient, c'en serait définitivement fini avec l'une des conquêtes de l'homme les plus originales, les plus fécondes et les plus valables, et avec les trésors de valeurs inappréciables qu'elle a su engendre.

Portions of the passage are cited in Omri, *Nationalism, Islam, and World Literature*, 41; I have modified his translation.

32. Al-Masʿadī frequently writes that the very act of questioning, particularly the nature of one's own existence, is what makes us human (*Collected Works*, 3:96–97).

CHAPTER 2

1. While initially published in 1979, *Talismano* was rereleased with modifications in 1987. Few copies of the first edition of *Talismano* remain. Consequently, I will be working from the revised 1987 version of the novel. Unless otherwise noted, citations in English are from the standard Jane Kuntz translation, while references in French are to the 1987 edition. Where indicated, I have made modifications to Kuntz's translation. Parenthetical citations that reference both editions feature the English page number(s) followed by the French. Unless otherwise indicated, all other translations from Arabic and French are my own.

2. Meddeb's account in many ways echoes Adonis's theory of modernity in *An Introduction to Arab Poetics* (trans. Catherine Cobham [London: Saqi, 1990]) discussed in the Introduction.

3. See Hoda El Shakry, "Abdelwahab Meddeb and the Po/Ethics of Sufism," *Expressions maghrébines* 16, no. 2 (Winter 2017): 95–115.

4. Said to have been built around the eighth century, the Tunis-based al-Zaytūna, from which some of the most prominent intellectuals of Islamic thought graduated, is among the oldest institutions of higher learning in the region.

5. In the words of the novel's brave English translator Jane Kuntz: "Prepositions and articles disappear, subject/verb phrases get collapsed into a gerund or an infinitive, and strings of long noun phrases stand in for sentences, lending the text a randomness that suits the narrative forward motion of the haphazard stroll through the city" (Kuntz, introduction to *Talismano*, trans. Kuntz [Champaign, Ill. Dalkey Archive Press, 2011], xi).

6. The word Islam, from the root *s-l-m*, translates to "submission, resignation, reconciliation (to the will of God)" (*Hans Wehr: A Dictionary of Modern Written Arabic*, 3rd ed. 1994, ed. J. Milton Cowan [Beirut: Librairie du Liban, 1980], 425–26).

7. The exact details of al-Ḥallāj's death remain disputed. It is said that his controversial teachings resulted in a number of complaints being issued against him by the reigning Muʿtazilites before he was excommunicated, arrested, and sent to prison for eight years by the Vizier Ibn ʿĪsā. Since he resumed his preaching upon release and had fallen into disfavor with the Vizier for both theological and political reasons, he was arrested and tried before a commission. They found him guilty of heresy and a *fatwa* was issued sentencing him to

death. His execution is said to have included hundreds of lashings, the gradual cutting off of his limbs, and a beheading, with his body finally being burned and the ashes thrown in the Tigris. Al-Hallāj is most notable for having declared *Anā al-ḥaqq*, or "I am truth/the real" (see De Lacy O'Leary, "Al-Hallaj," *Philosophy East and West* 1, no. 1 [April 1951]: 56–62).

8. Known as *Shaykh al-Ishrāq*, or the "Master of Illumination," Suḥrawardī, who was born in present-day Azerbaijan, was the founder of the school of philosophy known as *ishrāqī*, or "Illuminationism," which was a philosophical strain of Islamic mysticism that developed from Avicennan, Peripatetic, Platonic, as well as Zoroastrian thought (see Seyyed Hossein Nasr's "The Spread of the Illuminationist School of Suhrawardi," *Studies in Comparative Religion* 6, no. 3 [Summer 1972]: 111–22).

9. Ibn ʿArabi is a recurring figure in a number of Meddeb's works, such as the prose poetry collection *Tombeau d'Ibn Arabi*. He is also a prominent interlocutor in Meddeb's second novel, *Phantasia*.

10. The Ikhwān al-Ṣafāʾ (Brethren of Purity) were an eighth-century Muslim secret society in Basra, in present-day Iraq. They composed the *Rasāʾil al-Ikhwān al-Ṣafāʾ* [Treatises of the Brethren of Purity], an influential Islamic encyclopedia that contains fifty-two treatises on various philosophical concerns within the Islamic sciences.

11. First commissioned in the tenth century, al-Azhar is said to be the second-oldest continuously run university in the world. It is considered one of the leading institutions for the study of Sunni theology and shariʿa.

12. Said to be the oldest university in the world, al-Qarawiyyin was founded in the ninth century. Still following the traditional pedagogical methods of the madrasa, its scholars focus predominantly on the Islamic sciences, with a particular emphasis on Mālikī law, jurisprudence, and Arabic grammar and linguistics.

13. As I elaborate in my discussion of Driss Chraïbi's *Le passé simple* in Chapter 5, Sherifian lineage refers to the claim that the members of the Alaouite dynasty currently in power in Morocco are direct descendants of the Prophet Muhammad.

14. It is even said that upon Algeria's occupation in 1830, the literacy rates were higher than those in France due in large part to the efforts of *zāwiyas* (John Ruedy, *Modern Algeria: The Origins and Development of a Nation* [Bloomington: Indiana University Press, 2005], 103).

15. On the Islamic modernists, see Samira Haj, *Reconfiguring Islamic Tradition* Reform, Rationality, and Modernity (Stanford: Stanford University Press, 2008); and Fazlur Rahman, *Islam and Modernity: Transformation of an Intellectual Tradition* (Chicago: University of Chicago Press, 1982), 49–51.

16. Muḥammad ʿAbduh was an Egyptian jurist, legal reformer, scholar and leading members of the Islamic modernist movement. He was heavily influenced by Jamāl al-Dīn al-Afghānī (1838–1897), a fellow reformer and staunch anticolonialist who was a major figure of the Muslim intellectual tradition.

17. Al-Ṭāhir al-Ḥaddād was a Tunisian reformer most notable for his groundbreaking work on women's rights.

18. Shaykh Muḥammad al-Bashīr al-Ibrahīmī was an Algerian reformer who also promoted women's rights within Islam.

19. Muḥammad ʿAllāl al-Fāsī was a Moroccan writer-poet, politician, Islamic scholar, and religious reformer who founded the nationalist Istiqlāl or Independence party.

20. See the works of Shaden Tageldin, Samah Selim, Stephen Sheehi, Tarek El-Ariss, Muhsin al-Musawi, Elizabeth Holt, Boutheina Khaldi, and Jeffrey Sacks.

21. "Et ce que nous avons lapidé, ici nous exorcise; hantise de l'histoire qui se répète indéfinie spirale nous emportant vers l'apostasie. . . . Nos incursions et actes ne s'identifieront pas indéfiniment manière de troubler l'avers cohérent de l'État; nous n'en représentons pas l'envers, ni le double. Comprenez, que nous sommes autre, généreux et longanimes. Vos pareils, gens de dieu et de réformes, sont à rosser" (Meddeb, *Talismano* 1987, 229–30).

22. Bourguiba was instrumental in the formation of the splinter Neo-Dustūr party (al-Ḥizb al-Ḥurr al-Dustūrī al-Jadīd, or the New Constitutional Liberal Party) when he was ousted from the old-guard Dustūr party (al-Ḥizb al-Ḥurr al-Dustūrī or the Constitutional Liberal Party) in 1934. See Hoda El Shakry, "Printed Matter(s): Critical Histories and Perspectives on Tunisian Cultural Journals," *ALIF: A Journal of Comparative Poetics* 37 (2017): 151–53.

23. "L'idole [est un] simulacre pour se défaire à jamais de la résonance archaïque, célébration à déjouer pouvoir. Pour que le pouvoir soit irréconciliablement nôtre, il faut le tuer par l'éloquence trouble, à investir la ville par cathartique spectacle. L'idole ainsi fabriquée n'est rien en soi: elle n'alimente pas une fiction nouvelle à fourbir foi et croyance; elle achève un type de pouvoir, culte de la soumission. Elle exorcise non pas un passé réputé tyrannique, souvent sanguinaire, mais les mirifiques instincts qui se hérissent ataviques à chaque émanation de sang" (Meddeb, *Talismano* 1987, 109).

24. *Mujūn* is a classical genre of poetry of the Abbasid and Buwayhid eras notable for its playfulness, vulgarity, caricature, and crude references to sex and bodily functions.

25. Written in rhymed couplets, the *maqāma* frequently recounts the tales of beggars, rogues, criminals, and other such figures.

26. The ninth-century Iraqi intellectual al-Jāḥiẓ was a renowned prose writer, philosopher, and theologian infamous for his scandalous poems, essays, and prose on a variety of topics both "lofty" and "low."

27. The work inspired Mikhail Bakhtin's theory of the Rabelasian chronotope, which seeks to "destroy and rebuild the entire false picture of the world, to sunder the false hierarchal links between objects and ideas, to abolish the divisive ideational strata" (Bakhtin, "Forms of Time and Chronotope in the Novel," in *The Dialogic Imagination*, ed. Michael Holquist; trans. Caryl Emerson and Holquist [Austin: University of Texas Press, 1981], 169).

28. "[Je] découvre un noir de blanc vêtu en train de réciter le texte à venir, révélation rajeunie, besoin nouveau de la répétition du verbe non plus immuable mais transformé à l'appel d'un souffle autre qui ne célèbre plus le respect de la loi paraphée diversion uniformisant les conduites. Mais le balancement du buste, lecteur émerveillé, demeure d'une sensibilité toute coranique" (Meddeb, *Talismano* 1987, 101).

29. In an earlier meditation on the relationship between language and writing, Meddeb comments on the unique qualities of Chinese in which the signifier and signified uniquely coincide: "Their words are other deserts; they repudiate the memory of voices to better preserve the alliance with the objects they mean to designate." He also refers to a Chinese calligrapher as being "in harmony with the world" due to his craft (Meddeb, *Talismano*, 117).

30. Brigitte Weltman-Aron makes a parallel argument with respect to Assia Djebar, in Weltman-Aron, *Algerian Imprints: Ethical Space in the Work of Assia Djebar and Hélène Cixous* (New York: Columbia University Press, 2015), 61.

31. The first sura said to be revealed to the Prophet Muhammad, "Al-ʿalaq," opens:

READ in the name of thy Sustainer, who has created
—created man out of a germ-cell!
Read—for they Sustainer is the Most Bountiful One
who has taught [man] the use of the pen
—taught man what he did not know!
"Al-ʿalaq" ("The Clot") (Qurʾan 96:1–5 trans. Asad)

32. See Toshihiko Izutsu, *Sufism and Taoism: A Comparative Study of Key Philosophical Concepts* (Berkeley: University of California Press, 2016).

33. A noble title that etymologically means sovereignty or authority, "Sultan" has come to indicate the title of rulers (generally within the caliphate) who hold ultimate power.

34. On the various scripts within Arabic calligraphy and their usage, see Kadri ElAraby, "The Art and Design of Arabic Calligraphy," *Digest of Middle East Studies* 6, no. 1 (Winter 1997): 1–23; and Nico Van den Boogert, "Some Notes on Maghribi Script," *Manuscripts of the Middle East* (MME), no. 4 (1989): 30–43.

35. A renowned North African explorer who chronicled his world travels during the fourteenth century.

36. A fourteenth-century North African historiographer of both Arab and Muslim origins, Ibn Khaldūn is said to be instrumental in the founding of modern sociology, historiography, economics, and demography. References to his work appear across al-Tāhir Waṭṭār's *al-Zilzāl* and Assia Djebar's *L'amour, la fantasia*.

37. A thirteenth-century Turkish poet and Sufi mystic.

38. Meddeb's *Tombeau d'Ibn 'Arabi* is a tribute to the late philosopher and mystic. It consists of lyrical prose that directly engages both *Tarjuman al-Ashwāq* and the author's commentary on it.

39. See William Chittick, *The Sufi Path of Knowledge: Ibn 'Arabi's Metaphysics of Imagination* (Albany: State University of New York Press, 1989).

40. Following the philosophies of Aristotle, the Peripatetics were phenomenological in orientation and believed matter to be at the heart of all scientific and intellectual inquiry, including the soul. Peripatetics within Islamic philosophy include such figures as al-Kindī (Alkindus), al-Fārābī (Alpharabius), Ibn Sīnā (Avicenna), and Ibn Rushd (Averroes).

41. On the intersections between Islam, and particularly Sufism, and psychoanalysis, see Omnia El Shakry, *The Arabic Freud: Psychoanalysis and Islam in Modern Egypt* (Princeton, N.J.: Princeton University Press, 2017).

42. Annemarie Schimmel writes that "Ḥallaj describes the fate of the moth that approaches the flame and eventually gets burned in it, thus realizing the Reality of Realities. He does not want the light or the heat but casts himself into the flame, never to return and never to give any information about the Reality, for he has reached perfection" (*Mystical Dimensions of Islam* [Chapel Hill: University of North Carolina Press, 1975], 70).

43. Le point est le principe de toute ligne, et la ligne entière n'est que points réunis. La ligne ne peut donc se passer du point, ni le point de la ligne. Et toute ligne droite ou courbe, sort par mouvement de ce même point. Et tout ce sur quoi tombe le regard est un point entre deux points. C'est là l'indice que [le vide] apparaît à travers tout ce qu'on contemple. C'est pourquoi je déclare: Je ne vois nulle chose en laquelle je ne voie [vide!] (Meddeb, *Talismano* 1987, 110).

44. See Safdar Ahmed, *Reform and Modernity in Islam: The Philosophical, Cultural and Political Discourses among Muslim Reformers* (New York: I. B. Taurus, 2013).

45. [N]otre orientation vers des valeurs éculées ainsi que l'émergence des moribonds corps de métier ne constituent pas retour au vieil état des choses ni fantaisie à combler le vide d'une imagination restreinte: non: nous ne nous reconnaissons pas régressifs ni bien intentionnés face à la tradition. Nous

sommes plus modernes que vous ne croyez. Nous nous ébranlons à activer l'impensé (Meddeb, *Talismano* 1987, 189).

46. A nous livrer par l'écrit sans vous donner prise, à vous fatiguer l'oeil par l'arabesque des mots, à vous proposer les réseaux du voyage, à vous enjoindre fêlure à tout ce qui s'offre aux yeux, à vous secouer par la haute morale, à détruire parmi vous les plus vigoureuses des complexions, à me dépoussiérer, à me volatiliser, à vous compénétrer par imperceptible fente; texte poussière à recevoir comme Livre à l'envers, un texte rassasié, où quatre ou cinq idées se répètent, dans le jeu clinquant de la différence, s'édifiant désespérance de loi, s'insérant à l'expérience où des vivants à travers mon je se reconnaîtraient: écrit couché, à l'envers rêvé dans le Livre feu allographe qui désorigine la sensibilité, rassasié, de gauche à droite transcrit alors que le corps et les yeux suivent leurs cours méditatifs à lire dans le texte de droite à gauche, dans la même continuité horizontale s'éclaire le sense renversé: paroles d'exil, soleil qui se cache, homme qui disparaît, de l'ici à l'ailleurs on erre entre le cachant et l'émanant, couchant et levant, à privilégier le moment sanglant plus que la naissance illuminante, genèse de l'éphémère, cacher, coucher: maghreb; et par-delà voiles réapparaître au oui païen par le texte tant que les jours accourissent, afin d'affirmer sa présence sur les traces de l'abandon, par antithèse et graphie au physique inversée, par retour aux thèmes qui ne supportent pas mots: corps, jouissance, mort, désert; tant d'indicibles à transformer moments du dire en passant par le langage de la métaphore, à rendre archaïques, à soi-même, séculaires, pour répéter que c'est de femme qui viendra lumière à éclairer nos territoires: par l'astre Jupiter, pa la pierre chrosolithe, par Vénus, par hématite, la féminité fécondera les lits foulés par la disponibilité mâle; et que cette nouvelle ingérence ajoute au corps divisé sa parcelle orpheline (Meddeb *Talismano* 1987, 243–44).

CHAPTER 3

1. All English citations from *Al-zilzāl* reference the published William Granara English edition (London: Saqi, 2000). Where indicated, I have made modifications to his translations to preserve certain nuances in the Arabic. Parenthetical citations that reference both editions feature the English page number(s) followed by the Arabic. Unless otherwise noted, all other translations are my own.

The Arabic text of the epigraph reads:

تذهل المرضعة عما أرضعت. وتضع كل ذات حمل حملها. ويسكر الناس وما هم بسكارى. لا. إنما يذهب مدخر عما ادخر من زيت وسكّر وسميد، ويضع كل ذي سلة سلته، وكل ذي بضاعة بضاعته. ويسكت الناس لحظة عن الحديث. هذه هي صفة الزلزال في قسنطينة، فالمرضعة ذاهلة عما ترضع بعد، وهي في الشوارع تركض خلف المواد الغذائية. الأحمال في بطون بقرات إبليس هاته، ليس أعزّ من خمس لترات زيتاً، أو خمسة كيلو سكّراً. أما هؤلاء، فأي سكر أكثر مما هم فيه، إنهم على ما يبدو، في هذه الحال، يهيمون على وجوههم، منذ أمد طويل.

(Waṭṭār, *Al-zilzāl*, 83–84).

2. The referenced portion of *Al-ḥajj* (Qur'an 22:2) reads:
يَوْمَ تَرَوْنَهَا تَذْهَلُ كُلُّ مُرْضِعَةٍ عَمَّا أَرْضَعَتْ وَتَضَعُ كُلُّ ذَاتِ حَمْلٍ حَمْلَهَا وَتَرَى النَّاسَ سُكَارَى وَمَا هُم بِسُكَارَى وَلَكِنَّ عَذَابَ اللَّهِ شَدِيدٌ

3. The most prominent exegetes of Islamic eschatology include Muḥammad al-Bukharī (810–870), Abū Ḥamīd al-Ghazalī (1058–1111), Ibn al-Nafīs (1213–1288), and Ismail ibn Kathīr (1301–1373). For a discussion of the Islamic eschatological tradition, see David Cook, *Studies in Muslim Apocalyptic* (Princeton, N.J.: Darwin, 2002); Timothy Gianotti, *Al-Ghazali's Unspeakable Doctrine of the Soul: Unveiling the Esoteric Psychology and Eschatology of the Iḥyā'* (Leiden: Brill, 2001); and Abū Ḥamīd al-Ghazalī, *The Remembrance of Death and the Afterlife: —Kitāb dhikr al-mawt wa-mā ba'dahu*, book 40 of *The Revival of the Religious Sciences—Ihyā' 'ulūm al-dīn*, trans. T. J. Winter (Cambridge: Islamic Texts Society, 1989).

4. Beyond the discussions of Sufism in Chapters 1 and 2, see al-Qushayri, *Principles of Sufism*, trans. B. R. Von Schegell (Berkeley, Calif.: Mizan, 1990); Ahmet Karamustafa, *Sufism: The Formative Period* (Edinburgh: Edinburgh University Press, 2007); and Michael Sells, *Early Islamic Mysticism: Sufi, Qur'an, Mi'raj, Poetic and Theological Writings* (New York: Paulist Press, 1996).

5. The Bakhtinian eschatological chronotope transforms present and past events through their literary insertion into a voided future time-space. Bakhtin writes: "The future is perceived as the end of everything that exists, as the end of all being (in its past and present forms). . . . Eschatology always sees the segment of a future separating the present from the end as lacking value; this separating segment of time loses its significance and interest, it is merely an unnecessary continuation of an indefinitely prolonged present" (Mikhail Bakhtin, *The Dialogic Imagination*, ed. Michael Holquist; trans. Caryl Emerson and Holquist [Austin: University of Texas Press, 1981], 148).

6. My use of "Arabism" echoes James McDougall's definition of the term as "connoting a positive identification with 'being Arab' (culturally) and with 'Arab solidarity' (politically) and to denote the political programs organized around such (self-)identification" ("Dream of Exile, Promise of Home: Language, Education and Arabism in Algeria," *International Journal of Middle East Studies* 43, no. 2 [2011]: 266n5). A more neutral equivalent would be the term "Arabness," which is favored by some scholars and more closely resembles the French *arabité*. I have opted for "Arabism" because I believe it more precisely captures the social and political policies that promote "Arabness" as such. Similarly, my use of the term "Islamism" is not meant to imply any affinities with sensationalist representations of "political Islam" or "Islamic fundamentalism." Rather, it indicates a cultural, social, and historical identification with Islam as a source of religious identity.

7. The quotation in the heading was a popular nationalist slogan mobilized by the Front de Libération Nationale (FLN, or National Liberation Front) during Algeria's battle for independence.

8. One of the novel's protagonists, Zaydān, is investigated by the FLN for his involvement in the Algerian Communist Party, which is seen as a threat to the unity of Algeria's anticolonial nationalist efforts. For a more in-depth discussion of the novel *Al-lāz*, see Debbie Cox, "The Novels of Tahar Wattar: Command or Critique?," *Research in African Literature* 28, no. 3 (Fall 1997): 94–109; and Cox, "Symbolism and Allegory in the Algerian Arabic Novel," *Arabic and Middle Eastern Literatures* 1, no. 2 (1998): 193–204; Ronald Judy, "On the Politics of Global Language, or Unfungible Local Value," *Boundary 2* 24, no. 2 (Summer 1997): 101–43; and William Granara, "Mythologising the Algerian War of Independence: Tahir Wattar and the Contemporary Algerian Novel," *Journal of North African Studies* 4, no. 3 (Autumn 1999): 1–14.

9. This comment is from an interview that aired on the Franco-German station Arte in 1994 and over the BBC in the United Kingdom. All references to the interview are from my translation of the Arabic.

10. According to the organization Reporters sans frontières, at least fifty-seven journalists were murdered between the years 1993 and 1997 (see Julija Šukys, *Silence Is Death: The Life and Work of Tahar Djaout* [Lincoln: University of Nebraska Press, 2007], 29).

11. Some examples include Lahouari Addi, "Les Intellectuels qu'on assassin," *Esprit*, January 1995, 130–38; and Addi, "Algeria and the Dual Image of the Intellectual," in *The Century of the Intellectual: From the Dreyfus Affair to the Rushdie Affair*, ed. J. Jennings and T. Kemp-Welch (London: Routledge, 1997). The controversy is also discussed in Patricia Geesey, "Exhumation and History: Tahar Djaout's Les Chercheurs d'os," *French Review* 70, no. 2 (December 1996): 278; Madeleine Dobie, "Francophone Studies and the Linguistic Diversity of the Maghreb," *Comparative Studies of South Asia, Africa and the Middle East* 23, no. 1–2 (2003): 35; and Cox, "The Novels," 95.

12. The common account of "Salafism"—as an orthodox Islamic philosophy dating back to the medieval period that promotes following the practices, interpretations, and exegetical writings of the first three generations of Muslims known as *al-salaf al-ṣāliḥ* or the pious predecessors—is a narrative that has recently come under critical investigation. Henri Lauzière's "The Construction of *Salafiyya*: Reconsidering Salafism from the Perspective of Conceptual History" (*International Journal of Middle East Studies* 42, no. 3 [2010]: 369–89) thoughtfully demystifies a number of presumptions and misconceptions about Salafism, by offering a conceptual history that situates the philosophy more concretely in the twentieth century, and specifically in relation to the marketing efforts of the Salafiyya press and bookstore established in Cairo in 1909.

13. Mālikīs represent one of four schools of orthodox *fiqh* in Sunni Islam along with the Ḥanafīs, Shāfiʿīs, and Ḥanbalīs. They believe that Islamic jurisprudence should be based on the Qurʾan and the sunna of the Prophet Muhammad—which is defined as including both hadith and the legal rulings of the Four Rightly Guided Caliphs—and the practices of the *salaf*.

14. For a history of Sufism in Algeria, particularly the prominent Rahmaniyyah *ṭarīqa* (order) of the nineteenth century, see Julia Clancy-Smith, *Rebel and Saint: Muslim Notables, Populist Protest, and Colonial Encounters (Algeria and Tunisia, 1800–1904)* (Berkeley: University of California Press, 1994), 138–68.

15. On the relationship between the reformist schools of the Maghrib and Mashriq, see Charles Kurzman, *Modernist Islam, 1840–1940: A Sourcebook* (Oxford: Oxford University Press, 2002), 93. It is worth noting that the Islamic modernists Muḥammad ʿAbdu and Jamāl al-Dīn al-Afghānī were also concerned with the intersection of science and Islam. Their conceptualization of modernity linked Western progress to early Islam, thereby reorienting the axis of modernity outside of a Eurocentric worldview. For more on the Islamic modernists, see Samira Haj, *Reconfiguring Islamic Tradition: Reform, Rationality, and Modernity* (Stanford: Stanford University Press, 2008); and Fazlur Rahman, *Islam and Modernity: Transformation of an Intellectual Tradition* (Chicago: University of Chicago Press, 1982), 49–51.

16. The French educational system in Algeria was highly centralized and administered largely by the Jesuit missionaries Pères Blancs and Soeurs Blanches. Arabic was marginalized in the domains of education, cultural production, as well as state bureaucracy, and its instruction largely fell under the jurisdiction of Islamic schools or madrasas. For more on the pedagogical practices of these Qurʾanic schools, see Leon Carl Brown, "The Islamic Reformist Movement in North Africa," *Journal of Modern African Studies* 2, no. 1 (1964): 59; and Kurzman, *Modernist Islam, 1840–1940: A Sourcebook*, 93. An overview of France's policies with respect to education and language policy is offered in Farid Aitsiselmi and Dawn Marley, "The Role and Status of the French Language in North Africa," in *Studies in French Applied Linguistics*, ed. Dalila Ayoun (Amsterdam: John Benjamins, 2008). The data they reference is from M. Benrabah, *Langue et pouvoir en Algérie: Histoire d'un traumatisme linguistique* (Paris: Séguire, 1999), 79.

17. This conforms to Waṭṭār's representation of Bū al-Arwāḥ as an unreliable narrator. Such archetypal figures are common in satirical Arabic literature of both the classical and modern period. David Fieni, for example, compares the "picaresque" Shaykh Bū al-Arwāḥ with Badīʿ al-Zamān al-Hamadhānī's ninth-century *maqāmāt* (Fieni, "Decadent Orientalisms: Configuring the Decay of Colonial Modernity in French and Arabic" [Ph.D. diss., University of California, Los Angeles, 2006], 116).

18. As Debbie Cox demonstrates, this also features prominently in Waṭṭār's earlier novel *Al-lāz*, where he hybridizes various registers of Arabic (Qurʾanic, vernacular, and Modern Standard) and resignifies Qurʾanic words to connote more secular, nationalist, or political meanings (*Politics, Language, and Gender in the Algerian Arabic Novel* [London: Edwin Mellon, 2002], 108).

19. This tradition is discussed extensively in Fathi El-Shihibi, "Travel Genre in Arabic Literature: A Selective Literary and Historical Study" (Ph.D. diss., Boston University, 1998. Boca Raton, Fla.: Dissertation.com, 2006); Nabil Matar, *In the Lands of the Christians: Arabic Travel Writing in the Seventeenth Century* (New York: Routledge, 2003); and Robin Ostle, Ed de Moor, and Stefan Wild, eds., *Writing the Self* (London: Saqi, 1998).

20. In his critical introduction to the English translation of the novel, William Granara observes: "The basic structure of the novel is the journey (*rihla*), a popular subgenre in Arabic literature in all its phases" (Granara, *Earthquake*, 18). This point is further discussed in Granara, "Mythologising the Algerian War of Independence: Tahir Wattar and the Contemporary Algerian Novel," *Journal of North African Studies* 4, no. 3 (Autumn 1999).

21. The French colonial restructuring of Algeria resonates with the "Hausmannization" of Paris in the 1860s. On the geospatial policies of French colonial urbanization, architecture, and city planning, see Zeynep Çelik, Julia Clancy-Smith, and Frances Terpak, eds., *Walls of Algiers: Narratives of the City through Text and Image* (Seattle: University of Washington Press, 2009).

22. The Arabic text reads:

الوجوه أيضاً تتميّز في قسنطينة. الملامح، تختلف من شخص لآخر، القامات كذلك. زمن الاستعمار، كانت الملامح عامة: أوروبية، وعربية. أما الآن، فلا. ملامح الشاوي الصاعد من أعين البيضاء (أو من أعين مليلة)، أو (باتنة)، أو (خنشلة)، أو (شلغوم العيد) . . . الملامح، كالروائح، تعلم عن نفسها بنفسها، بشكل صارخ في هذه المدينة.

(Waṭṭār, *Al-zilzāl*, 10–11).

23. The Arabic text reads:

لعل هذا هو تاريخ المدينة من يوم كانت. انتهت بانتهاء البربر وابتدأت بابتداء الرومان، وظلت تبتدئ وتنتهي بين البربر والرومان ومختلف الأجناس حتى جاء العرب. استأنفت تاريخها معهم حتى جاء الأتراك. انتهت وابتدأت، حتى جاء الفرنسيون. وها هي تنتهي وتبتدئ من جديد. إن الزلزال الذي يضع حداً لحياة هذه العاهرة لم يحدث بعد. وحين يحدث ينتقم من كل ماضيها الأسود الملطّخ.

(Waṭṭār, *Al-zilzāl*, 75–76).

24. The Arabic text reads:

ابن خلدون يخلد في النار على عبارته، فالعرب الذين جاؤوا بالدين الحنيف، لا يمكن أن يكونوا شعار لخراب الحياة . . . لكن ها هو الواقع يصدقه، فلم يقتصروا على تخريب الحياة فقط، وإنما انطلقوا إلى الدين أيضاً يخربونه.

- العربي يبني بيد ويخرب بأخرى.

[...] هؤلاء ليسوا عرباً. وليسوا بربراً، ولا حتى وندالاً أو تتاراً أو مغولاً أو أقباطاً. هؤلا إما أن يكونوا روساً سلّطهم الله على البلاد ليحطموا مقوماتها، وإما أن يكونوا بلا أصل ولا فصل ولا دين أو ملّة، فيوم كنا نعمل بدافع العروبة والدين، وبضمير العربي الحر، إلى جانب ابن باديس وأهل الفضل والعلم من صحابته وتلاميذه كنا نعمر ولا نخربن نعمر الألسنة بلغة الضاد، لغة القرآن الكريم، نعمر الأفئدة بالدين، بالحديث والسنّة، وما كان عليه السلف.

(Waṭṭār, *Al-zilzāl*, 33–34).

25. The Arabic text reads:

ملأى بالبضائع، وتختزن فيها ملايين الأطنان من المؤن، ومئات الآلاف من قوارير الغاز، وملايين الملايين من أطنان رصاص وإسمنت القنوات والمجاري [...]. من هذا العالم السفلي، حيث تناسب المياه، هاربة في كل قطرة من قطراتها، بذرة من طين وأكلاس الصخرة المسكينة.

(Waṭṭār, *Al-zilzāl*, 37).

26. The Arabic text reads:

الذهول، والهلع، وامتلاء النفس باللون الداكن، تلكم هي الحالة التي وصف بها تعالى، قيام الساعة، وهي حالة شاء تعالى أن يخصّ بها الزلزال الذي استعاره سبحانه للتعبير عن قيام الساعة.

(Waṭṭār, *Al-zilzāl*, 14–15)

27. The Arabic text reads:

اللون الداكن يتحرّك في القلب، بل المادة السائلة، تشرع في الذوبان. الحرارة ترتفع. الركبتان يسارع إليهما الوهن. العنق يودّ التلوي. الرأس فوقه ثقيل. الذراعان تصبحان عبئاً كبيراً على الكتفين.

(Waṭṭār, *Al-zilzāl*, 82–83).

28. While there are some discrepancies, most historians and scholars of Islam believe that the Prophet Muhammad was betrothed to ʿĀʾisha when she was six and he around fifty-three, although it is said that the marriage was not consummated until she was nine.

29. It is worth noting that the Prophet Muhammad's first wife, Khadīja, who was nearly twenty years his senior, was his first convert to Islam and used her social status and financial resources to help him promote the new religion. Furthermore, Muhammad's closest companions, the four caliphs who followed him, were all bound to the Prophet through marriages: Abū Bakr and ʿUmar were his fathers-in-law, while his daughters married ʿAlī and ʿUthmān. This demonstrates the significance of marital bonds for the propagation of Islam in its early history.

30. Some accounts of the Prophet Muhammad's life claim that he told his followers to take half of their religion from ʿĀʾisha, although this is contested by conservative exegetical schools. For more detailed discussions of the life of ʿĀʾisha and her place within various discursive, exegetical, and historiographical traditions, see Nadia Abbott, *Aishah the Beloved of Mohammed* (Chicago: University of Chicago Press, 1942); miriam cooke, "Women, Religion, and the Postcolonial Arab World," *Cultural Critique*, no. 45 (Spring 2000): 150–84;

and Hoda Elsadda, "Discourses on Women's Biographies and Cultural Identity: Twentieth-Century Representations of the Life of ʿA'isha Bint Abi Bakr," *Feminist Studies* 27, no. 1 (Spring 2001): 37–64.

31. As the daughter of the Prophet's companion Abū Bakr and an opponent of ʿAlī ibn Abī Ṭālib's claim to the caliphate, ʿĀ'isha is rather critically represented in much Shiʿa religious scholarship. The above-cited sources elaborate on this issue.

32. My reading of Waṭṭār's novel recalls the works of the Moroccan feminist Fatima Mernissi and the Algerian novelist Assia Djebar, to whom I turn shortly. Their texts actively read female agency back into hegemonic historical narratives, particularly with respect to early Islamic history, the colonial encounter, and anti-imperial revolutionary activities (see Fatima Mernissi, *Women's Rebellion* [London: Zed, 1996]; and Mernissi, *Forgotten Queens* [Minneapolis: University of Minnesota Press, 1993]; as well as Assia Djebar, *Loin de Médine* [Paris: Albin Michel, 1991]; and Djebar, *L'amour, la fantasia* [Paris: Jean-Claude Lattes, 1985]).

33. The temporal and spatial ruination that marks the city of Constantine resonates with Ann Laura Stoler's theorization of the unique historicity of imperial formations (see Stoler, "Imperial Debris: Reflections on Ruins and Ruination," *Cultural Anthropology* 23, no. 2 [May 2008]: 191–219).

34. Allegory then functions, in the words of Gil Hochberg, as a "form of representation that contains a representational crisis: it connects the 'personal story' with the 'public (national) story' but at the same time it shows the link between the two stories to be a type of illusionary link, one that is 'too much of a link'" ("National Allegories and the Emergence of Female Voice in Moufida Tlatli's *Les silences du palais*," *Third Text* 14, no. 50 [Spring 2000]: 39). Hochberg's analysis offers a productive reworking of the debate between Fredric Jameson and Aijaz Ahmad over the question of national allegory.

CHAPTER 4

1. All English citations from *L'amour, la fantasia* and *Loin de Médine* reference the published Dorothy S. Blair English editions. Where indicated, I have made modifications to her translation to preserve certain nuances in the French. Parenthetical citations that reference both editions feature the English page number(s) followed by the French. Unless otherwise noted, all other translations are my own.

Epigraph: L'Afrique du Nord, du temps de l'Empire français,—comme le reste de l'Afrique de la part de ses coloniaux anglais, portugais ou belges—a subi, un siècle et demi durant, dépossession de ses richesses naturelles, déstructuration de ses assises sociales, et, pour l'Algérie, exclusion dans l'enseignement de ses deux langues identitaires, le berbère séculaire, et la langue arabe dont la qualité poétique ne pouvait alors, pour moi, être perçue que dans les versets coraniques qui me restent chers. . . . En ce sens, le monolinguisme français, institué en Algérie coloniale, tendant à dévaluer nos langues maternelles, nous poussa encore davantage à la quête des origines.

Académie française: The oldest of the five *académies* of the Institut de France, the Académie française is the governing body in France on all issues pertaining to the French language. The description of the *immortels* highlights the sacred position of the French language: "The Académie française . . . brings together poets, novelists, men of the theater, philosophers, doctors, scientists, anthropologists, art critics, soldiers, statesmen and men of the Church—all of whom have particularly highlighted the French language. In its diverse constitution, it offers an accurate image of the talent, intelligence, culture, imagination, literature and science underlying the genius of France. . . . Their moral authority with respects to language is rooted in customs, traditions and splendor. . . . The election to the French Academy is often viewed by the public as a supreme consecration (Académie française, n.p.).

2. Apuleius, or Apulée in French (125–180), was a Latin novelist, writer, and public intellectual of Amazigh descent from present-day Algeria. A prominent figure of Latin Christianity and Western theology, Tertullianus, or Tertullien in French (160–225), was a prolific writer from Roman Carthage. Similarly, St. Augustine, or Augustin in French (358–430), was a theologian and philosopher born in Roman Africa (present-day Algeria). Speculated to be of Amazigh descent, St. Augustine converted to Christianity, which was the religion of his mother.

3. On *le mythe Kabyle*, see James McDougall, "Myth and Counter-Myth: 'The Berber' as National Signifier in Algerian Historiographies," *Radical History Review*, no. 86 (Spring 2003): 67; and Mohand Tilmatine, "French and Spanish Colonial Policy in North Africa: Revisiting the Kabyle and Berber Myth," *International Journal of the Sociology of Language*, no. 239 (May 2016): 95–119. On the literary revival of Roman Africa by "Latinists," see Mohamed-Salah Omri, "History, Literature, and Settler Colonialism in North Africa," *Modern Language Quarterly* 66, no. 3 (September 2015): 273–98.

4. Djebar was also the first Algerian woman to be accepted into the elite École Normale Supérieure in Paris.

5. The majority of literary criticism on *L'amour, la fantasia* approaches the novel through feminist politics (Gafaiti, Gauch, Murdoch, Orlando, Ringrose, and Steadman), questions of selfhood and identity (Mortimer, Murray, and Zimra), or the relationship between language, (post)colonialism, and exile (Bensmaïa, Calle-Gruber, Donadey, Gracki, Hiddleston, Hochberg, Lionnet, N. Rahman, Siassi, Tageldin, Thiel, Walker, and Zimra). Few scholars have focused on the question of Islam in the novel (Erickson, Wehr, and Ouedghiri).

6. It is said that Djebar was trying to transition to writing fiction in Arabic during her hiatus but was unable to gain sufficient proficiency to do so.

7. On the film's formal innovations, see Réda Bensmaïa, "La nouba des femmes du Mont Chenoua: Introduction to the Cinematic Fragment," *World Literature Today* 70, no. 4 (Autumn 1996): 877–84.

8. The interviews were conducted in Djebar's native region of Cherchell during the 1970s.

9. The footnote is omitted from Blair's translation.

10. The word Islam derives from the Arabic root *s-l-m*, whose diverse meanings range from: to surrender, submit, be safe, rescue, protect from harm, salute, accept or commit (*Al-mawrid: Arabic-English, English-Arabic Dictionary* [Beirut: al-ʿIlm li-l-Malāyīn, 2007], 641).

11. As Djebar was writing *L'amour, la fantasia*, tensions surrounding the ethnolinguistic and religious homogenization of Algeria were percolating but had not quite escalated to the violence that plagued the 1990s. She examines this subject in depth in her later novel *Le blanc de l'Algerie*. An experimental memoir, the book is a tribute to the hundreds of Berberophone and Francophone intellectuals whose lives were taken in the 1990s.

12. Abraham's dream is referenced in Qur'an 37:102–11. Muslims generally believe the son in the parable to be Ishmael, as opposed to Isaac in Christianity and Judaism.

13. *La prise de l'Imprenable . . . Images érodées, délitées de la roche du Temps. Des lettres de mots français se profilent, allongées ou élargies dans leur étrangeté, contre les parois des cavernes, dans l'aura des flammes d'incendies successifs, tatouant les visages disparus de diaprures rougeoyantes . . . Et l'inscription du texte étranger se renverse dans le miroir de la souffrance, me proposant son double évanescent en lettres arabes, de droite à gauche redévidées; elles se délavent ensuite en dessins d'un Hoggar préhistorique . . . Pour lire cet écrit, il me faut renverser mon corps, plonger ma face dans l'ombre, scruter la voûte de rocailles ou de craie, laisser les chuchotements immémoriaux remonter, géologie sanguinolente. Quel magma de sons pourrit là, quelle odeur de putréfaction s'en échappe? Je tâtonne, mon odorat troublé, mes oreilles ouvertes en huîtres, dans la crue de la douleur ancienne. Seule dépouillée, sans voile, je fais face aux images du noir. . . . Hors de puits des siècles d'hier, comment affronter les sons du passé?. . . Quel amour se cherche, quel avenir s'esquisse malgré l'appel des morts, et mon corps tintinnabule de long éboulement des générations-aïeules* (Djebar, *L'amour, la fantasia*, 69).

14. This point is explored in much of the criticism on *L'amour, la fantasia* informed by feminist theory (see Lindsey Moore, *Arab Muslim, Woman: Voice and Vision in Postcolonial Literature and Film* [New York: Routledge, 2008], 66–68).

15. Like many of the region's indigenous inhabitants, the nomadic Berberophone Touareg were largely Islamicized in the seventh century. As the

French occupation extended into the central Sahara in the nineteenth century, a number of violent clashes with the Touareg, particularly those in Ahaggar, resulted in the gradual annexing of their territories. The veiling of Touareg men and their matriarchal social structure may serve as an intentional contrast to the novel's frequent references to the veiling of Muslim women. Djebar's description of herself in the passage as "*sans voile*" supports this reading. On the Touareg, see James McDougall, *History and the Culture of Nationalism in Algeria* (Cambridge: Cambridge University Press, 2006), 186–88.

16. See Mohammad Abdullah Enan, *Ibn Khaldun: His Life and Works* (Kuala Lumpur: The Other Press, 2007). Scholars have further demonstrated the appropriation of Ibn Khaldūn in orientalist historiography. Abdelmajid Hannoum, for example, offers a structuralist reading of the translation and transmission of Ibn Khaldūn's work in relation to French colonial ideology in the Maghreb (Hannoum, "Translation and the Colonial Imaginary: Ibn Khaldûn Orientalist," *History and Theory* 42, no. 1 [February 2003]: 61–81).

17. Cortège d'autres invasions, d'autres occupations. . . . Peu après le tournant fatal que représente la saignée à blanc de la dévastation hilalienne, Ibn Khaldoun, de la même stature qu'Augustin, termine une vie d'aventures et de méditation par la rédaction de son autobiographie. Il l'intitule "Ta'arif", c'est à dire "Identité". Comme Augustin, peu lui importe qu'il écrive, lui, l'auteur novateur de "l'Histoire des Berbères", une langue installée sur la terre ancestrale dans des effusions de sang! Langue imposée dans le viol autant que dans l'amour (Djebar, *L'amour, la fantasia*, 301).

18. Car il s'agit bien d'un 'retour' à la langue écrite . . . la culture arabe repose sur l'enseignement (et donc l'écriture lue et recopiée) du Livre; alors qu'au Maghreb, il y a une des plus anciennes cultures écrites, avec les femmes comme détentrices privilégiées de l'écriture, l'alphabet tamazigh des Touaregs (originally cited in Jeanne-Marie Clerc, *Assia Djebar: Écrire, transgresser, resister* [Paris: L'Harmattan, 1997], 65).

19. Je compris plus tard que j'avais, au village, participé à la fin d'un enseignement séculaire, populaire. A la ville, grâce à un mouvement nationaliste de 'musulmans modernistes', se forgeait une jeunesse nouvelle, de culture arabe. Ces medersas ont pullulé depuis. Si j'avais fréquenté l'une d'elles . . . j'aurais trouvé naturel ensuite d'enturbanner ma tête, de cacher me chevelure, de couvrir mes bras et mes mollets, bref de mouvoir mon corps au-dehors comme une nonne musulmane! (Djebar, *L'amour, la fantasia*, 258).

20. Djebar uses the French term *cloîtrées*, or cloistered, to describe the practice of shielding women from the gaze of unrelated males by sequestering them in a domestic space reserved for women, often referred to as a harem.

21. This is exacerbated by the implicit orientalism of the novel's collective representation of veiled women living in the harem. In the second installa-

tion of the quartet, *Ombre sultane* [A sister to Sheherazade, 1987], for example, Djebar contrasts the gendered subjectivity of two Algerian women—the "liberated" Isma and the "cloistered" Hajila—by employing alternating first- and second-person narratives. Eventually, Isma facilitates Hajila's escape from the prison-like harem and her journey toward "freedom."

22. Tandis que l'homme continue à avoir droit à quatre épouses légitimes, nous disposons de quatre langues pour exprimer notre désir, avant d'ahaner: le français pour l'écriture secrète, l'arabe pour nos soupirs vers Dieu étouffés, le libyco-berbère quand nous imaginons retrouver les plus anciennes de nos idoles mères. La quatrième langue, pour toutes, jeune ou vieilles, cloîtrées ou à demi émancipées, demeure celle du corps (Djebar, *L'amour, la fantasia*, 254).

23. Après plus d'un siècle d'occupation française—qui finit, il y a peu, par un écharnement—, un territoire de langue subsiste entre deux peuples, entre deux mémoires; la langue française, corps et voix, s'installé en moi comme un orgueilleux préside, tandis que la langue maternelle, toute en oralité, en hardes dépenaillées, résiste et attaque, entre deux essoufflements. Le rythme du "rebato" en moi s'éperonnant, je suis à la fois l'assiégé étranger et l'autochtone partant à la mort par bravade, illusoire effervescence du dire et de l'écrit (Djebar, *L'amour, la fantasia*, 299–300).

24. "Elle lit," c'est à dire, en langue arabe, "elle étudie". Maintenant je me dis que ce verbe "lire" ne fut pas par hazard l'ordre lancé par l'archange Gabriel, dans la grotte, pour la révélation coranique . . . "Elle lit", autant dire que l'écriture à lire, y compris celle des mécréants, est toujours source de révélation: de la mobilité du corps dans mon cas et donc de ma future liberté (Djebar, *L'amour, la fantasia*, 254).

25. J'interviens pour saleur le peinture qui, au long de mon vagabondage, m'a accompagnée en seconde silhouette paternelle. Eugène Fromentin me tend une main inattendue, celle d'une inconnue qu'il n'a jamais pu dessiner [. . .]. Plus tard, je me saisis de cette main vivante, main de la mutilation et du souvenir et je tente de lui faire porter le "qalam" (Djebar, *L'amour, la fantasia*, 313).

26. The sura continues:

اقْرَأْ وَرَبُّكَ الْأَكْرَمُ {٣}
الَّذِي عَلَّمَ بِالْقَلَمِ {٤}
عَلَّمَ الْإِنْسَانَ مَا لَمْ يَعْلَمْ {٥}

Read—for they Sustainer is the Most Bountiful One
who has taught [man] the use of the pen
—taught man what he did not know!
"Al-ʿalaq" ("The Germ-Cell" or "The Clot") (Qur'an 96:3–5 trans. Asad)

27. Effacer la tablette, c'était comme si, après coup, l'on ingérait une portion du texte coranique. L'écrit ne pouvait continuer à se dévider devant nous, lui-même copie d'un écrit censé immuable, qu'en s'étayant, pause après pause, sur cette absorption. . . . Cette langue que j'apprends nécessite un corps en posture, une mémoire qui y prend appui. La main enfantine, comme dans un entraînement sportif, se met, par volonté quasi adulte, à inscrire. "Lis!" Les doigts œuvrant sur la planche renvoient les signes au corps, à la fois lecteur et serviteur (Djebar, *L'amour, la fantasia*, 260).

CHAPTER 5

1. All English citations from *Le passé simple* reference the published Hugh A. Harter English edition (Washington, D.C.: Three Continents, 1990). Where indicated, I have made modifications to his translations to preserve certain nuances in the French. Parenthetical citations that reference both editions feature the English page number(s) followed by the French. Unless otherwise noted, all other translations are my own.

Epigraph: S'il n'y avait eu *que* le Protectorat et le colonialisme, tout eût été simple. C'est du coup que mon passé, notre passé eût été simple. Non, monsieur Sartre, l'enfer ce n'est pas les autres. Il est aussi en nous-mêmes.

2. On the reception of the novel, see Kadra-Hadjadji, *Contestation et révolte dans l'oeuvre de Driss Chraïbi* (Algiers: E.N.A.L., 1986), 53–64.

3. The Moroccan cultural journal *Souffles-Anfas* (1966–1971) was run by Abdellatif Laâbi and a small collective of Marxist-Leninist intellectuals spread across Paris and Morocco. Published in corresponding French and Arabic editions, *Souffles-Anfas* (Breaths) sought to bring national issues into dialogue with broader debates on decolonization and globalization. Due to its incendiary political content, Laâbi was arrested, tortured, and sentenced to a ten-year prison term. He was then exiled to France for "crimes of opinion."

4. Chraïbi is rewriting the famous line from Sartre's 1944 existentialist play *Huis clos* (translated as *No Exit*): "*L'enfer, c'est les autres*" (Hell is other people).

5. The "1952 Generation" references a group of Francophone writers from the Maghreb publishing in the 1950s. Many of these authors, particularly Chraïbi, were criticized for their alleged neglect of nationalist and anticolonialist concerns. Other works of this generation include Mouloud Feraoun's *Le fils de pauvre* (Algeria, 1954); Mohammed Dib's *La grande maison* (Algeria, 1952); Mouloud Mammeri's *La colline oubliée* (Algeria, 1952); Albert Memmi's *La statue de sel* (Tunisia, 1953); Ahmed Sefrioui's *La boîte à merveilles* (Morocco, 1954); Kateb Yacine's *Nedjma* (Algeria, 1956); and Malek Haddad's *Je t'offrirai une gazelle* (Algeria, 1959).

6. Le temps privilégié du récit, le seul apte à construire une chronologie événementielle (http://www.etudes-litteraires.com/indicatif-passe-simple.php).

7. A *ṭarīqa* is a Sufi school or order led by a spiritual guide, or *murshid*, who oversees members who are referred to as either *murīds* (those desiring God's knowledge) or *faqīrs* (those in need of God's knowledge from the root *f-q-r* or poverty).

8. Similar views were expressed in a number of right-wing French publications such as *Rivarol* (February 17, 1955).

9. The PDI was created in the 1940s under the name Ḥizb al-Istiqlāl (Independence Party).

10. Non content d'avoir d'un trait de plume insulté son père et sa mère, craché sur toutes les traditions nationales, y compris la religion dont il se réclame aujourd'hui, M. Chraïbi s'attaque maintenant au problèm marocain. Au nom d'un Islam qu'il a bafoué, au nom d'un intérêt soudain pour une cause qui n'a jamais été la sienne. . . . Ce judas de la pensée marocaine n'éprouve jamais le besoin de parler des valeurs de son peuple. Dénigreur passionné, il préfère s'accrocher aux valeurs des autres qui pourtant ne sont valables pour nous que dans la mesure oú nous respectons et aimons les nôtres.

11. Il n'a pas fait un bilan sociologique de l'ordre colonial, par contre, il a peut-être démontré les causes tangibles qui approfondissaient et nourissaient la colonisation. En ce sens, il est vraisemblablement le seul écrivain maghrébin qui ait eu le courage de mettre tout un peuple devant ses lâchetés, qui lui ait étalé son immobilisme, les ressorts de son hypocrisie, de cette auto-colonisation et oppression exercée les uns sur les autres, le féodal sur l'ouvrier agricole, le père sur ses enfants. Le mari sur son épouse-objet, le patron libidineux sur son apprenti.

12. Much of the critical literature on *Le passé simple* is delimited by an overemphasis on the autobiographical elements of the novel (see Isaac Yetiv, *La thème de l'aliénation dans le roman maghrébin d'expression française: 1952–1956* [Sherbrooke: CELEF, 1972]; and Lia Brozgal *Against Autobiography: Albert Memmi and the Production of Theory* [Lincoln: University of Nebraska, 2013]). Muḥammad Barrāda writes that the novel is an autobiography, in which Chraïbi observes his "society as if from outside" ("The New Cultural and Imaginative Discourse in Morocco: Utopic Change," in *Contemporary North Africa: Issues of Development and Integration*, ed. Halim Barakat [London: Croom Helm, 1985], 233).

13. Laïla Ibnlfassi, for example, employs a Lacanian framework to analyze the novel, arguing that the father, mother, and brother Hamid all function as psychic placeholders for the character and author Driss. Hédi Abdel-Jaouad, on the other hand, posits that patricidal fantasies and the desire to emancipate the mother in Maghrebi fiction "is founded essentially on the ruins of castrating Maghrebian patriarchy" (15). He further argues that by consecrating the mother in written form, these "son-writers" privilege oral-

ity, or *parole*, over the written word, or *langue*. An exception in this regard is Jarrod Hayes, who offers a queer reading that addresses the novel's often-neglected homoerotic references in relation to broader questions of national politics (see Charles Bonn and Yves Baumstimler, *Psychanalyse et texte littéraire au Maghreb* [Paris: L'Harmattan, 1992]; Läila Ibnlfassi, "Chraïbi's *Le passé simple* and a Theory of Doubles," in *African Francophone Writing: A Critical Introduction*, ed. Ibnlfassi and Nicki Hitchcott [Oxford: Berg, 1996]; Hédi Abdel-Jaouad, "'Too Much in the Sun': Sons, Mothers, and Impossible Alliances in Francophone Maghrebian Writing," *Research in African Literatures* 27, no. 3 [Autumn 1996]: 15–33; as well as Jarrod Hayes's *Queer Nations: Marginal Sexualities in the Maghreb* [Chicago: University of Chicago Press, 2000], 81–82, 263–64; and "Rachid O. and the Return of the Homopast: The Autobiographical as Allegory in Childhood Narratives by Maghrebian Men," *Sites: The Journal of Twentieth-Century/Contemporary French Studies Revue d'études français* 1, no. 2 [1997]: 497–526).

14. Ellen McLarney posits that the Oedipal overtones of the novel function "symbolically to portray political tensions within the 'family' of the Moroccan nation, with the 'father' as king," with Driss's patricidal fantasies serving as a call to regicide against the Moroccan monarchy (McLarney, "Politics of *Le passé simple*," *Journal of North African Literature* 8, no. 2 [Summer 2003]: 2).

15. While a number of critics (particularly at the time of the novel's release) focused more broadly on *Le passé simple*'s "negative" representation of Islam, recent scholarship has paid little attention to this question. Carine Bourget and Houaria Kadra-Hadjadji deal predominantly with the broader politics of Islam in Chraïbi's oeuvre rather than his thematic and textual engagement with the Qur'an and hadith.

16. From the Arabic *shurafa'*, the term denotes descendants of the Prophet Muhammad. The first Sherifian dynasty in Morocco was established by Idris Ibn ʿAbdallah (788–793), followed by his son Idris II (793–828). Responsible for the Arabization of Northern Morocco, the dynasty ruled the Western Maghreb until 985. Their power was legitimized by the lineage of Idris I, who claimed descendance from the Prophet through ʿAli ibn Abi Talib and his wife Fatima (see C. R. Pennell, *Morocco since 1830 A History* [New York: New York University Press, 2000]; Mohamed El Mansour, "The Sanctuary [*Hurm*] in Precolonial Morocco," in *In the Shadow of the Sultan: Culture, Power, and Politics*, ed. Rahma Bourqia and Susan Gilson Miller, 49–73 [Cambridge: Harvard University Press, 1999]; and Rahma Bourqia, "The Cultural Legacy of Power in Morocco," ibid., 243–58).

17. For a detailed analysis of the trilogy, see Jacqueline Kaye and Abdelhamid Zoubir, *The Ambiguous Compromise: Language, Literature and National Identity in Algeria and Morocco* (London: Routledge, 1990).

18. Yusuf Ali's translation uses the image of thread: "and seek what Allah Hath ordained for you, and eat and drink, until the white thread of dawn appear to you distinct from its black thread; then complete your fast Till the night appears." (Qurʾan 2:187 trans. Ali)

19. The sura "Al-naḥl" ["The Bee"] reads:

إِنَّ إِبْرَاهِيمَ كَانَ أُمَّةً قَانِتًا لِلَّهِ حَنِيفًا وَلَمْ يَكُ مِنَ الْمُشْرِكِينَ {٠٢١}
شَاكِرًا لِّأَنْعُمِهِ اجْتَبَاهُ وَهَدَاهُ إِلَى صِرَاطٍ مُّسْتَقِيمٍ {١٢١}

Verily, Abraham was a man who combined within himself all virtues, devoutly obeying God's will, turning away from all that is false, and not being of those who ascribe divinity to aught beside God: [for he was always] grateful for the blessings granted by Him who had elected him and guided him onto a straight way. (Qurʾan 16:120–21 trans. Asad).

20. The Qur'an lists the following figures as Abraham's progeny: David, Solomon, Job, Joseph, Moses, Aaron, Zachariah, John, Jesus, Elijah, Ishmael, Elisha, Jonah and Lot (6:83–87).

21. Vous faites vos cinq prières par jour et votre chapelet pèse un kilogramme. Tout le monde vous respecte. Vous avez une barbe de patriarche. Vous êtes un homme de Dieu. . . . Vous êtes saint. Descendant direct du Prophète. . . . Bien dissimulés dans ce carré de feutre pieux, *il y a cent grammes de kif*. Le spirituel et le temporel en mêmes temps, n'est pas? C'est la vie. Dieu est grand! (Chraïbi, *Le passé simple*, 165).

22. The Lycée Lyautey in Casablanca that Driss Ferdi attends in the novel is the same school where Chraïbi studied. Founded by Louis Hubert Gonzalve Lyautey (1854–1934), the *lycée* was the most elite educational institution under the Moroccan Protectorate. A French army general and the first resident-general in Morocco (1912–1925), Lyautey was concerned with the cultivation of an indigenous elite. In fact, Chraïbi was one of three Muslim Moroccan students to attend the school at the time (see Nicholas Harrison, "Representativity [with reference to Chraïbi]," *Paragraph* 24, no. 3 [November 2001]: 35; and McLarney, "Politics of *Le passé simple*," 7).

23. For references to Le Seigneur's dogma, see Chraïbi, *Le passé simple*, 17, 22.

24. Notre rôle de père est un rôle de guide. Apprends tout ce que tu peux et le mieux possible, afin que tout ce que tu auras appris te soit une arme utile pour tes examens d'abord et pour la compréhension du monde occidental ensuite. Car nous avons besoin d'une jeunesse capable d'être entre notre léthargie orientale et l'insomnie occidentale, capable aussi d'assimiler la science actuelle et de l'enseigner à nos futures generations. Mais ne te laisse jamais tenter par ce que tu auras appris, par ces mirages dont jusqu'ici tu n'as jamais entendu parler

et qui te paraîtraient suffisants pour les considérer comme dogmes. N'oublie pas en effet que toute la civilisation actuelle repose sur des postulats (Chraïbi, *Le passé simple*, 23).

25. The "Makhzen" is a rather complex term with highly specific resonances in Moroccan history. In the simplest of terms, it refers to the centralized power of the sultanate, or state. Etymologically, the Arabic word means a warehouse or storeroom, hence McLarney's apt comparison to the *grenier* in *Le passé simple*. The term's use in Morocco predates the Protectorate and has become synonymous with both the abstract and hegemonic power of the state, as well as the material resources that it provides its citizens. For a discussion of the politics of the term "Makhzen" in relation to the concepts of *Dār al-mulk* and *Dawla* respectively, see Abdellah Hammoudi, "The Reinvention of *Dar al-mulk*: The Moroccan Political System and Its Legitimation," in *In the Shadow of the Sultan: Culture, Power and Politics in Morocco*, ed. Rahma Bourqia and Susan Gilson Miller, 129–75 (Cambridge: Harvard University Press, 1999); and Rahma Bourqia, "The Cultural Legacy of Power in Morocco," 243–58.

26. Thami El Glaoui and ʿAbd al-Ḥayy al-Kitānī created a petition in March 1953 with more than three hundred signatories that "demanded the abdication of the Sultan for 'unorthodox religious practices'" (see Egya N. Sangmuah, "Sultan Ben Youssef's American Strategy and the Diplomacy of North African Liberation, 1943–61," *Journal of Contemporary History* 27, no. 1 [January 1992]: 138; Amal Vinogradov and John Waterbury, "Situations of Contested Legitimacy in Morocco: An Alternative Framework," *Comparative Studies in Society and History* 13, no.1 [January 1971]: 53; and Jamil M. Abun-Nasr, *A History of the Maghreb* [Cambridge: Cambridge University Press, 1987], 391–92). El Glaoui is referenced in *The Simple Past*, 30 and 73.

27. From *murābiṭ* (one who is garrisoned/attached), a *marabout* can be a Qurʾanic teacher or scholar, a Sufi guide, or saint.

28. Driss declares, "*je suis actif*" in response to Si Kettani's sexual proposal (Chraïbi, *Le passé simple*, 95).

29. This harkens to the "*Droit de Seigneur*" discussed earlier.

30. Un matin vous vous êtes togé dans un drap presque blanc et vous êtes allé de porte en porte, de carrefour en carrefour, du mosquée en mosquée, hurlant que vous aviez vu en songe le Prophète discuter de la situation mondiale avec Franklin Delano Roosevelt. On vous a donné une zaouïa où vous vous êtes retiré précipitamment et une pension substantielle que vous avez acceptée avec le dédain des vanités de ce monde. Par la suite, vous avez eu d'autres rêves que l'on s'empressa de bénir par autant de dons concrets, notamment une charge de jurisconsulte et une Cadillac. Le Résidence vous nomma conseiller général du Makhzen et le Tout-Fès voulut vous avoir pour hôte (Chraïbi, *Le passé simple*, 87).

31. A *zāwiya* is a Sufi lodge or school of instruction.

32. The passage seems to reference the political and economic ties of the United States with the French Protectorate. There are also references to the U.S. presence in Morocco during World War II and the capitalist manipulation of the economy through the dumping of confiscated tea on the market (53).

33. Pandolfo adds that *la ligne mince* functions as a "classificatory boundary between East and West, black and white, tradition and modernity" that "materializes the fracture at the core of Driss's identity" in the traumatic image of a wound or cut (Pandolfo, "The Thin Line of Modernity," 120–21).

34. *Ligne Mince*, *Ligne Mince*, je t'appelle comme un enfant insomniaque appellerait une berceuse maternelle. . . . Et c'est la *Ligne Mince* par quoi j'échappe. Elle est tombée dans cette chambre comme un flash. Seigneur, regardez votre pantin. Derrière mes paupières closes désespérément dans ma tension de trouver le sommeil, c'est d'abord comme un fil de toile d'araignée, un fil si mince, si impalpable qu'il en est irréel. Ce fil est une lettre, un chiffre ou une ligne brisée. Il ne bouge pas, mais je le vois grossir, oh! si lentement, si doucement, si imperceptiblement au début. Et, en se précisant, en grossissant, lettre, ligne brisée ou chiffre devient matériel et bouge, pendule, danse de plus en plus vite. Et la *Ligne Mince* devient aussi épaisse que le doigt, plus grosse que le bras, prend l'allure d'un piston de moteur, d'une hélice d'avion, d'une trajectoire de fusée, devient aussi énorme qu'une montagne, toujours avec sa forme de chiffre, de lettre ou de ligne brisée. Et à mesure que la vitesse et la grosseur de la *Ligne* atteignent le paroxysme, sa matérialité devenue visible et palpable acquiert une sorte de son, d'abord sourd, puis de plus en plus net, puis pareil à un sifflement de balle, puis aussi précis, fort, violent, cataracteux que le bruit d'une roue d'auto sur une route goudronnée, sur un chemin pavé, sur une route rocailleuse, pour être en fin de compte une gigantesque clameur d'un train en marche. Et tout cela est derrière mes paupières closes désespérément dans ma tension de trouver le sommeil, dedans mes yeux injectés d'épouvante, dans mon cerveau tout entier assourdi par ce tintamarre, écrasé par ce poids, haché par cette vitesse. Puis la gamme des bruits descend d'un ton, puis d'un autre, d'un autre encore; la vitesse diminue; la montagne devient bloc, le bloc poutre, letter ou chiffre, derrière mes paupières closes désespérément dans ma tension de trouver le sommeil, n'est plus qu'une *Ligne Mince* sans sonorité ni mouvement, pareille à un fil de toile d'araignée, un fil si mince, si impalpable qu'il en est irréel (Chraïbi, *Le passé simple*, 63–65).

35. Elle me dit: tu es un nègre. Tu es un nègre depuis des générations croisé de blanc. Tu es en passe *de franchir la ligne*. De perdre ta dernière goutte de sang authentiquement nègre. Ton angle facial s'est ouvert et tu n'es plus crépu, plus lippu. Tu as été issu de l'Orient et, de par ton passé douloureux,

tes imaginations, ton instruction, tu vas triompher de l'Orient. Tu n'as jamais cru en Allah, tu sais disséquer les légends, tu penses en français, tu es lecteur de Voltaire et admirateur de Kant. Seulement le monde occidental pour lequel tu es destiné te paraît semé de bêtises et de laideurs, à peu de chose près les mêmes laideurs et les mêmes bêtises que tu fuis. De plus, tu le pressens hostile, il ne va pas t'accepter d'emblée. Et . . . tu as des reculs. Voilà pourquoi je t'apparais. Depuis le premier jour où je te suis apparue, tu n'es rien d'autre qu'une plaie (Chraïbi, *Le passé simple*, 105–6).

36. There are different combinations of letters known as *Muqaṭṭaʿāt*, meaning shortened or abbreviated, that open twenty-eight different suras in the Qurʾan. The main theories on their meaning are that the letters are an abbreviation for entire sentences, symbols for God, or the Prophet Muhammad; others posit that they are a means of calling attention to the Prophet during his revelations; and finally, a more controversial reading proposes that they indicate the initials of various scribes who transcribed the Qurʾan under the supervision of the Prophet. For an in-depth discussion of the *Muqaṭṭaʿāt*, see Qurʾan trans. Asad 1133–34.

37. Mon Dieu oui, vous parlez juste. Voyez, je vous accepte encore . . . et, même lorsque vous tonnez vos malédictions ou nous détaillez les châtiments du Jugement dernier, vous vous exprimez par rythmes incantatoires. Voyez, mon Dieu: Haj Fatmi Ferdi m'a appris à vous aimer—dans la peur du corps et la désolation de l'âme. Il a appliqué votre loi, une femme qu'il a torturée, si bien torturée, grave, ponctuel, digne, que, cette torture en moins, elle tomberait en poussière; des fils qu'il lie, ligote, taille, écrase, le devoir et l'honneur dit-il . . . je vous aime encore pourtant. Alors—quoique de vous à moi, de vous qui déterminez à moi le déterminé, une prière soit inutile—faites que je vous aime encore longtemps. Ces versets que je psalmodie dans votre maison et dans les oreilles de vos fidèles, je les dis . . . parce que vous devez être autre chose que l'Allah des m'sids et des entraves. Je vous répète que je suis entravé (Chraïbi, *Le passé simple*, 107).

38. Le héros du *Passé simple* s'appelle Driss Ferdi. C'est peut-être moi. En tout cas, son désespoir est le mien. Désespoir d'une foi. Cet Islam en quoi il croyait, qui parlait d'égalité des règnes, de la part de Dieu en chaque individu de la creation, de tolérance, de liberté et d'amour, il le voyait adolescent ardent formé dans les écoles françaises, réduit au pharisaïsme, système social et arme de propagande. A tout prendre, il s'embarquait pour la France: il avait besoin de croire, d'aimer, de respecter quelqu'un ou quelque chose [. . .]. Choisir? J'ai déjà choisi mais je voudrais tellement n'avoir plus à le faire. Car, si j'ai choisi vivre en France—et peut-être d'y mourir, mais cela dépend pas de moi—je continue à participer à ce monde de mon enfance et à cet Islam en lequel je crois de plus en plus.

39. Le sujet est "Liberté, Egalité, Fraternité." Je ne suis pas pleinement qualifié pour en parler. Par contre, je puis aisément lui substituer un sujet de remplacement et qui m'est autrement familier: "La théocratie musulmane." Usant de tel théorèm des triangles semblables, je présume que le résultat sera le même, à peu de chose près (Chraïbi, *Le passé simple*, 208).

CHAPTER 6

1. Citations to *Luʿbat al-nisyān* reference Issa J. Boullata's translation. Where indicated, I have made modifications to his translation to preserve certain nuances in the Arabic. Parenthetical citations that reference both editions feature the English page number(s) followed by the Arabic. Unless otherwise noted, all other translations are my own.

2. Barrāda briefly studied at the Sorbonne in Paris from 1970 to 1973.

3. A number of Barrāda's critical works were published in Cairo, and he regularly attended Pan-Arabist conferences, such as the October 1961 Rome conference "Al-adab al-ʿarabī al-muʿasir" [Contemporary Arabic literature].

4. Other variations include heterologic (*raznorechivoe*) and heterological (*raznorechivyi*).

5. Among his many examples of speech genres, Bakhtin lists militaristic speech, scientific statements, rhetorical speech (both political and judicial), as well as everyday speech. Each distinct sphere follows its own "lexical, phraseological, and grammatical resources of the language," while adhering to "the national unity of language" (Bakhtin, *Speech Genres*, 60). Although the novel takes theoretical precedence in "Discourse in the Novel," Bakhtin emphasizes the heterologic dimensions of other speech genres, both oral and written, across his critical writings (see *Rabelais and His World*; *Problems of Dostoevsky's Poetics*; and *Speech Genres*).

6. Tzvetan Todorov translates the Bakhtinian neologism as *hétérologie* and distinguishes it from both *hétéroglossie* and *hétérophonie* (*Mikhaïl Bakhtine: Le principe dialogique—suivi de: Écrits du Cercle Bakhtine* [Paris: Éditions du Seuil, 1981], 88–93). Karine Zbinden argues that Todorov's translation seeks to highlight the etymological distinction between *logos* (word) and *glotta* (tongue or natural language) (Zbinden, *Bakhtin between East and West: Cross-Cultural Transmission* [London: Legenda—Modern Humanities Research Association and Maney Publishing, 2006], 77).

7. Barrāda's critical oeuvre—particularly *ʾAsʾilat al-riwāya, ʾasʾilat al-naqd* [The question of the novel, the question of (literary) criticism] and *Al-riwāya al-ʿarabiyya wa rihān al-tajdīd* [The Arabic novel and the wager of renewal]—engage not only with the work of Bakhtin but also that of Barthes, Jakobson, Todorov, and Lukács.

8. For an in-depth discussion of literary experimentation in Moroccan fiction and criticism—by Barrāda as well as Muḥammad Amanṣūr, Aḥmad al-Madīnī, and Saʿīd Yaqṭīn—see Anouar El Younssi, "'Al-Tajrib' (Experimentalism) in the Moroccan New Novel and the Debate over Legitimacy" (Ph.D. diss., Pennsylvania State University, 2016).

9. The Arabic text reads:

ذلك أن الرواية شكل تعبيري إنساني، وجد منذ القديم، واغتنى بإضافات عديدة من لدُن مبدعين ينتمون إلى ثقافات وحضارات متباينة [...] بل هناك شكل مفتوح، مستوعب لمختلف الإضافات، يتوفر على مكونات نصية وجمالية تتعدى "الأصل" الإثني أو الثقافي لأنها مُكونات تعتمد السرد والتخييل والحبكة وتعدد اللغات والاصوات، وهي جميعها عناصر مشتركة في التراث الروائي الإنساني المتفاعل باستمرار.

10. Portions of this passage are cited in El Younssi, "'Al-Tajrib' (Experimentalism) in the Moroccan New Novel and the Debate over Legitimacy" 105–6, although our translations differ. The Arabic text reads:

أصبح النقاش حول استيراد الشكل متجاوزاً، وأسهمت الترجمة في تقديم تنويعات عديدة للشكل والنقد العالميين، كما تبلور وعي يرى بأن جميع الثقافات أسهمت في بلورة الأشكال التعبيرية وإغنائها . . .

11. The Arabic text reads:

وإحياء عناصر من السرد التراثي، واصطناع لغة المؤرخين القدامى ومعجم الصوفيين. والمزج بين الأجناس الأدبية في رحاب النص الروائي.

12. In a paper published under the title "The New Cultural and Imaginative Discourse in Morocco: Utopic Change," Barrāda theorizes new developments in Moroccan literature and criticism through the lens of utopian discourse.

13. The Arabic text reads:

ومصدر الإشكال هو في تحديد معنى الجدة والجديد، إذ غالباً ما تتضمن هذه الكلمة ومشتقاتها قيمة إيجابية بالنسبة إلى ما هو قديم. لكن، في مجال الإبداع الأدبي والفني، يصعب أن نقرن الجديد، آلياً، بالتميز والأفضلية على ما هو "قديم"، أي سابق زمنياً في التحقق. ذلك أن أعمالاً أدبية وفنية لها عمر طويل وتحمل قدامة قرون وعقود، تظل محافظة على "جدتها" من خلال تحريك مشاعر وأفكار متلقين يعيشون في زمن راهن وجديد.

14. The Arabic text reads:

يرجع تشظي الشكل الروائي إلى اهتزاز الشكل الواقعي الكلاسيكي المعتمد على سرد خطي، والتزام منظور أحادي.

15. Portions of this passage are also quoted in El Younssi, "'Al-Tajrib' (Experimentalism) in the Moroccan New Novel and the Debate over Legitimacy," 20–21, although our translations differ. The Arabic text reads:

تغدو الكتابة في نظرنا هي مجال تجلّي وعي الكاتب بمختلف الأجناس الأدبية، وبوظيفة اللغة والشكل في تحريك وتغيير المقاييس الجمالية; إنها تمثل جماع تفاعل وعي الكاتب مع شروطه التاريخية...

16. The Arabic text reads:

عندما أفكر في المظاهر الأساسية للإبداع الأدبي العربي في هذه الحقبة، تلفت نظري، قبل كل شيء، ظاهرة التعدد اللغوي بوصفها تجليا للإبداع المغيّر لمفهوم الأدب ولحمولاته الأيديولوجية وأيضا لطريقة قرائته. وقد أصبح قولاً مشاعاً التأكيد على أن تحقّق النص الأدبي إنما يتمّ باللغة وعبرها. ولكن ما سأحاول طرحه هنا، يتوخّى تدقيق علاقة المنتج الأدبي باللغة—وخاصة في الرواية—من منظور حتمية التعدد اللغوي داخل كل نص روائي، واعتبار التعددية مكوّناً داخلياً ملتصقاً بالرَّحم المولّد للنص في تحققه الشكلي والخِطابي والأيديولوجي.

17. As discussed in relation to Maḥmūd al-Masʿadī's *Mawlid al-nisyān* and Al-Ṭāhir Waṭṭar's *Al-zilzāl*, the number seven is significant in the Qurʾan and Islam more broadly.

18. The term *al-rāwī* can also mean storyteller or relator.

19. The text does not specify the narrator of the final "Illumination," although it is suggested that it is an extended family member or friend of the wedding party. Issa Boullata writes that it is likely the "implied author" (introduction to *The Game of Forgetting* [Austin: University of Texas at Austin Press, 1996], 7).

20. See the discussion of Sufi poetics in the Introduction.

21. The Arabic text reads:

كان معجبة بطريقة ذلك العالم في تفسير الحديث [...] يقرأ السارد الحديث بِعَنْعناته اللاّتنتهي، وهو يتدخل ليوضح نسب كل صحابي أو تابع، وليوثّق الأشخاص والأفكار والمراجع، ثم يبدأ في التفسير منتقلا من التاريخ إلى الجغرافية إلى السيرة النبوية إلى النوادر الفكاهات [...] مع سيدْ المدني بالحسني، يسترجع الكلامُ والتّلفظ قوتهما، وتَتَسَلْطَنُ صيغة الحكي [...] كان عالمنا يسترسل في حديثه كأنه في خَلْوة مع جماعة أصدقاء بدون تكلّف أو إغلاق...

(Muḥammad Barrāda, *Luʾbat al-nisyān*, 44–45).

22. The Arabic text reads:

فإنني أتساءل عمّا إذا لم أكن نَوْعاً من الرقابة يمارسها الكاتب من خلال ما أقوله؛ فالمفروض أنني أعرف أكثر ممّا يعرفه باقي الرواة، وأن لكلامي وزناً بصفتي مُطلعاً على الخَلفِيّات وعلى بعض التفاصيل التي خصّني بها الكاتب، ويمكنني أن أستعملها لأزحزح ما حكاه الآخرون.

(Muḥammad Barrāda, *Lu'bat al-nisyān*, 53).

23. The Arabic text reads:

هو التفريط في مقوماتنا الروحية وتعاليمنا المقدسة، حتى لم نعد نعرف ماإذا كنا نعيش بمجتمع إسلامي أو بإحدى ملحقات الميتروبول [...] والذين ما يزالون متشبثين بالتعاليم الصحيحة والسنة المحمدة يجدون أنفسهم غرباء وسط الحشود المتهافتة على الربح والزنا، لا تتورع عن الغش والكذب والربا [...] هل هذه هي المحجة البيضاء؟ هل تعثرون في حياتكم العملية على شيء من العدالة وعفة النفس والتكافل والتسامح وجميع الفضائل التي جسدها محمد بن عبد الله وأوصى بها سلالات المؤمنين؟

(Muḥammad Barrāda, *Luʾbat al-nisyān*, 125).

24. Islamic reformist movements are also referenced in the novel on pages 65–66 and 114.

25. The Arabic text reads:

فنحن لا نستطيع أن نحتمي من التحولات التي هي جوهر الحياة، بالعودة إلى نموذج تحقق في عصرنا الذهبي [...] أعتقد أن نقطة المنطق هي جعل الموروث الحضاري والثقافي والديني في علاقة حوار وتفاعل مع أسئلة الحاضر ومع المعضلات التي تولدها التحولات وتناقضاتها. ولا يمكن أن ننطلق من إلغاء ما نعيشه عن طريق افتراض حلول مسبقة قائمة في حقبة سالفة لها خصوصيتها ومستواها التاريخي المعين.

(Muḥammad Barrāda, *Luʿbat al-nisyān*, 126).

26. For a detailed discussion of the Day of Judgment in the Qurʾan, see Chapter 3.

27. In one example on page 138 (144 in the Arabic), Barrāda blends the Qurʾanic sura 3:140 with a sentence that mixes Moroccan dialect with MSA by leaving out Qurʾanic quotation marks. Boullata adds the Qurʾanic citation into the English translation.

28. See Chapter 5.

EPILOGUE

1. The Arabic text of the epigraph reads:

فالإنسان هو أن يوفي بالأمانة التي أوكله الله بها باعتبار أنّه يحاول في إيمانه بالله أن يكون صورة منه يخلق ويبتكر ما يستطيع من أفكار.

[...]

أليس الأدب نوعا من الفلسفة التي تصدر عن تحليل عقلي لمشكلة الوجود بل تساهم في التفكير في هذه المواضيع بالوجدان أي يضطلع به الإنسان من مأساة باطنية ومن تأمّل لا عن طريق المنطق والتحليل الفلسفي بل عن طريق الشعور والتعبير عن الشعور. فالأدب من هذه الناحية يمكن أن يسمّى" فلسفة وجدانية".

2. While recent scholarship has begun to problematize the ways in which discourses of the *nahḍa* can reify a fixed notion of Arab modernity tied to post-Enlightenment European thought, the intellectual history of the Maghreb is often, at best, relegated to a footnote.

3. Pan-Arabist ideology was first popularized in the late nineteenth and early twentieth centuries by such figures as the Lebanese intellectual Jurjī Zaydān (1861–1914) and the Sharif of Mecca Ḥusayn ibn ʿAlī (1854–1931), who sought independence from Ottoman rule. In the 1930s, Pan-Arabism gained cachet as an intellectual movement when Syrian thinkers of the Arab Baʿth [Renaissance] Party, such as Constantin Zurayq, Zakī al-Arsūzī, and Michel ʿAflaq, fused the concept with Marxist thought. The formation of the Arab League in 1945 and 1950s Nasserism gave the movement political legs in the midcentury.

4. Socialist (*ishtirākiyya*) and Marxist ideologies were championed by such critics as Salāma Mūsā (1887–1958) and Luwīs ʿAwaḍ (1915–1990) in Egypt, as well as ʿUmar Fakhūrī (1895–1946) and Raʾīf Khūrī (1912–1967) in Lebanon.

5. Verena Klemm writes that they were guided by the principles of dialectical materialism, as "defined by Andrej Ždanov, Stalin's leading cultural ideologist, and introduced by Maksim Gork'iy during the first Congress of Soviet Writers in 1934" ("Different Notions of Commitment [*Iltizām*] and Committed Literature [*al-adab al-multazim*] in the Literary Circles of the Mashriq," *Arabic and Middle Eastern Literatures* 3, no. 1 [2000]: 59n8).

6. For an in-depth discussion of these questions, see Yoav Di-Capua, *No Exit: Arab Existentialism, Jean-Paul Sartre, and Decolonization* (Chicago: University of Chicago Press, 2018); and David DiMeo, *Committed to Disillusion: Activist Writers in Egypt in the 1960s-1980s* (Cairo: American University in Cairo Press, 2016).

7. Started in Beirut in 1957 by Yūsuf al-Khāl and the Syrian poet and critic Adonis, *Shiʿr* promoted a model of artistic production supposedly not driven by didacticism or party-line politics. This was called into question during the debate with *Al-ādāb*, when al-Khāl and Adonis were accused of being mouthpieces for the SNPP, or Syrian Socialist Nationalist Party.

8. Badawī also addressed the subject in his doctoral dissertation "Al-zamān al-wujūdī" [Existential time].

9. Many on the left—such as Suhayl Idrīs and the Egyptian Maḥmūd Amīn al-ʿĀlim—were unconvinced by Ḥusayn's literary-political didacticism, and he came to represent the old guard of the Arab bourgeois literary establishment (Di-Capua, *No Exit*, 1064).

10. The play was written between 1939 and 1940 but not serialized until 1955.

11. Marcel's "theistic existentialism" more closely aligned with Kierkegaardian than Sartrean existentialism; Kierkegaard emphasized individual choice in relation to Christian ethics and thought.

12. The Arabic text reads:

وهي وجودية قوامها ايمان الانسان بنفسه الى أبعد حدود الايمان، بحيث يجعل الانسان بنفسه مقياسا للخير والشر، ويحمل الانسان وحده تبعة أعماله ولا يُسأل عنها الا امام نفسه، قبل ان يسأل عنها امام الجماعة وقوانينها [...] فاما الوجودية التي [...] أسلمت في تونس على يد الاستاذ المسعدي فهي تجعل لثقة الانسان بنفسه حدودا اهمها وأقواها وأضخمها هذا الحد الديني [...] وهي قوة الله الَّذي يراقب الضمير ويعلم خائنة الاعين وما تخفي الصدور

13. For al-Masʿadī's views on Sartre and Camus specifically, see *Collected Works*, 3:368.

14. The Arabic text reads:

ذلك أن الالتزام في الأدب لا يعدو، في معناه الصحيح عندي، أن يكون الأديب ملتزما لجوهريّ الشؤون منصرفا عن بهرج اللفظ والصنعة. الالتزام هو ان يكون الأدب جماع قصة الإنسان وخلاصة ما يستنبطه من أعمق أعماقه وصميم أحشائه. هو ان يكون الأدب رسالة الإنسان إلى الإنسان، رسالة يستوحيها من الجانب الإلهي من فكره وروحه و من هذا الوجدان أو الحدس الإلهي الذي هو الفكر وما فوق الفكر والعقل وما فوق العقل والخيال مع العلم والمعرفة مع الانطلاق والكيان مُجربا في كليته وشموله

15. The Arabic text reads:

فإن كان التفكير الفلسفي الوجودي يوضح الفكرة، والأدب الالتزامي يعبر عن السلوك والموقف فأن هذا وذاك كليهما واقع في نطاق مشكلة الوجود ومصير الإنسان ومنزلته من الكون وسلوكه في الحياة ومآله بعد الحياة

16. Portions of the passage are cited in Omri, *Nationalism, Islam, and World Literature: Sites of Confluence in the Writings of Mahmūd al-Masʿadī* (London: Routledge, 2006), 42, although I have modified his translation of those sections.

The Arabic text reads:

ان الانسان جوهر فرد. ذلك ما ينبغي له ان يكون وذلك هو سر شرفه الأسنى في الوجود. بل انه لمن الحق المبين أن الإنسان ما اشتدت فردية جوهره إلا اشتد اتصاله بإنسانيته ووفاؤه لرسالته في الكون على أن الأديب قد يجد اكتمال انسانيته في الاتجاه بفرديته إلى التعمق في الذات والتيه في أبعادها فيبدو منقطعا الى "الفن للفن" أو إلى "الحياة في البرج العاجية" كما يقال، ولكنه لا يزال مع ذلك ومن خلال فنه ذلك وحياته تلك يجتذبنا إلى إنسانيته الكاملة، ويرفعنا أفرادا وأقواما إلى منازل الشرف والسمو.

17. See al-Masʿadī, "Islam, nationalisme et communisme" (*Collected Works*, 4:323–34); "la liberté de l'écrivain" (ibid., 4:335–41); and "*al-ʿurūba wa-l-islām fi al-dhātiyya al-qawmiyya al-tūnisiyya*" (ibid., 2:181–83).

Bibliography

'Abbasid Belles Lettres. Edited by Julia Ashtiany, T. M. Johnstone, J. D. Latham, and R. B. Serjeant. Cambridge: Cambridge University Press, 1990.

Abbott, Nadia. *Aishah, the Beloved of Mohammed.* Chicago: University of Chicago Press, 1942.

Abdel Haleem, M. A. S. "Grammatical Shift for Rhetorical Purposes: *Iltifāt* and Related Features in the Qur'ān." *Bulletin of the School of Oriental and African Studies* 55, pt. 3 (1992): 407–32.

Abdel-Jaouad, Hédi. "'Too Much in the Sun': Sons, Mothers, and Impossible Alliances in Francophone Maghrebian Writing." *Research in African Literatures* 27, no. 3 (Autumn 1996): 15–33.

Abdul-Raof, Hussein. "The Linguistic Architecture of the Qur'an." *Journal of Qur'anic Studies* 2 no. 2 (2010): 37–51.

———. *Schools of Qur'anic Exegesis: Genesis and Development.* London: Routledge, 2010.

Aboul-Ela, Hosam. "Is There an Arab (Yet) in This Field? Postcolonialism, Comparative Literature, and the Middle Eastern Horizon of Said's Discourse Analysis." *MFS Modern Fiction Studies* 56, no. 4 (Winter 2010): 729–50.

———. "Our Theory Split." Roundtable: Theory and Arabic Literature in the United States. *International Journal of Middle East Studies* 43, no. 4 (2011): 725–27.

Abun-Nasr, Jamil M. *A History of the Maghreb in the Muslim Period.* Cambridge: Cambridge University Press, 1987.

Addi, Lahouari. "Algeria and the Dual Image of the Intellectual." In *Intellectuals in Politics: From the Dreyfus Affair to Salman Rushdie*, edited by J. Jennings and T. Kemp-Welch. London: Routledge, 1997.

———. "Les Intellectuels qu'on assassine." *Esprit* 208, no. 1 (January 1995): 130–38.

Adonis. *Al-naṣṣ al-qur'ānī wa-āfāq al-kitāba.* Beirut: Dār al-ādāb, 1993.

———. *An Introduction to Arab Poetics.* Translated by Catherine Cobham. London: Saqi, 1990. First French edition 1985.

———. *Sufism and Surrealism.* Translated by Judith Cumberbatch. London: Saqi, 2005. First Arabic edition 1995.

Agrama, Hussein Ali. "Secularism, Sovereignty, Indeterminacy: Is Egypt a Secular or a Religious State?" *Comparative Studies in Society and History* 52, no. 3 (2010): 495–523.

Ahmed, Leila. "Women and the Advent of Islam." *Signs* 11, no. 4 (Summer 1986): 665–91.

Ahmed, Safdar. *Reform and Modernity in Islam: The Philosophical, Cultural and Political Discourses among Muslim Reformers.* New York: I. B. Taurus, 2013.

Aitsiselmi, Farid, and Dawn Marley. "The Role and Status of the French Language in North Africa." *Studies in French Applied Linguistics*, edited by Dalila Ayoun. Amsterdam: John Benjamins, 2008.

Ali, Maulana Muhammad. *A Manual of Hadith*. English and Arabic edition. 2nd ed. London: RoutledgeCurzon, 1951.

Al-Kassim, Dina. "The Faded Bond: Calligraphesis and Kinship in Abdelwahab Meddeb's *Talismano.*" *Public Culture* 13, no. 1 (2001): 113–38.

Allan, Michael. *In the Shadow of World Literature: Sites of Reading in Colonial Egypt.* Princeton, N.J.: Princeton University Press, 2016.

———. "Scattered Letters: Translingual Poetics in Assia Djebar's *L'Amour, la fantasia.*" *Philological Encounters* 2, no. 1 (2016): 1–19.

Allen, Roger. *The Arabic Literary Heritage: The Development of Its Genres and Criticism.* Cambridge: Cambridge University Press, 1998.

Appadurai, Arjun. "Disjuncture and Difference in the Global Cultural Economy." *Public Culture* 2, no. 2 (Spring 1990): 1–24.

———. "Grassroots Globalization and the Research Imagination." *Public Culture* 12, no. 1 (Winter 2000): 1–19.

Apter, Emily. "Literary World-Systems." In *Teaching World Literature*, edited by David Damrosch, 44–60. New York: Modern Language Association, 2009.

Asad, Talal. *Formations of the Secular: Christianity, Islam, Modernity.* Stanford: Stanford University Press, 2003.

Asad, Talal, Wendy Brown, Judith Butler, and Saba Mahmood. *Is Critique Secular? Blasphemy, Injury, and Free Speech.* Berkeley: Townsend Center for the Humanities, 2009.

Badawī, ʿAbd al-Raḥmān. *Al-insāniyya wa-l-wujūdiyya fī al-fikr al-ʿarabī.* Cairo: Maktabat al-Nahḍa al-Miṣriyya, 1947.

Al-Baghdadi, Nadia. "Registers of Arabic Literary History." *New Literary History* 39, no. 3 (Summer 2008): 437–61.

Bakhtin, Mikhail. M. *Al-khiṭāb al-riwāʾī.* Translated by Muḥammad Barrāda. Cairo: Dār al-Fikr, 1987.

———. *The Dialogic Imagination*. Edited by Michael Holquist. Translated by Caryl Emerson and Holquist. Austin: University of Texas Press, 1981.

———. "Discourse in the Novel." In *The Dialogic Imagination*, edited by Michael Holquist. Translated by Caryl Emerson and Holquist. Austin: University of Texas Press, 1981.

———. *Esthétique et théorie du roman*. Translated by Daria Olivier. Paris: Gallimard, 1978.

———. "Forms of Time and Chronotope in the Novel." In *The Dialogic Imagination*, edited by Michael Holquist. Translated by Caryl Emerson and Holquist. Austin: University of Texas Press, 1981.

———. *Problems of Dostoevsky's Poetics*. Translated by Caryl Emerson. Minneapolis: University of Minnesota Press, 1984.

———. *Rabelais and His World*. Translated by Helen Iswolsky. Bloomington: Indiana University Press, 1984.

———. *Speech Genres and Other Late Essays*. Edited by Caryl Emerson and Michael Holquist. Translated by Vern W. McGee. Austin: University of Texas Press, 1986.

Barrāda, Muḥammad [Berrada, Mohamed]. *The Game of Forgetting*. Translated by Issa J. Boullata. Austin: University of Texas Press, 1996.

——— [Berrada, Mohamed]. "The New Cultural and Imaginative Discourse in Morocco: Utopic Change." In *Contemporary North Africa: Issues of Development and Integration*, edited by Halim Barakat, 231–49. London: Croom Helm, 1985.

———. *Al-riwāya al-ʿarabiyya wa-rihān al-tajdīd*. Dubai: Majallat Dubayy al-Thaqāfiyya, 2011.

———. *Al-riwāya dhākira maftūḥa*. Cairo: Āfāq, 2008.

———. *As'ilat al-riwāya, as'ilat al-naqd*. Casablanca: al-Rābiṭa, 1996.

———. *Faḍā'āt riwā'iyya*. Rabat: Manshūrāt Wizārat al-Thaqāfa, 2003.

———. "Generation Drive." Translated by Hoda El Shakry and Maya Boutaghou. In *Souffles-Anfas: A Critical Anthology from the Moroccan Journal of Culture and Politics*, edited by Olivia Harrison and Teresa Villa-Ignacio. Stanford: Stanford University Press, 2016.

———. *Luʿbat al-nisyān*. 1987. 2nd ed. Rabat: Dār al-Amān, 1992.

Barthes, Roland. "Death of the Author." 1977. In *Image, Music, Text*, translated by Stephen Heath. New York: Hill and Wang, 1998.

Bashier, Salman H. *Ibn al-ʿArabī's Barzakh: The Concept of the Limit and the Relationship between God and the World*. Albany: State University of New York Press, 2004.

Benrabah, M. *Langue et pouvoir en Algérie: Histoire d'un traumatisme linguistique*. Paris: Séguire, 1999

Bensmaïa, Réda. *Experimental Nations: Or, the Invention of the Maghreb*. Princeton, N.J.: Princeton University Press, 2003.

———. "La nouba des femmes du Mont Chenoua: Introduction to the Cinematic Fragment." Translated by Jennifer Curtiss Gage. *World Literature Today* 70, no. 4 (Autumn 1996): 877–84.

bin Tyeer, Sarah R. *The Qur'an and the Aesthetics of Premodern Arabic Prose*. London: Palgrave Macmillan, 2016.

Bonebakker, S. A. "*Adab* and the Concept of *Belles-Lettres*." In *The Cambridge Encyclopedia of Arabic Literature: 'Abbasid Belles Lettres*, edited by Julia Ashtiany, T. M. Johnstone, J. D. Latham, and R. B. Serjeant, 16–30. Cambridge: Cambridge University Press, 1990.

Bonn, Charles, and Yves Baumstimler, dir. *Psychanalyse et texte littéraire au Maghreb*. Paris: L'Harmattan, 1992.

Boullata, Issa. Introduction to *The Game of Forgetting*, by Mohamed Berrada [Muḥammad Barrāda]. Austin: University of Texas Press, 1996.

———, ed. *Literary Structures of Religious Meaning in the Qur'an*. London: Routledge, 2000.

Bourget, Carine. *Coran at Tradition islamique dans la literature maghrébine*. Paris: Éditions Karthala, 2002.

Bourqia, Rahma. "The Cultural Legacy of Power in Morocco." In *In the Shadow of the Sultan: Culture, Power, and Politics in Morocco*, edited by Bourqia and Susan Gilson Miller, 243–58. Cambridge: Harvard University Press, 1999.

Brown, Leon Carl. "The Islamic Reformist Movement in North Africa." *Journal of Modern African Studies* 2, no. 1 (1964): 55–63.

Brown, Wendy. "Idealism, Materialism, Secularism?" *The Immanent Frame*. http://blogs.ssrc.org/tif/2007/10/22/idealism-materialism-secularism/.

Brozgal, Lia Nicole. *Against Autobiography: Albert Memmi and the Production of Theory*. Lincoln: University of Nebraska Press, 2013.

Calle-Gruber, Mireille. "Écrire de main morte ou l'art de la césure chez Assia Djebar." *L'Esprit Créateur* 48, no. 4 (Winter 2008): 5–14.

Çelik, Zeynep, Julia Clancy-Smith, and Frances Terpak, eds. *Walls of Algiers: Narratives of the City through Text and Image*. Seattle: University of Washington Press, 2009.

Chaker, Salem. "Berber Challenge in Algeria, the State of the Question." *Race, Gender and Class* 8, no. 3 (2001): 135–56.

Chittick, William. *The Sufi Path of Knowledge: Ibn 'Arabi's Metaphysics of Imagination*. Albany: State University of New York Press, 1989.

Chraïbi, Driss. *L'âne*. Paris: Éditions Denoël, 1956.

———. *Une enquête au pays*. Paris: Éditions du Seuil, 1981.

———. *L'Homme du Livre*. Casablanca: Balland-Eddif, 1995.

———. "Je renie *Le passé simple*." *Démocratie*, February 4, 1957.

———. *La mère du printemps (L'oum-er-bia)*. Paris: Éditions du Seuil, 1982.
———. *Muhammad*. Washington, D.C.: Three Continents, 1998.
———. *Naissance à l'aube*. Paris: Éditions du Seuil, 1986.
———. *Le passé simple*. Paris: Denoël, 1954.
———. "Questionnaire: établi par Abdellatif Laâbi." *Souffles* 5 (1967): 5–10.
———. *The Simple Past*. Translated by Hugh A. Harter. Washington, D.C.: Three Continents, 1990.
Clancy-Smith, Julia. *Rebel and Saint: Muslim Notables, Populist Protest, and Colonial Encounters (Algeria and Tunisia, 1800–1904)*. Berkeley: University of California Press, 1994.
Clerc, Jeanne-Marie. *Assia Djebar: Écrire, transgresser, résister*. Paris: L'Harmattan, 1997.
Cook, David. *Studies in Muslim Apocalyptic*. Princeton, N.J.: Darwin, 2002.
cooke, miriam. "Women, Religion, and the Postcolonial Arab World." *Cultural Critique*, no. 45 (Spring 2000): 150–84.
Corbin, Henry. *Creative Imagination in the Sūfism of Ibn 'Arabī*. Translated by Ralph Manheim. Princeton, N.J.: Princeton University Press, 1969.
Courville, Mathieu E. *Edward Said's Rhetoric of the Secular*. London: Continuum, 2009.
Cox, Debbie. "The Novels of Tahar Wattar: Command or Critique?" *Research in African Literatures* 28, no. 3 (Fall 1997): 94–109.
———. *Politics, Language, and Gender in the Algerian Arabic Novel*. London: Edwin Mellon, 2002.
———. "Symbolism and Allegory in the Algerian Arabic Novel." *Arabic and Middle Eastern Literatures* 1, no. 2 (1998): 193–204.
Damrosch, David. "Foreword: Literary Criticism and the Qur'an." *Journal of Qur'anic Studies* 16, no. 3 (2014): 4–10.
Davis, Ruth. "Beyond Spatiality: Theorising the Local and Untranslatability as Comparative Critical Method." In *Approaches to World Literature*, vol. 1, edited by Joachim Küpper, 59–84. Berlin: Walter de Gruyter, 2013.
———. "Cultural Policy and the Tunisian Ma'lūf: Redefining a Tradition." *Ethnomusicology* 41, no. 1 (Winter 1997): 1–21.
Dib, Mohammed. *La grande maison*. Paris: Éditions du Seuil, 1952.
Di-Capua, Yoav. "Arab Existentialism: An Invisible Chapter in the Intellectual History of Decolonization." *American Historical Review* 117, no. 4 (2012): 1061–91.
———. *No Exit: Arab Existentialism, Jean-Paul Sartre, and Decolonization*. Chicago: University of Chicago Press, 2018.
DiMeo, David. *Committed to Disillusion: Activist Writers in Egypt in the 1960s-1980s*. Cairo: American University in Cairo Press, 2016.
Djebar, Assia. *L'amour, la fantasia*. Paris: Jean-Claude Lattes, 1985.

———. *Le blanc de l'Algérie.* Paris: Éditions Albert Michel, 1995.
———. Dialogue with Lyone Trouillot. *2005 PEN World Voices Festival of International Literature.* https://pen.org/postcolonial-passages-assia-djebar-lyone-trouillot/.
———. "Discours de reception." Prononcé dans la séance publique. Paris: Palais de l'Institut. June 22, 2006. http://www.academie-francaise.fr/discours-de-reception-et-reponse-de-pierre-jean-remy.
———. *Fantasia: An Algerian Cavalcade.* Translated by Dorothy S. Blair. Portsmouth, N.H.: Heinemann, 1993.
———. *Far from Medina: Daughters of Ishmael.* Translated by Dorothy S. Blair. London: Quartet, 1994.
———. *Loin de Médine.* Paris: Albin Michel, 1991.
———. *Nulle part dans la maison de mon père.* Paris: Fayard, 2007.
———. *Ombre sultane.* Paris, Jean Claude Lattès, 1987.
———. *La soif.* Paris: R. Julliard, 1957.
———. *Vaste est la prison.* Paris: A. Michel, 1995.
Dobie, Madeleine. "Francophone Studies and the Linguistic Diversity of the Maghreb." *Comparative Studies of South Asia, Africa and the Middle East* 23, no. 1–2 (2003): 32–40.
Donadey, Anne. "The Multilingual Strategies of Postcolonial Literature: Assia Djebar's Algerian Palimpsest." *World Literature Today* 74, no. 1 (Winter 2000): 27–36.
———. *Recasting Postcolonialism: Women Writing between Worlds.* Portsmouth, N.H.: Heinemann, 2001.
Döring, Tobias, and Mark Stein, eds. *Edward Said's Translocations: Essays in Secular Criticism.* New York: Routledge, 2012.
Dziri, Mostafa. "Celui par qui le scandale arrive." *Souffles* 5 (1967): 12–17.
El Aissati, Abderrahman. "Ethnic Identity, Language Shift, and the Amazigh Voice in Morocco and Algeria." *Race, Gender and Class* 8, no. 3 (2001): 57–69.
El Mansour, Mohamed. "The Sanctuary (*Hurm*) in Precolonial Morocco." In *In the Shadow of the Sultan: Culture, Power, and Politics*, edited by Rahma Bourqia and Susan Gilson Miller, 49–73. Cambridge: Harvard University Press, 1999.
El Shakry, Hoda. "Abdelwahab Meddeb and the Po/Ethics of Sufism." *Expressions maghrébines* 16, no. 2 (Winter 2017): 95–115.
———. "Heteroglossia and the Poetics of the *Roman Maghrébin.*" *Contemporary French and Francophone Studies: SITES* 20, no 2 (2016): 8–17.
———. "Lessons from the Maghreb." In *Arabic Literature in the Classroom: Teaching Methods, Theories, Themes, and Texts*, edited by Muhsin J. al-Musawi, 109–29. New York: Routledge, 2017.

———. "Printed Matter(s): Critical Histories and Perspectives on Tunisian Cultural Journals." *ALIF: A Journal of Comparative Poetics* 37 (2017): 140–68.

El Shakry, Omnia. *The Arabic Freud: Psychoanalysis and Islam in Modern Egypt*. Princeton, N.J.: Princeton University Press, 2017.

El Younssi, Anouar. "Al-Tajrib" (Experimentalism) in the Moroccan New Novel and the Debate over Legitimacy." Ph.D. diss., Pennsylvania State University, 2016.

ElAraby, Kadri M. G. "The Art and Design of Arabic Calligraphy." *Digest of Middle East Studies* 6, no. 1 (Winter 1997): 1–23.

El-Ariss, Tarek. *Trials of Arab Modernity: Literary Affects and the New Political*. New York: Fordham University Press, 2013.

El-Awa, Selwa M. S. *Textual Relations in the Qur'ān: Relevance, Coherence and Structure*. London: Routledge, 2006.

El-Desouky, Ayman A. "Between Hermeneutic Provenance and Textuality: The Qur'an and the Question of Method in Approaches to World Literature." *Journal of Qur'anic Studies* 16 no. 3 (2014): 11–38.

Elhariry, Yasser. "Abdelwahab Meddeb, Sufi Poets, and the New Francophone Lyric." *PMLA* 131, no. 2 (March 2016): 255–68.

Elmarsafy, Ziad. *The Enlightenment Qur'an: The Politics of Translation and the Construction of Islam*. Oxford: Oneworld, 2009.

———. *Sufism in the Contemporary Arabic Novel*. Edinburgh: Edinburgh University Press, 2012.

Elsadda, Hoda. "Discourses on Women's Biographies and Cultural Identity: Twentieth-Century Representations of the Life of 'A'isha Bint Abi Bakr." *Feminist Studies* 27, no. 1 (Spring 2001): 37–64.

Enan, Mohammad Abdullah. *Ibn Khaldūn: His Life and Works*. Kuala Lumpur: The Other Press, 2007.

Erickson, John. *Islam and Postcolonial Narrative*. Cambridge: Cambridge University Press, 1998.

Ernst, Carl W. "Between Orientalism and Fundamentalism: Problematizing the Teaching of Sufism." In *Teaching Islam*, edited by Brannon Wheeler, 108–23. Oxford: Oxford University Press, 2002,

———. *Sufism: An Introduction to the Mystical Tradition of Islam*. 1997. Boston: Shambhala, 2011.

Esack, Farid. *The Qur'an: A User's Guide*. Oxford: Oneworld, 2005.

Feraoun, Mouloud. *Le fils de pauvre*. Paris: Éditions du Seuil, 1954.

Fernando, Mayanthi L. *The Republic Unsettled: Muslim French and the Contradictions of Secularism*. Durham, N.C.: Duke University Press, 2014.

Fieni, David. "Decadent Orientalisms: Configuring the Decay of Colonial Modernity in French and Arabic." Ph.D. diss., University of California, Los Angeles, 2006.

Fontaine, Jean. "Arabic Language Tunisian Literature (1956–1990)." *Research in African Literatures* 23, no. 2 (Summer 1992): 183–93.

Fudge, Bruce. *Qur'ānic Hermeneutics: Al-Ṭabrisī and the Craft of Commentary.* London: Routledge, 2011.

Gafaiti, Hafid. "The Blood of Writing: Assia Djebar's Unveiling of Women and History." *World Literature Today* 70, no. 4 (Autumn 1996): 813–22.

Gauch, Suzanne. *Liberating Shahrazad: Feminism, Postcolonialism, and Islam.* Minneapolis: University of Minnesota Press, 2006.

Geesey, Patricia. "Exhumation and History: Tahar Djaout's Les Chercheurs d'os." *French Review* 70, no. 2 (December 1996): 271–79.

al-Gharībī, Khālid. *Jadaliyyat al-aṣāla wa-l-muʿāṣira fī adab al-Masʿadī: Al-sudd, Ḥadatha Abū Hurayra qāl, Mawlid al-Nisyān, Al-Sindbād, wa-l-ṭahara.* Tunis: Ṣāmid, 1994.

al-Ghazālī, Abū Ḥāmid. *The Remembrance of Death and the Afterlife—Kitāb dhikr al-mawt wa-mā baʿdahu.* Book 40 of *The Revival of the Religious Sciences—Ihyāʾ ʿulūm al-dīn.* Translated by T. J. Winter. Cambridge: Islamic Texts Society, 1989.

Gianotti, Timothy. *Al-Ghazali's Unspeakable Doctrine of the Soul: Unveiling the Esoteric Psychology and Eschatology of the Iḥyāʾ.* Leiden: Brill, 2001.

Gourgouris, Stathis. "Detranscendentalizing the Secular." *Public Culture* 20, no. 3 (2008): 437–45.

———. *Lessons in Secular Criticism.* New York: Fordham University Press, 2013.

Gracki, Katherine. "Writing Violence and the Violence of Writing in Assia Djebar's Algerian Quartet." *World Literature Today* 70, no. 4 (Autumn 1996): 835–43.

Graiouid, Said. "We Have Not Buried the Simple Past: The Public Sphere and Post-Colonial Literature in Morocco." *Journal of African Cultural Studies* 20, no. 2 (December 2008): 145–58.

Granara, William. "Ali al-Duʿaji (1909–1949)." In *Essays in Arabic Literary Biography: 1850–1950*, edited by Roger Allen, 79–86. Wiesbaden: Harrassowitz Verlag, 2010.

———. "Mythologising the Algerian War of Independence: Tahir Wattar and the Contemporary Algerian Novel." *Journal of North African Studies* 4, no. 3 (Autumn 1999): 1–14.

Guerin, Adam. "Racial Myth, Colonial Reform, and the Invention of Customary Law in Morocco, 1912–1930." *Journal of North African Studies* 16, no. 3 (2011): 361–80.

Haddad, Malek. *Je t'offrirai une gazelle.* Paris: Juillard, 1959.

Haj, Samira. *Reconfiguring Islamic Tradition: Reform, Rationality, and Modernity.* Stanford: Stanford University Press, 2008.

Hammoudi, Abdellah. "The Reinvention of *Dar al-Mulk*: The Moroccan Political System and Its Legitimation." In *In the Shadow of the Sultan: Culture, Power and Politics in Morocco*, edited by Rahma Bourqia and Susan Gilson Miller, 129–75. Cambridge: Harvard University Press, 1999.

Hannoum, Abdelmajid. "Translation and the Colonial Imaginary: Ibn Khaldûn Orientalist." *History and Theory* 42, no. 1 (February 2003): 61–81.

Hans Wehr: A Dictionary of Modern Written Arabic. 3rd ed. 1994. Compiled by J. Milton Cowan. Beirut: Librairie du Liban, 1980.

Hanssen, Jens, and Max Weiss, eds. *Arabic Thought in the Liberal Age: Towards a Critical History of the Nahda*. Cambridge: Cambridge University Press, 2016.

Harrison, Nicholas. "Representativity (with reference to Chraïbi)." *Paragraph* 24, no. 3 (November 2001): 30–43.

Harrison, Olivia C. "Cross-Colonial Poetics: *Souffles-Anfas* and the Figure of Palestine." *PMLA* 128, no. 2 (March 2013): 353–69.

Hart, William D. *Edward Said and the Religious Effects of Culture*. Cambridge: Cambridge University Press, 2000.

Hayes, Jarrod. *Queer Nations: Marginal Sexualities in the Maghreb*. Chicago: University of Chicago Press, 2000.

———. "Rachid O. and the Return of the Homopast: The Autobiographical as Allegory in Childhood Narratives by Maghrebian Men." *Sites: The Journal of Twentieth-Century/Contemporary French Studies Revue d'études français* 1, no. 2 (1997): 497–526.

Hiddleston, Jane. *Assia Djebar: Out of Algeria*. Liverpool: Liverpool University Press, 2006.

Hillauer, Rebecca. *Encyclopedia of Arab Women Filmmakers*. Translated by Allison Brown, Deborah Cohen, and Nancy Joyce. Cairo: American University in Cairo Press, 2005.

Hochberg, Gil Z. "'Colonial Hospitality': False Hosts and Ill-Mannered Guests in Assia Djebar's *L'amour, la fantasia*." *Nottingham French Studies* 40, no. 2 (Autumn 2001): 84–95.

———. "National Allegories and the Emergence of Female Voice in Moufida Tlatli's *Les silences du palais*." *Third Text* 14, no. 50 (Spring 2000): 33–44.

Holmberg, Bo. "*Adab* and Arabic Literature." In *Literary History: Towards a Global Perspective*, vol. 1: *Notions of Literature across Times and Cultures*, edited by Anders Pettersson, Gunilla Lindberg-Wada, Margareta Petersson, and Stefan Helgesso, 180–205. Berlin: Walter de Gruyter, 2006.

Ḥusayn, Ṭāhā. "*Al-adab bayna al-ittiṣṣāl wa-l-infiṣāl*." *Al-jumhūriyya* 29 (May 1957). Republished in *Al-sudd* (Tunis: al-Dār al-Tūnisiyya li-l-Nashr, 1974), 243–44.

———. *Fi al-shiʿr al-jāhilī*. Cairo: Dār al-muʿārif, 1981.

Ibnlfassi, Laïla. "Chraïbi's *Le passé simple* and a Theory of Doubles." In *African Francophone Writing: A Critical Introduction*, edited by Ibnlfassi and Nicki Hitchcott. Oxford: Berg, 1996.

Izutsu, Toshihiko. *Sufism and Taoism: A Comparative Study of Key Philosophical Concepts*. Berkeley: University of California Press, 2016.

Jameson, Fredric. "Third World Literature in the Era of Multinational Capitalism." *Social Text*, no. 15 (Autumn 1986): 65–88.

Judy, Ronald A. T. "On the Politics of Global Language, or Unfungible Local Value." *Boundary 2* 24, no. 2 (Summer 1997): 101–43.

Jurjānī, ʿAlī ibn Muḥammad [al-Sayyid al-Sharīf] al-. *Kitāb al-taʿrīfāt*. Beirut: Dār al-Kutub al-ʿIlmiyya, 1983.

Kadra-Hadjadji, Houaria. *Contestation et révolte dans l'oeuvre de Driss Chraïbi*. Algiers: E.N.A.L., 1986.

Karamustafa, Ahmet T. *Sufism: The Formative Period*. Edinburgh: Edinburgh University Press, 2007.

Kaye, Jacqueline, and Abdelhamid Zoubir. *The Ambiguous Compromise: Language, Literature and National Identity in Algeria and Morocco*. London: Routledge, 1990.

Khatibi, Abdelkébir. *Al-riwāya al-maghribiyya*. Translated by Muḥammad Barrāda. Rabat: al-Markaz al-Jāmiʿī li-l-Baḥth al-ʿIlmī, 1971.

———. *Maghreb pluriel*. Paris: Denöel, 1983.

———. *Roman maghrébin*. Paris: François Maspero, 1968.

Klemm, Verena. "Different Notions of Commitment (*iltizām*) and Committed Literature (*al-adab al-multazim*) in the Literary Circles of the Mashriq." *Arabic and Middle Eastern Literatures* 3, no. 1 (2000): 51–62.

Kristeva, Julia. "Word, Dialogue and Novel." In *The Kristeva Reader*, edited by Toril Moi. New York: Columbia University Press, 1986.

Kuntz, Jane. Introduction to *Talismano*, by Abdelwahab Meddeb, translated by Kuntz. Champaign, Ill.: Dalkey Archive Press, 2011.

Kurzman, Charles, ed. *Modernist Islam, 1840–1940: A Sourcebook*. Oxford: Oxford University Press, 2002.

Laâbi, Abdellatif. "Défense du *Passé simple*. *Souffles*, no. 5 (May 1967): 18–21.

Lang, George. "Jihad, Ijtihad, and Other Dialogical Wars in *La mère du printemps, Le harem politique*, and *Loin de Médine*." In *The Marabout and the Muse: New Approaches to Islam in African Literature*, edited by Kenneth W. Harrow. Portsmouth, N.H.: Heinemann, 1996.

Lapidus, Ira M. "Knowledge, Virtue, and Action: The Classical Muslim Conception of *Adab* and the Nature of Religious Fulfillment in Islam." In *Moral Conduct and Authority: The Place of* Adab *in South Asian Islam*, edited by Barbara Daly Metcalf. Berkeley: University of California Press, 1984.

Laroui, Abdallah. *La crise des intellectuels arabes: Traditionalisme ou historicisme?* Paris: Libraire François Maspero, 1974.

Lauzière, Henri. "The Construction of *Salafiyya*: Reconsidering Salafism from the Perspective of Conceptual History." *International Journal of Middle East Studies* 42, no. 3 (2010): 369–89.

Lee, Susanna. *A World Abandoned by God: Narrative and Secularism.* Lewisburg, Pa.: Bucknell University Press, 2006.

Lester, Toby. "What Is the Koran?" *Atlantic*, January 1999, https://www.theatlantic.com/magazine/archive/1999/01/what-is-the-koran/304024/.

Lionnet, Françoise. "Ces voix au fil de soi(e): Le détour du poétique." In *Assia Djebar: Littérature et transmission*, edited by Wolfgang Asholt, Mireille Calle-Gruber, and Dominique Combe, 23–36. Paris: Presses Sorbonne Nouvelle, 2010.

Lukács, Georg. *The Theory of the Novel: A Historico-Philosophical Essay on the Forms of Great Epic Literature.* Translated by Anna Bostock. Cambridge: MIT Press, 1971.

Mahmood, Saba. "Ethics and Piety." In *A Companion to Moral Philosophy*, edited by Didier Fassin, 223–41. Malden: Wiley-Blackwell, 2012.

———. *Politics of Piety*. Princeton: Princeton University Press, 2005.

Malti-Douglas, Fedwa. *Structures of Avarice: The Bukhaā in Medieval Arabic Literature.* Leiden: Brill, 1985.

Mamelouk, Douja. "Ali al-Duʿaji and *al-ʿAlam al-Adabi* [The literary world]: A Voice of the Tunisian Avant-Garde under Colonial Rule (1930–1936)." *Journal of North African Studies* 21, no. 5 (2016): 794–809.

Mammeri, Mouloud. *La colline oubliée.* Paris: Plon, 1952.

Marx-Scouras, Danielle. "A Literature of Departure: The Cross-Cultural Writing of Driss Chraïbi." In "North African Literature," special issue, *Research in African Literatures* 23, no. 2 (Summer 1992): 131–44.

al-Masʿadī, Maḥmūd. *Al-aʿmāl al-kāmila* [Collected works]. Vols. 1–4. Edited by Maḥmūd Ṭarshūna. Tunis: Dār al-Janūb li-l-Nashr, 2003.

———. *Mawlid al-nisyān* [*The Genesis of Forgetfulness*]. Tunis: al-Dār al-Tūnisiyya li-l-Nashr, 1974.

Matar, Nabil, ed. *In the Lands of the Christians: Arabic Travel Writing in the Seventeenth Century*. New York: Routledge, 2003.

Al-mawrid: Arabic-English, English-Arabic Dictionary. Compiled by Munir Baalbaki and Dr. Rohi Baalbaki. Beirut: al-ʿIlm li-l-Malāyīn, 2007.

Mbembe, Achille. *On the Postcolony*. Berkeley: University of California Press, 2001.

McDougall, James. "Dream of Exile, Promise of Home: Language, Education, and Arabism in Algeria." *International Journal of Middle East Studies* 43, no. 2 (2011): 251–70.

———. *History and the Culture of Nationalism in Algeria.* Cambridge: Cambridge University Press, 2006.

———. "Myth and Counter-Myth: 'The Berber' as National Signifier in Algerian Historiographies." *Radical History Review*, no. 86 (Spring 2003): 66–88.

McLarney, Ellen. "Politics of *Le passé simple*." *Journal of North African Studies* 8, no. 2 (Summer 2003): 1–18.

Meddeb, Abdelwahab. *Instants soufis*. Paris: Éditions Albin Michel, 2015.

———. *Islam and the Challenge of Civilization.* Translated by Jane Kuntz. New York: Fordham University Press, 2013.

———. *La maladie de l'Islam*. Paris: Éditions du Seuil, 2002.

———. *Pari du civilisation*. Paris: Éditions du Seuil. 2009.

———. *Portrait du poète en soufi*. Paris: Éditions Belin, 2014.

———. *Sortir de la malédiction: L'Islam entre civilisation et barbarie*. Paris: Éditions du Seuil, 2008.

———. *Talismano*. Paris: Éditions Sindbad, 1987.

———. *Talismano*. Translated by Jane Kuntz. Champaign. Ill.: Dalkey Archive Press, 2011.

———. *Tombeau d'Ibn Arabi*. Saint-Clément-de-Rivière: Éditions Fata Morgana, 1995.

———. "Wanderer and Polygraphist." Translated by Pierre Joris. *boundary 2* 26, no. 1 (Spring 1999): 191–95.

Meddeb, Abdelwahab, Pierre Joris, and Frank Berberich. "Islam and its Discontents: An Interview with Frank Berberich." *MIT Press* 99 (Winter 2002): 3–20.

Memmi, Albert. *La statue de sel*. Paris: Corrêa, 1953.

Mernissi, Fatima. *The Forgotten Queens of Islam*. Minneapolis: University of Minnesota Press, 1993.

———. *Women's Rebellion and Islamic Memory*. Translated by Emily Agar. London: Zed, 1996.

Mikhail, Mona N. "Existential Themes in a Traditional Cairo Setting." In *Naguib Mahfouz: From Regional Fame to Global Recognition*, edited by Michael Beard and Adnan Haydar. Syracuse, N.Y.: Syracuse University Press, 1993.

Mirdehghan, Mahinnaz, Keivan Zahedi, and Fatemeh Nasiri. "Iltifat, Grammatical Person Shift and Cohesion in the Holy Quran." *Global Journal of Human Social Science Research* 12, no. 2 (2012): 45–50.

Mitchell, Timothy. "The Stage of Modernity." In *Contradictions of Modernity*, edited by Mitchell, 1–34. Minneapolis: University of Minnesota Press, 2000.

Moore, Lindsey. *Arab, Muslim, Woman: Voice and Vision in Postcolonial Literature and Film*. New York: Routledge, 2008.

Moosa, Ebrahim. *Ghazālī and the Poetics of the Imagination*. Chapel Hill: University of North Carolina Press, 2005.

Mortimer, Mildred. "Assia Djebar's *Algerian Quartet:* A Study in Fragmented Autobiography." *Research in African Literatures* 28, no. 2 (Summer 1997): 102–17.

Mufti, Aamir. "Auerbach in Istanbul: Edward Said, Secular Criticism, and the Question of Minority Culture." *Critical Inquiry* 25, no. 1 (Autumn 1998): 95–125.

Murdoch, H. Adlai. "Woman, Postcoloniality, Otherness: Djebar's Discourses of *Histoire* and *Algérianité*." *L'Esprit Créateur* 48, no. 4 (Winter 2008): 15–33.

Murray, Jenny. *Remembering the (Post)Colonial Self: Memory and Identity in the Novels of Assia Djebar*. Bern: Peter Lang, 2008.

al-Musawi, Muhsin. "Beyond the Modernity Complex: ʿAbd al-Ḥakīm Qāsim's Re-Writing of the Nahḍah Self-Narrative." *Journal of Arabic Literature* 41, no. 1/2 (2010): 22–45.

———. "Engaging Tradition in Modern Arab Poetics." *Journal of Arabic Literature* 33, no. 2 (2002): 172–210.

Nasr, Seyyed Hossein. "The Spread of the Illuminationist School of Suhrawardi." *Studies in Comparative Religion* 6, no. 3 (Summer 1972): 111–22.

Naylor, Phillip C. *France and Algeria: A History of Decolonization and Transformation*. Gainesville: University of Florida Press, 2000.

Neuman, Justin. *Fiction beyond Secularism*. Evanston, Ill.: Northwestern University Press, 2014.

Neuwirth, Angelika. *Scripture, Poetry, and the Making of a Community: Reading the Qur'an as a Literary Text*. New York: Oxford University Press, 2014.

Neuwirth, Angelika, and Michael A. Sells, eds. *Qur'ān Studies Today*. London: Routledge, 2016.

Neuwirth, Angelika, Nicolai Sinai, and Michael Marc, eds. *The Qur'ān in Context: Historical and Literary Investigations into the Qur'ānic Milieu*. Leiden: Brill, 2010.

Nöldeke, Theodor. *Geschichte des Qorâns*. Göttingen: Verlag der Dieterichschen Buchhandlung, 1860.

al-Nowaihi, Magda M. "Committed Postmodernity: Mohamed Berrada's *The Game of Forgetting*." *Middle East Critique* 8, no. 15 (1999): 1–24.

Ouedghiri, Meryem. "Writing Women's Bodies on the Palimpsest of Islamic History: Fatima Mernissi and Assia Djebar." *Cultural Dynamics* 14, no. 1 (2002): 41–64.

O'Leary, De Lacy. "Al-Hallaj." *Philosophy East and West* 1, no. 1 (April 1951): 56–62.

Omri, Mohamed-Salah. "History, Literature, and Settler Colonialism in North Africa." *Modern Language Quarterly* 66, no. 3 (September 2015): 273–98.

———. "Interview with Mahmud al-Masʿadi." *Comparative Critical Studies* 4, no. 3 (2007): 435–40.

———. *Nationalism, Islam and World Literature: Sites of Confluence in the Writings of Mahmūd al-Masʿadī.* London: Routledge, 2006.

———. "Notes on the Traffic between Theory and Arabic Literature." Roundtable: Theory and Arabic Literature in the United States. *International Journal of Middle East Studies* 43, no. 4 (2011): 731–33.

Orlando, Valerie. *Nomadic Voices of Exile: Feminine Identity in Francophone Literature of the Maghreb.* Athens: Ohio University Press, 1999.

Ostle, Robin, Ed de Moor, and Stefan Wild, eds. *Writing the Self: Autobiographical Writing in Modern Arabic Literature.* London: Saqi, 1998.

Pandolfo, Stefania. *Impasse of the Angels: Scenes from a Moroccan Space of Memory.* Chicago: University of Chicago Press, 1997.

———. "The Thin Line of Modernity: Some Moroccan Debates on Subjectivity." In *Questions of Modernity*, edited by Timothy Mitchell, 115–47. Minneapolis: University of Minnesota Press, 2000.

Prendergast, Christopher, ed. *Debating World Literature.* London: Verso, 2004.

Pennell, C. R. *Morocco since 1830: A History.* New York: New York University Press, 2000.

Perkins, Kenneth. *A Modern History of Tunisia.* 2005. 2nd ed. Cambridge: Cambridge University Press, 2014.

Phillips, Christina. "The Game of Remembering: A Study of Narrative Strategies and the Postmodern Theme in Muḥammad Barrāda's Novel *Mithl Ṣayf Lan Yatakarrar: Maḥkiyyāt.*" *Middle Eastern Literatures: Incorporating Edebiyat* 14, no. 1 (2011): 71–87.

Qur'an. *The Holy Qur'an.* Translated by Yusuf Ali. Brentwood, Md.: Amana, 1983.

———. *The Message of the Qur'an.* Translated and with commentary by Muhammad Asad. Bristol: Book Foundation. 2003.

al-Qushayri. *Principles of Sufism.* Translated by B. R. Von Schlegell. Berkeley: Mizan, 1990.

Rahman, Fazlur. *Islam and Modernity: Transformation of an Intellectual Tradition.* Chicago: University of Chicago Press, 1982.

Rahman, Najat. *Literary Disinheritance: The Writing of Home in the Work of Mahmoud Darwish and Assia Djebar.* Lanham, Md.: Lexington, 2008.

"La révolte d'un jeune homme ou le Maroc mis à nu." *Bulletin de Paris* 65 (January 7, 1955): 9–10.

Ringrose, Priscilla. *Assia Djebar: In Dialogue with Feminisms.* Amsterdam: Rodopi, 2006.

Roberge, Jonathan. "What Is Critical Hermeneutics?" *Thesis Eleven* 106, no. 1 (2011): 5–22.

Robbins, Bruce. "Secularism, Elitism, Progress, and Other Transgressions: On Edward Said's 'Voyage In.'" *Social Text*, no. 40 (Fall 1994): 25–37.

Rouighi, Ramzi. "The Andalusi Origins of the Berbers?" *Journal of Medieval Iberian Studies* 2, no. 1 (2010): 93–108.

———. "The Berbers of the Arabs." *Studia Islamica*, nouvelle édition/n.s. 1 (2011): 67–101.

———. *The Making of a Mediterranean Emirate: Ifrīqyā and Its Andalusis 1200–1400*. Philadelphia: University of Pennsylvania Press, 2011.

Ruedy, John. *Modern Algeria: The Origins and Development of a Nation*. 2nd ed. Bloomington: Indiana University Press, 2005.

Sacks, Jeffrey. "Futures of Literature: Inhitat, Adab, Naqd." *diacritics* 37, no. 4 (Winter 2007): 32–55.

Safranski, Rüdiger. *Goethe: Life as a Work of Art*. Translated by David Dollenmayer. New York: Liveright, 2017.

Said, Edward. *Orientalism*. New York: Vintage, 1979.

———. *The World, the Text, and the Critic*. Cambridge: Harvard University Press, 1983.

Salama, Mohammad. *The Qur'an and Modern Arabic Literary Criticism: From Ṭahā to Naṣr*. London: Bloomsbury Academic, 2018].

Saleh, Walid A. *The Formation of the Classical Tafsīr Tradition: The Qur'ān Commentary of Al-Tha'labī (D. 427/1035)*. Leiden: Brill, 2004.

Salem, Norma. *Habib Bourguiba, Islam and the Creation of Tunisia*. London: Croom Helm, 1984.

Sangmuah, Egya N. "Sultan Ben Youssef's American Strategy and the Diplomacy of North African Liberation, 1943–61." *Journal of Contemporary History* 27, no. 1 (January 1992): 129–48.

Scharfman, Ronnie. "Nomadism and Transcultural Writing in the Works of Abdelwahab Meddeb." *L'Esprit Créateur* 41, no. 3 (Fall 2001): 105–13.

———. "Thanotography: Writing and Death in Abdelwahab Meddeb's *Talismano*." *SubStance* 21, no. 3 issue 69 (1992): 85–102.

Schimmel, Annemarie. *Mystical Dimensions of Islam*. Chapel Hill: University of North Carolina Press, 1975.

Sefrioui, Ahmed. *La boîte à merveilles*. Paris: Éditions du Seuil, 1954.

Selim, Samah. "The Nahda, Popular Fiction, and the Politics of Translation." *MIT Electronic Journal of Middle East Studies* 4 (Fall 2004): 71–89.

———. "Toward a New Literary History." Roundtable: Theory and Arabic Literature in the United States. *International Journal of Middle East Studies* 43 (2011): 734–36.

Sellman, Johanna. "Narration and Vernacular in Mohamed Berrada's *Luʿbat al-nisyan.*" In *Facts, Fiction, and African Creative Imaginations*, edited by Toyin Falola and Fallou Ngom, 304–14. London: Routledge, 2010.

Sells, Michael A. *Approaching the Qur'ān: The Early Revelations*. 1999. 2nd ed. Ashland, Ore.: White Cloud, 2006.

———. *Early Islamic Mysticism: Sufi, Qur'an, Miʿraj, Poetic and Theological Writings*. New York: Paulist Press, 1996.

Shaikh, Saʿdiyya. *Sufi Narratives of Intimacy: Ibn ʿArabi, Gender, and Sexuality*. Chapel Hill: University of North Carolina Press, 2012.

Sheehi, Stephen. *Foundations of Arab Modernity*. Gainesville: University Press of Florida, 2004.

———. "Inscribing the Arab Self: Butrus al-Bustani and Paradigms of Subjective Reform." *British Journal of the Middle Eastern Studies* 27, no. 1 (2000): 7–24.

———. "Towards a Critical Theory of al-Nahḍah: Epistemology, Ideology and Capital." *Journal of Arabic Literature* 43, no. 2/3 (2012): 269–98.

el-Shihibi, Fathi A. "Travel Genre in Arabic Literature: A Selective Literary and Historical Study." Ph.D. diss., Boston University, 1998. Boca Raton, Fla.: Dissertation.com, 2006.

Siassi, Guilan. "Itineraries of Desire and the Excesses of Home: Assia Djebar's Cohabitation with "la langue adverse." *L'Esprit Créateur* 48, no. 4 (Winter 2008): 56–68.

Siegel, Irene. "Authorizing Narrative: Negotiations of Belonging in North African Literature." Ph.D. diss., University of California, Berkeley, 2009.

Sinai, Nicolai. "When Did the Consonantal Skeleton of the Quran Reach Closure? Part I." *Bulletin of SOAS* 77, no. 2 (2014): 273–92.

Somekh, Sasson. *The Changing Rhythm: A Study of Najīb Maḥfūẓ's Novels*. Vol. 1. Leiden: Brill, 1973.

Steadman, Jennifer Bernhardt. "A Global Feminist Travels: Assia Djebar and Fantasia." *meridians: feminism, race, transnationalism* 4, no. 1 (2003): 173–99.

Stefanidis, Emmanuelle. "The Qur'an Made Linear: A Study of the *Geschichte des Qorâns*' Chronological Reordering." *Journal of Qur'anic Studies* 10, no. 2 (2008): 1–22.

Stoler, Ann Laura. "Imperial Debris: Reflections on Ruins and Ruination." *Cultural Anthropology* 23, no. 2 (May 2008): 191–219.

Šukys, Julija. *Silence Is Death: The Life and Work of Tahar Djaout*. Lincoln: University of Nebraska Press, 2007.

Tageldin, Shaden M. "Proxidistant Reading: Toward a Critical Pedagogy of the Nahḍah in U.S. Comparative Literary Studies." *Journal of Arabic Literature* 43, no. 2/3 (2012): 227–68.

———. "Which *Qalam* for Algeria? Colonialism, Liberation, and Language in Djebar's *L'amour, la fantasia* and Mustaghānimī's *Dhākirat al-Jasad.*" *Comparative Literature Studies* 46, no. 3 (2009): 467–97.

Tilmatine, Mohand. "French and Spanish Colonial Policy in North Africa: Revisiting the Kabyle and Berber Myth." *International Journal of the Sociology of Language*, no. 239 (May 2016): 95–119.

Todorov, Tzvetan. *Mikhaïl Bakhtine: Le principe dialogique—suivi de: Écrits du Cercle Bakhtine*. Paris: Éditions du Seuil, 1981.

Van den Boogert, Nico. "Some Notes on Maghribi Script." *Manuscripts of the Middle East* (MME), no. 4 (1989): 30–43.

Vatin, Jean-Claude. "Revival in the Maghreb: Islam as an Alternative Political Language." In *Islamic Resurgence in the Arab World*, edited by Ali E. Hillal Dessouki. New York: Praeger, 1982.

Vinogradov, Amal, and John Waterbury. "Situations of Contested Legitimacy in Morocco: An Alternative Framework." *Comparative Studies in Society and History* 13, no. 1 (January 1971): 32–59.

Von Denffer, Ahmad. *ʿUlum al-Qur'an: An Introduction to the Sciences of Qur'an*. 1985. Leicestershire, UK: Islamic Foundation, 1996.

Wadud, Amina. *Qur'an and Woman: Rereading the Sacred Text from a Woman's Perspective*. Oxford: Oxford University Press, 1999.

Walker, Muriel. "Femme d'écriture française: La francographie djebarienne." *L'Esprit Créateur* 48, no. 4 (Winter 2008): 47–55.

Ware, Rudolph T. *The Walking Qur'an: Islamic Education, Embodied Knowledge, and History in West Africa*. Chapel Hill: University of North Carolina Press, 2014.

Waṭṭār, al-Ṭāhir. *Al-lāz*. Algiers: SNED, 1974.

———. *Al-zilzāl*. Beirut: al-Dār al-ʿArabiyya li-l-ʿUlūm, 2007.

———. *The Earthquake*. Translated by William Granara. London: Saqi, 2000.

———. Interview. https://www.youtube.com/watch?v=CUtvpzcBqlk.

Wehrs, Donald. *Islam, Ethics, Revolt: Politics and Piety in Francophone West African and Maghreb Narrative*. Lanham, Md.: Lexington, 2008.

Weltman-Aron, Brigitte. *Algerian Imprints: Ethical Space in the Work of Assia Djebar and Hélène Cixous*. New York: Columbia University Press, 2015.

Wild, Stefan, ed. *The Qur'an as Text*. Leiden: Brill, 1996.

Yacine, Kateb. *Nedjma*. Paris: Éditions du Seuil, 1956.

Yetiv, Isaac. *La thème de l'aliénation dans le roman maghrébin d'expression française: 1952–1956*. Sherbrooke: CELEF, 1972.

Zadeh, Travis. "Quranic Studies and the Literary Turn." *Journal of the American Oriental Society* 135, no. 2 (April-June 2015): 329–42.

Zbinden, Karine. *Bakhtin between East and West: Cross Cultural Transmission*. London: Legenda—Modern Humanities Research Association and Maney Publishing, 2006.

Ždanov, A. A. "Soviet Literature—The Richest in Ideas, the Most Advanced Literature." Speech to Soviet Writers Congress, 1934. https://www.marxists.org/subject/art/lit_crit/sovietwritercongress/zdhanov.htm.

Zimra, Clarissa. "Disorienting the Subject in Djebar's *L'Amour, la fantasia.*" In "Another Look, Another Woman: Retranslations of French Feminism,' special issue, *Yale French Studies*, no. 87 (1995): 149–79.

———. "Mapping Memory: Architectural Metaphors in Djebar's Unfinished Quartet." *L'Ésprit Créateur* 43, no. 1 (Spring 2003): 58–68.

———. "Not So Far from Medina: Assia Djebar Charts Islam's 'Insupportable Feminist Revolution." *World Literature Today* 70, no. 4 (Autumn 1996): 823–34.

Index

adab: as critical lens, 4–5; education and, 22, 41–42, 104; as ethical, literary, and social community, 56, 77, 146, 150–51; history of, 19; orientalism and, 17; polysemy of, 17–18, 20
Adonis (poet), 16, 27–28
aesthetics, 37, 75, 165; ethics and, 17, 41–42, 80, 95; *iʿjāz al-Qurʾan* and, 20, 23–24; postmodernist, 142; Qurʾanic, 5, 19; Sufi, 59; vulgarity and, 68–69
agency, 12–13, 134, 165, 194fn32
ʿĀʾisha (wife of the Prophet Muhammad), 15, 96, 97, 193fn28, 193fn30, 194fn31
Algeria, 86–87, 91–92, 94–95, 97, 100; Arabization of, 86, 107–08; colonialism and, 33, 92, 100, 103, 105, 113–14; ethnolinguistic landscape of, 88, 107, 111–12, 115, 196fn11; national identity of, 84–85, 93, 98–99, 102–03, 107, 196fn11; postrevolutionary, 83, 106; Sufism in, 65; women and, 110–11
Amazigh, 31–32, 85, 92, 101, 108, 110, 125. *See also* Berber
L'Amour, la fantasia (Djebar), Algerian national identity and, 107, 110–11, 196fn11; Amazigh identity in, 108–11; anticlericalism and, 105, 110; Arabic in, 107–09, 111–12, 115; embodiment in, 102, 105, 111, 114–16; French in, 108, 111–13, 115; hadith and, 104–05, 116; *ijtihād* and, 103, 106, 111, 114, 116; love in, 106–07; orality in, 102, 105, 108, 112, 116; piety in, 105–06, 114; polyphony and, 102–03, 116; scholarship on, 195fn5; women and, 107, 110, 113
anthropology, 5, 9, 11, 22, 46, 132
apocalypse. *See under* eschatology: apocalypse and
Appadurai, Arjun, 4, 13, 175fn27
Arab (ethnic identity), 6–7, 87, 110
Arabic: Algerian vernacular, 88, 91, 102, 111, 115; concern for "purity" of, 88, 93, 98; education and/in, 39, 85, 87–88, 111; literary or formal, 43, 115, 157; Modern Standard (MSA), 89, 148, 154, 192fn18; Moroccan vernacular, 148, 209fn27; national identity and, 7, 32, 86, 89, 99, 100–01, 107; Qurʾanic, 18, 89, 93, 112; relationship with French, 62–63, 71–74, 86, 107–09, 111–15, 136, 142, 144
Arab-Islamic heritage, 15–16, 60, 88, 105, 107–08, 125. *See also turāth*
Arabism, 85–87, 89, 92, 93, 98–99, 160, 165. *See also* pan-Arabism
Arabization, 7, 107–08, 110, 130, 140. *See also taʿrīb*
Asad, Talal, 11–12, 22, 172fn7
aṣāla, 16, 38, 157
asynchronicity, xvi, 16, 24, 89, 145–46, 148
avant-garde, 16, 27, 40–41, 141
authenticity, 4, 38, 42, 150, 157, 166. *See also aṣāla*

Bakhtin, Mikhail, 14, 34, 85, 89, 141–44, 172, 173fn11, 175fn28
Barrāda, Muḥammad, 141–43; *Asʾilat al-riwāya, asʾilat al-naqd* (Questions of the novel, questions of [literary] criticism), 142, 146, 206fn7; *Faḍāʾāt riwāʾiyya* (Novelistic spaces), 142; *Al-riwāya al-ʿarabiyya wa-rihān al-tajdīd* (The Arabic novel and the wager of renewal), 142, 157; *Al-riwāya dhākira maftūḥa* (The novel: An open memory), 142; translations into Arabic, 142–43. *See also Luʿbat al-nisyān*
Barthes, Roland, 14, 34, 142
bāṭin. *See* Sufism
barzakh, 38, 45–46, 49, 132, 138, 140

Hoda El Shakry is Assistant Professor of Comparative Literature at the University of Chicago.

Printed and bound by CPI Group (UK) Ltd, Croydon, CR0 4YY
09/06/2025
14685656-0003